Understanding Computer Science

By: Roger S. Walker, Ph.D., P.E.
Professor and Chairman
Computer Science & Engineering Dept.
University of Texas at Arlington
Staff Consultant, Texas Instruments Information
Publishing Center

Managing Editor: Gerald Luecke
Mgr. Technical Products Development
Texas Instruments Information Publishing Center

Editor: Charles W. Battle
Ben Korte

TEXAS INSTRUMENTS

P.O. BOX 225012, MS-54 • DALLAS, TEXAS 75265

This book was developed by:

The Staff of the Texas Instruments Information Publishing Center
P.O. Box 225012, MS-54
Dallas, Texas 75265

For marketing and distribution inquire to:

Orm F. Henning
Marketing Manager
P.O. Box 225012, MS-54
Dallas, Texas 75265

Word Processing:

Barbara Morgan, Vicki Seale

Typesetting:

Judy Lipsett

Artwork and layout by:

Schenck Design Associates, Inc.
Plunk Design

ISBN 0-89512-161-1
Library of Congress Catalog Number: 84-51251

Second Edition

About the cover:

Represented on the cover are the components of modern day computers: individual integrated circuits, an assembled printed circuit card, flat interconnection cable, a keyboard, floppy disks and a computer print-out.

Table of Contents

Preface

We are living in the computer age. Computers sort our mail, calculate and print our paychecks, maintain our bank accounts and print the monthly statements, control home appliances, control automobile engines, and on and on. Many facets of our daily lives are touched somewhere, somehow by a computer.

You may have access to a computer at school, in your company, or even at home. You may have written a computer program. Whatever your status, if you are interested in understanding computers — how they work, how they are programmed, how they are used — then you should find this book helpful.

Computer science is the study of computers and their uses. It includes the design and construction of hardware and the design and use of software. In this book we are primarily concerned with the design and use of software — the way a computer is programmed to make it do specific tasks.

After a history of computer developments that traces computer capability and a short summary of hardware operation, the discussion of software begins. First, learning how to tell a computer what to do (programming) then understanding how to design programs to make them more efficient and easier to modify. Second, learning about the programming languages that have been developed, something of their characteristics and differences. And third, studying examples of how software is used to operate a system (operating system); manage resources such as keyboards, memories, printers; structure data in storage; translate human instructions to machine language, and analyze systems to determine resources required to do a specific task. The book concludes with a look into the future.

This book, like others in the series, is designed to build understanding step-by-step. Try to master each chapter before going on to the next one. A quiz is provided at the end of each chapter for personal evaluation of progress. Answers are also included.

If you have access to a computer, you may want to try out the programming techniques as you learn them. If you are interested in more detail on the way hardware works, two additional books in this series, *Understanding Digital Electronics* and *Understanding Microprocessors* will provide more complete study on the digital computer.

Contrary to common belief computers do not operate by themselves, they need people. People interested in computer science. We hope that this book contributes to your appreciation of this exciting and expanding field.

R.S.W.

About Computers and Computer Science

INFLUENCE OF THE COMPUTER ON OUR DAILY LIVES

The flashing red lights of the police patrol car pierced the darkness as officers Bill Jones and Tom Smith whipped around the corner to pursue the bright yellow Corvette that had just run through a red light. Bill accelerated the patrol car to catch up with the Corvette which had already begun to slow down as the driver had seen the flashing lights. Tom used the police radio to call the dispatcher and told her the Corvette license number. Using the keyboard in front of her, the dispatcher punched in the license number to their local computer. The local computer connected itself to the statewide computer network so it could have access to the central data files maintained by the state department of motor vehicles. The local computer requested a search of the stolen vehicle file and the current registered owner of that license number. Within seconds, the CRT screen in front of the dispatcher displayed a readout that the number had not been reported as stolen, and then gave a description of the vehicle and the name and address of the registered owner. The dispatcher relayed this information to Tom in the patrol car. By this time, the Corvette had pulled over and stopped and Bill had stopped behind it. Tom got out and approached the Corvette cautiously. He asked the driver for his driver's license and checked the name and address against the one that the dispatcher had given him. The name and address matched, so Tom asked the driver why he had run the red light. He mumbled something about being late for a date with a new girlfriend. Tom issued a ticket to the driver, told him to drive more carefully, and then returned to the patrol car. As the Corvette pulled away, Tom said, "Boy, that computer system down at the station sure makes our job easier and faster". "Yeah," Bill replied, "and I hear that they are going to equip our patrol cars with a minicomputer that will be able to connect to the station computer by radio so we can do our own vehicle checkout without bothering the dispatcher. That will free her to devote attention to more important things." As he started to pull away from the curb, Bill continued, "Let's go in here for a coffeebreak". "Ok", replied Tom as he grabbed the mike to check-out with the dispatcher.

They entered the small cafe and took a booth by the front window. From his position, Bill could see the traffic lights at the intersection. Bill said, "You know, Tom, the timing of those traffic signals is controlled by a computer, not just a clock timer like they used to be. Loops buried in the street sense the presence of cars and feed traffic flow information into the computer so it can adjust timing of the lights to maximize traffic flow. It seems that everywhere I look these days, there's a computer making our daily life easier, safer, and more enjoyable.

"Yes, I know what you mean." Tom said. "We have a microwave oven (*Figure 1-1*) at home and it sure does make cooking a lot easier. It has a microcomputer in it with a memory so we can actually program cooking times and temperatures by pressing control keys and numbers on the keypad. And my son says he doesn't know how I ever made it through school without the hand-held electronic calculator (*Figure 1-2*). He's going to be an engineer and he's even bought one of those programmable ones to use for his engineering courses. It's amazing how they can do so much in such a little space, and, really, its not very expensive considering the number of things it can do. It's like having a computer in your hip pocket."

**Figure 1-1.
Microwave Oven.**
(Courtesy of Litton Microwave Cooking Products)

Bill replied, "I just bought a new car that has a microcomputer in it. There are sensors or measuring devices mounted at various places that monitor the outside temperature, engine temperature, engine speed, exhaust oxygen level, spark advance, and exhaust gas recirculation rate. The electrical outputs of these sensors are wired to the computer inputs. The computer looks at every one of these inputs 10 times per second and adjusts the air/fuel ratio entering the engine cylinders for the most efficient fuel mileage and lowest exhaust emissions."

"You're right, Bill, about computers being all around us in our daily life. We could go on and on with examples we know about and I'm sure they're being used for things we don't even know about or haven't even thought about," Tom said.

You probably know about and can think of other examples of computer uses yourself; because, as Bill and Tom discussed, they are all around us. They affect our daily lives now, and their effect will no doubt increase in the future.

But how did this happen? How did these computer systems come about? They came about by people seeing a problem, analyzing the problem, and recognizing that the computer could be used to help solve the problem.

Computers greatly simplify such tasks as the management of large amounts of data, the performing of complex calculations, and the execution of repetitive control functions.

People recognized that the use of the computer has many benefits. A few of these are: The computer system is ideal for solving the problems of storing a large amount of data with easy and quick access to any particular piece (as the vehicle registration), for long, detailed calculations (as the hand-held calculator), and for routine or repetitive control functions, (as the microwave oven, the traffic control signal, or the automobile engine). As more problems were solved, more applications came to mind. As more applications came to mind, new hardware was developed for more cost effective solutions to more and more applications. Always, however, people were required to analyze the problem, and provide computer applied solutions. That's what this book is about — how people can apply computers to solve problems.

**Figure 1-2.
Hand-Held Calculator.**

WHAT IS COMPUTER SCIENCE?

Computer science is the study of computers and their uses (*Figure 1-3*). It includes the physical computer or hardware. It includes software — computer programming and languages. It includes the data base and systems analysis.

**Figure 1-3.
Definition of Computer
Science.**

WHAT IS A COMPUTER?

A "computer" is essentially a device that accepts some form of input data, manipulates the data, and produces an output or peforms an action as a result of the operation. Today, the term generally refers to electronic digital computers.

In the most general sense as shown in *Figure 1-4*, a computer is a device which senses or accepts input data, performs operations or computations (decides) on the data in a prearranged sequence or program, and provides the result as an output or action. This broad definition includes purely mechanical devices, combination electro-mechanical units and, so-called modern day electronic computers which include units that handle all their information internally electronically but have attached mechanical units for inputting, printing, and storing informaion. Computers further divide into two basic types — analog and digital. Current use of the word "computer" almost always refers to the electronic digital computer which uses solid-state electronic circuits. It is this computer and its use that this book covers. For reference, however, a brief definition of the analog computer is included.

**Figure 1-4.
Generalized Computer
Process.**

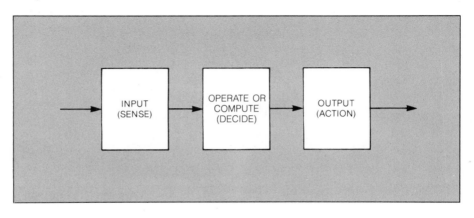

What Is An Analog Computer?

An analog computer processes inputs of continuously varying quantities.

An analog computer as shown in *Figure 1-5* operates on inputs of continuously varying quantities rather than on on-off or incrementally-stepped quantities which are the inputs for the digital computer. An example of a simple mechanical analog computer is the moving pointer type automobile speedometer. It receives as input the continuously variable rotational speed of the driveshaft and provides as output the pointer movement across the dial which indicates the speed of the car. An example of the use of an electronic analog computer is that of controlling a flight simulator for training pilots. The computer responds to the cockpit simulator control movements made by the pilot to physically change the attitude of the simulator so that the pilot feels as if he were controlling an actual airplane.

**Figure 1-5.
Analog Computer.**

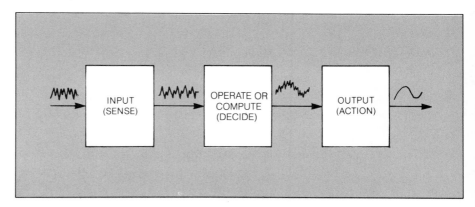

What Is A Digital Computer?

A digital computer processes inputs of incrementally stepped quantities.

A digital computer as shown in *Figure 1-6* operates on inputs that are on-off or incrementally-stepped quantities which are represented by numerical digits. Almost all electronic digital computers use binary digits to represent data. The term "bit" is an acronym for "binary digit". A bit is an independent piece of information that in binary digital systems can have one of two values, a 0 or a 1.

**Figure 1-6.
Digital Computer.**

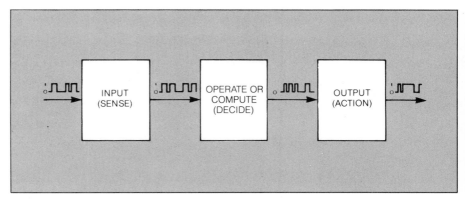

Figure 1-7.
Basic Computer System.

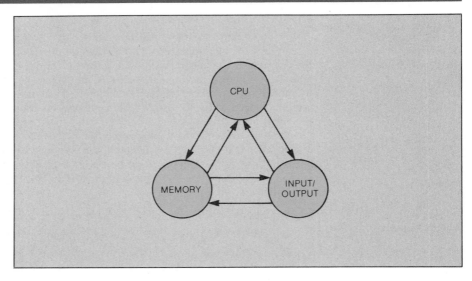

Three main subsystems —
an input/output unit, a
central processing unit,
and memory — make up
an electronic digital
computer.

Electronic digital computers consist of three main subsystems or modules as illustrated in *Figure 1-7*. The I/O unit, the central processing unit (CPU) and memory. The input/output module has two functions. The input function provides the means for you to enter or read in programs, commands and data to the CPU, and the output function provides the means for the CPU to return the answers to you.

The memory module is where programs or the sequence of instructions that tell the CPU what to do are stored. Also, the data to be processed is read into memory and held until ready for use, and the results of computations by the CPU are stored in memory until ready for output. If the memory space in the computer is not large enough, memory may be added by using auxiliary storage units. These units are separate pieces of equipment and typically consist of magnetic disc units and magnetic tape units. They are normally used to store large quantities of data during processing, and for storing both data and programs to keep on file between uses. These auxiliary storage devices and input/output equipment are often referred to as a group by the term "peripheral equipment".

The CPU is the heart of the computer. It reads the program instructions that are stored in memory, performs the computation, data movement, or other operation required by the instruction, and supervises the entire operation of the computer system.

How Are Computers Classified?

Computers are classified by physical size and computational power. These usually go hand-in-hand during any one period of technological development since more space is required to handle larger numbers or larger quantities of data. The general classifications currently used are, in order of decreasing size:

1) Large-scale general purpose computer   3) Minicomputer
2) Midicomputer   4) Microcomputer

Figure 1-8.
Large Scale General
Purpose Computer
System.
(Courtesy of International
Business Machines
Corporation)

The large scale, general purpose computer system (*Figure 1-8*) is most often used in large business corporations, government agencies, and universities where large volumes of data must be processed and a lot of program flexibility is needed to handle the many varied jobs. These machines are very expensive, both to purchase or lease and to operate. The price of these machines is usually several million dollars. They require air conditioning for close temperature control and many people to operate and maintain them.

When comparing computer system prices, you should know that computer costs are compared on the basis of bits-per-second-per-dollar. That is, a system that costs a million dollars and processes a lot of data in a few seconds may be more cost effective in bits-per-second-per-dollar than a smaller system that costs a half-million dollars but takes several minutes to process the same quantity of data. On the other hand, a roomful of computers that process data in a millionth of a second is certainly not required to control a manufacturing operation that operates once a second.

A computer's size and cost tend to be proportional to its computational power. Different tasks call for different types of computers.

Midicomputers (*Figure 1-9*) and minicomputers (*Figure 1-10*) are typically used in applications that don't require the fast computational speed or large memory capacity available on large scale systems. These computers have program flexibility, but they are sometimes programmed for a specific job and many times used only for that job. The midicomputers, however, are just as often used for general data processing functions. The minicomputers normally don't require air conditioning and usually a full-time person is not required for operation or maintenance. The price of a midicomputer system ranges from a few to several hundred thousand dollars, depending on the quantity of peripheral equipment. The minicomputer system price ranges from a few thousand to around one hundred thousand dollars, also depending mainly on peripheral equipment.

Figure 1-9.
Midicomputer System.
(Courtesy of Digital Equipment Corporation)

Figure 1-10.
Minicomputer System.

The microcomputer is a product of a recent development in semiconductor technology — the microprocessor. The microprocessor (*Figure 1-11a*) is a complete CPU that is contained on one integrated circuit chip in a package approximately 1.5 inches (3.8 cm) by 0.5 inches (1.3 cm). When memory and I/O interface circuits are included with this microprocessor, this permits the microcomputer to be very small as illustrated by the board computer in *Figure 1-11b*.

**Figure 1-11.
Microprocessor and
Microcomputer.**

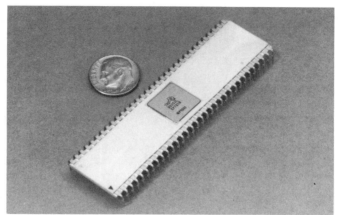

a. Microprocessor in a Package.

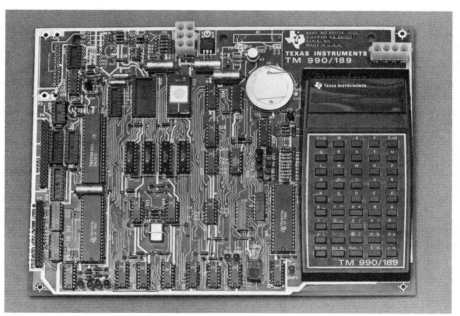

b. Microcomputer on a Board.

**Figure 1-12.
Microcomputer on a
Chip.**

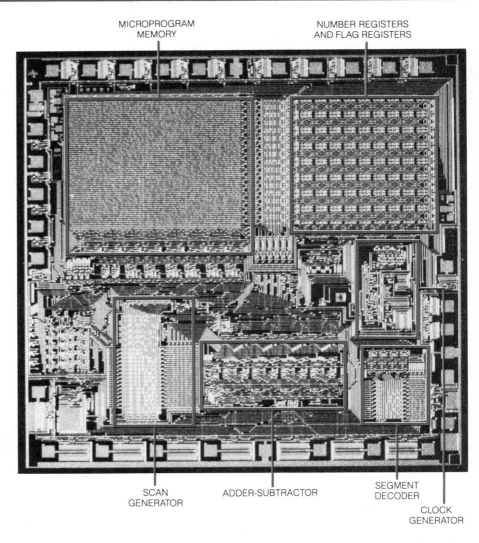

MICROPROGRAM
MEMORY

NUMBER REGISTERS
AND FLAG REGISTERS

SCAN
GENERATOR

ADDER-SUBTRACTOR

SEGMENT
DECODER

CLOCK
GENERATOR

Due to their small size,
low cost, and versatility,
microcomputers lend
themselves to specialized
applications such as microwave oven control.

Microcomputers have a relatively low cost of a few dollars to tens
of thousands of dollars and they are often used for a specific application.
The digital control unit that is used in some microwave ovens is a low-cost
complete microcomputer on a chip, as shown in *Figure 1-12*. These units
have input/output functions, memory, and a microprocessor CPU all in one
package. The keypad or control panel on the oven permits you to input
commands that tell the CPU what you want the oven to do. A permanently
stored program in the memory directs the CPU to read and process your
instructions to control the heating operation of the oven. The controlled
heating is the output function of the microcomputer.

HISTORICAL BACKGROUND

Let's look at what has happened in the past to bring computers to their present position of prominence. When man wanted to increase his capacity to add beyond counting on his fingers, making marks on walls or the floor, or grouping rocks, he began developing machines.

One of the oldest devices was the abacus which was developed around 2000 BC. This machine is still used in Japan, China, and other Asian countries. In fact, there have been cases where a very efficient abacus user could keep up with, or even beat, a person using a mechanical calculator when both were adding the same columns of figures. The abacus consists of several fixed vertical rods strung with moveable beads within a rectangular frame and with a horizontal bar across the rods (*Figure 1-13*). Each of the two beads above the cross bar have a value of five and each of the five beads below the cross bar have a value of one. Beginnning on the right hand side and moving left; the first rod represents the units digit, the second rod represents the tens digit, then follows the hundreds digit, thousands digit, and so on. The abacus is cleared or set to zero by moving all beads away from the cross bar. Numbers are entered by moving the appropriate beads to the cross bar, beginning with the rightmost digit and working left. In *Figure 1-13*, the number 1740 has been entered in the abacus.

The abacus, an early fore-runner of the computer, has been in existence for 4000 years.

**Figure 1-13.
Abacus.**

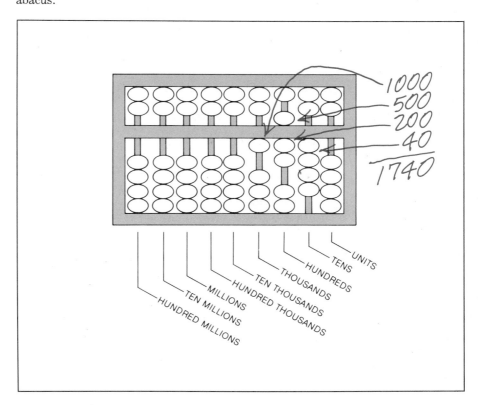

Mechanical Calculators

Mechanical calculators
were developed during the
17th, 18th, and 19th
centuries.

Although the abacus worked very well, and still does, man
continued to search for better and faster machines to do his calculations,
since this was the tedious and time consuming part of mathematics. Some
developments in the 1600's deserve mention here as part of the continuing
evolution. John Napier, a Scottish mathematician, published a paper in 1617
which described the use of specially marked rods to perform multiplication
and division. The rods were carved from ivory and were often referred to
as "Napier's Bones". (Napier's work in mathematics led to the much later
development of the slide rule which was the primary "machine" for
complex calculations for many years.) In 1642, Blaise Pascal invented the
first actual "adding machine" which resembled the mechanical desk
calculators that were popular in the 1960's. It was a complex arrangement
of wheels, gears, and windows for displaying the numbers. A more
advanced machine of similar kind was developed in the late 1600's by
Gottfried Leibnitz. His machine could mechanically add, subtract, multiply,
divide, and even extract square roots. However, it was not until 1820 that
the first *commercial* machines became available that could handle the four
basic mathematical operations of addition, subtraction, multiplication, and
division.

Punched Cards and Mechanical Computers

Later in the 19th century,
mechanical computers that
read instructions and data
from punched cards
appeared.

In the early 1800's, several people contributed to major advances
in man's continuing quest for calculating machines that could do more. One
contributor, although not primarily interested in mathematics, was Joseph
Jacquard. He invented a loom for weaving cloth that was controlled by
instructions that were stored in code on punched cards. This idea of
punched card storage was used to store both instructions and numbers or
data by Charles Babbage. In 1835, he invented a mechanical mathematical
digital computer that was called an analytical engine. He used the punched
cards to program his machine, which was capable of using the results of
one calculation as input for another calculation, and was capable of
handling repetitive calculations or loops. An even more significant
accomplishment of the analytical engine was the capability to jump around
in the program instructions rather than taking them in the entered
sequence. Modern day programmers call these loops or conditional
transfers. You will learn more about loops and conditional transfers in later
chapters of this book because the computers of today are based on many of
the principles used in the Babbage design.

You probably have guessed by now that the idea of using the
punched card for data and program storage really caught on. You probably
see some kind of punched card at least once a week. The type that's most
widely used now, often called an IBM card, was developed by Herman
Hollerith in the 1890's (*Figure 1-14*). He also developed the Hollerith code
for the card punching sequence and an *electrical* machine for reading and
sorting the cards.

Always before, only mechanical means were used to read the cards, so this was another "first". Herman Hollerith set the groundwork for a company that later evolved into International Business Machines (IBM).

**Figure 1-14.
IBM® Card.**

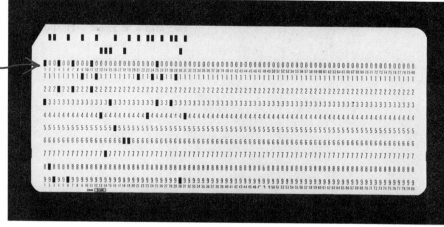

The holes are "read" electronically.

The 1940's saw the development of electro-mechanical computers that read information from paper tape and punched cards.

Electro-Mechanical Computers

Now, back to the computer evolution. With electricity commonly available, men began developing electro-mechanical machines rather than purely mechanical ones. You probably know that an electro-mechanical device is one that uses electricity to produce mechanical movement. An example is the electric bell. The relay and the solenoid were the electro-mechanical devices that were used in electro-mechanical computers. The first electro-mechanical computer, called the Mark I, was developed by Howard Aiken and others at Harvard University in 1944. It was a large machine — about 15.5 meters (51 feet) long by 2.4 meters (8 feet) high. Instructions were fed in on punched paper tape and data was input on punched cards. The output results were recorded on cards by an electric typewriter. The Mark I could multiply two numbers in about three seconds. In 1947, the Mark II could perform the same multiplication in about one-fourth of a second. This was 12 times faster and, at the time, a great step forward. But contrast that with the present day computers that can perform hundreds of thousands of mathematical calculations in one second!

Electronic Computers

Well, obviously something happened. How could calculating speeds be increased by so much? If you guessed that it was the electronic age with all its phenomenal breakthroughs, you're right. The electronic age got under way with the vacuum tube. You know what that is, because in the first television sets, the vacuum tube was usually the culprit that caused your TV to quit right in the best part of your favorite program. Its that glass bulb, heated by a filament, in which electrons flow from cathode to

®IBM is a registered trademark of International Business Machines Corporation

ENIAC, the first electronic computer, used vacuum tubes. Its operators programmed the machine by manually positioning plugs and switches.

anode in a vacuum. The first *electronic* digital computer used vacuum tubes and could perform multiplication in about 2.8 milliseconds. (A millisecond is one-thousandth of one second.) It was developed by J. Presper Eckert, John W. Mauchly and others at the Moore School of Engineering at the University of Pennsylvania in 1946. Their machine was called ENIAC, an acronym for Electronic Numerical Integrator and Computer. The U.S. Army Ordance Corps used ENIAC to calculate artillery firing tables. ENIAC was programmed by manually changing plug-in connections and setting switches which, as you can imagine, required a lot of time.

Parallel Transfers and Stored Programs

The concepts of transferring data in parallel and storing programs in machine memory enormously improved the speed and flexibility of computers.

During this same period, John Von Neumann, working at the Institute for Advanced Study in Princeton, New Jersey, published a paper describing a number of concepts which had a major impact on the computer evolution. One of these concepts was to move or transfer data bits in parallel rather than in series. In a serial machine, data bits are transferred in and out of the machine and within the machine one at a time like a bucket brigade (*Figure 1-15a*). In a parallel machine, several data bits are transferred all at the same time at a signal, similar to releasing the horses at the starting gate of a horse race (*Figure 1-15b*). You can easily see that much operating time is saved if you move eight data bits in one second rather than in 8 seconds. (Of course, in a real computer data bits are transferred at a much faster rate than one per second.)

Well, this parallel transfer of data was a great idea and is used today. But another concept in Von Neumann's paper was even more important in advancing computer technology. This was the concept of storing the computer program in the machine's memory. This idea was developed and refined and is used in the computers of today because the stored program permits tremendous flexibility in the use of a particular machine for many different applications and greatly speeds up the computer operation. By using stored programs, a computer can be performing scientific calculations one second, change to sorting a list of names the next, and change again to updating the quantity changes in a parts inventory. As you probably realize, the stored program concept was among the most significant developments that made the computer a commercial success.

**Figure 1-15.
Data Transfer Methods.**

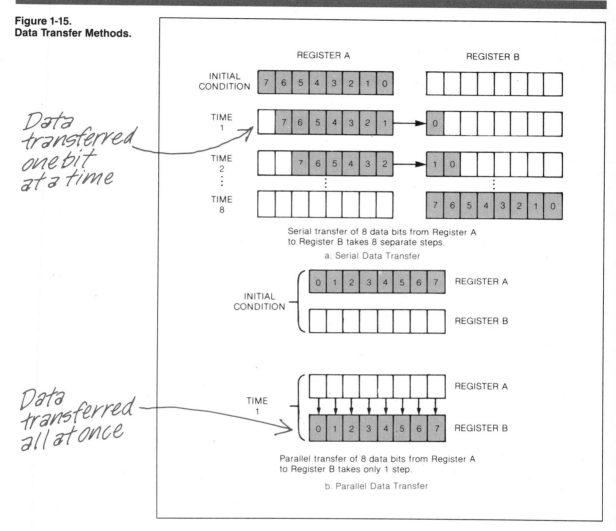

Data transferred one bit at a time

Data transferred all at once

The Computer Age

The electronic industry in general was making rapid advances and, with these new ideas for computers being refined, the beginning of the computer industry was signaled by the first mass-produced electronic digital computer — the UNIVAC I. The UNIVAC I was first built in 1951 by the same group that developed the ENIAC. Since then, computer technology has advanced very rapidly. Improvements in electronic circuits, particularly the integrated circuit which was developed by semiconductor manufacturers like Texas Instruments, and more efficient methods of programming have resulted in computers that are faster, more reliable, physically smaller, less expensive, and use less power. And, as you are well aware, the use of computers is not limited to big businesses.

Technology has progressed so rapidly that many modern calculators have the computing power of the early large computers.

The Texas Instruments Programmable 59 (*Figure 1-16*) is a mass-produced, hand-held, battery powered, programmable calculator that sells for something more than 100 dollars and has as much computational power as the first generation large computers of the 1950's.

Stop and think — this has all happened in just 30 years! And it's not stopping here, because we are still in the midst of the computer evolution. It has already had a tremendous effect on our lives and in the future the effect will be even greater!

**Figure 1-16.
Programmable Hand-
Held Calculator.**

DEVELOPMENT OF ELECTRONIC DIGITAL COMPUTERS

Now you've seen how man's search for better and faster means of calculating brought us into the age of electronic digital computers and you took a quick glance at the advancement in electronic computers. Let's now examine these developments in more detail by dividing the computer age into parts that are often referred to as "computer generations" just as you may refer to your family by generations.

First Generation Computers

As was said previously, this generation began in 1951 with the first mass-produced electronic computer, the UNIVAC I, which was sold by a company named Remington Rand. The first UNIVAC I was installed for and used by the U.S. Bureau of Census. For several years, people used "UNIVAC" anytime they referred to a computer, like some people use "Coke" to refer to any kind of soft drink. That continued until competition arrived when International Business Machines (IBM) began building and selling computers. The first IBM computer was the 701 and was first installed in 1953. In the next year, the IBM 650 became available, and it was the most popular computer for several years. So "IBM" was used to refer to computers.

The vacuum tubes used in first-generation computers of the 1950's caused problems of high power consumption, heat, and unreliability.

The vacuum tubes used in the first generation machines required a lot of electrical power and generated so much heat that many tons of air conditioning were required for cooling. The air conditioning itself also required much electrical power. Reliability of these early machines was so poor that "down time" often exceeded operating time. ("Down time", as you probably know, is the term used to describe the time that a machine is not capable of performing its job.) These machines did not have much internal memory and computation speed was typically about two milliseconds (0.002 seconds) for multiplication.

Second Generation Computers

This generation was ushered in by the changeover from vacuum tubes to transistors in commercial computers around 1959. The transistor as shown in *Figure 1-17* was less expensive, was more reliable, required less power, produced less heat, and was much smaller than even the miniature vacuum tubes that had been developed.

**Figure 1-17.
Transistor.**

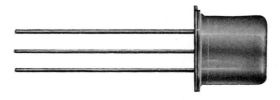

Second-generation computers, introduced in the late 1950's, used transistors in place of tubes. These machines were smaller, more reliable, and more economical to operate than the earlier vacuum-tube computers.

Because of the small size and low heat production, circuit density could be increased; that is, the components could be placed closer together. This, of course, allowed the total machine to be smaller, and also encouraged the use of small plug-in printed circuit cards that could be easily replaced to reduce maintenance time. These same things also contributed to designs that were easier to manufacture. The net result of all these factors was that the second generation computer was smaller, more reliable, less expensive, and used less electrical power for the same computational power as a first generation machine. Several other companies "jumped on the bandwagon" to design and build computers during the second generation period. Some manufacturers concentrated their efforts on the general purpose computer while others devoted their attention to scientific computers which were designed for "super" accuracy and efficiency in performing mathematical calculations. Because of the intense competition in the computer market, many different variations in computer design were tried, Some succeeded while others failed. *Table 1-1* shows some of the most widely used second generation computers. RCA concentrated on business applications, IBM and Univac on business and scientific, and Control Data on scientific and the highest speed computers.

Table 1-1.
Widely Used Second-Generaiton Computers.

MANUFACTURER	MODEL	SIZE	PRIMARY APPLICATION
IBM	1620	Small	Scientific
IBM	1401	Small to Medium	Business
IBM	7094	Large	Scientific and Business
CDC	1604	Medium to Large	Scientific
CDC	3600	Large	Scientific
RCA	501	Medium	Business
UNIVAC	1108	Large	Scientific and Business

Third Generation Computers

The third computer generation, which began in the late 1960's, saw the development of upwardly compatible "families" of computer models. All models within a family could run identical programs with little or no modification.

It is generally agreed that the third generation began around 1966 when manufacturers introduced the concept of a family of computers of which the IBM System/360 was the first example. The System/360 family included a small business machine, designated model 30, and other models up to large, powerful machines for both business and scientific application. Each model had a unique number and, in general, the higher the number, the greater the computational power. A problem with second generation machines had been that programs developed for smaller machines would not run or work properly on larger machines, even those built by the same company. This was the main reason for the development of the family concept. Now, a company could purchase or lease a small machine at first; then, as the company grew, a larger machine in the same family could be purchased or leased, and programs developed for the small machine could be executed or run on the larger machine with little or no modification to the programs. This is referred to as upward compatibility.

The first integrated circuits appeared in third-generation computers.

Another feature that signaled the beginning of the third generation computers was the use of miniature circuit modules and integrated circuits. The miniature hybrid circuit modules, called solid logic technology by IBM, had the bare chip transistor (rather than in a package) and chip capacitors mounted on a small ceramic substrate on to which resistors and conductors had been screened and fired. The whole module was about 0.5 in.(127 mm) square. However, most computer manufacturers soon switched to using the integrated circuit (IC). The IC was invented by Jack Kilby at Texas Instruments in 1958 and TI and many other semiconductor manufacturers have developed and manufactured a wide variety of all types of circuits since that time. A typical IC as shown in *Figure 1-18* is a small package which varies in size, but typically is about 1 in.(25.4 mm) long, 0.5 in.(12.7 mm) wide, and 0.125 in.(3.4 mm) thick. Inside is a very small silicon chip with many interconnected transistors and other components (*Figure 1-12*). The first IC's contained only a few components, but as the technology improved, higher levels of integration were achieved. (We'll talk more about this a little later.) So we see that a third generation computer using IC's was much smaller, more reliable, less expensive, and used less electrical power for the same computational power as a second generation machine.

**Figure 1-18.
IC Package.**

Fourth Generation Computers

Microprocessors — CPU's on a chip — came into use in fourth-generation computers of the 1970's.

The distinction between the third and fourth generation is not as clear as it was between the preceding generations. Some people thought that the fourth generation began with the IBM System/370 family (an updated version of the System 360), but many other people felt that the fourth generation began with the advent of the microprocessor. The microprocessor is a complete central processing unit (CPU) on one integrated circuit chip. More recent technological advances have permitted memory and input/output functions to be included on the same chip so that a total microcomputer is on one chip. The first microprocessor was a 4-bit processor. It appeared on the market in 1971, but was rapidly followed by an 8-bit microprocessor. Now, 16-bit microprocessors are available.

The next step is 32 bits. The number of bits a processor can accommodate is an indication of its capabilities or computational power. More bits provide greater power if other things are equal. These first microprocessors were limited in their computational performance, but by the late 1970's the microprocessors were as powerful and sophisticated as the CPU's in the second generation or even some of the third generation computers. Some of the more widely used microprocessors are shown in *Table 1-2*.

**Table 1-2.
Widely Used
Microprocessors.**

NUMBER OF BITS	MANUFACTURER	TYPE NUMBER
4	Texas Instruments	1000
4	Intel	4004
8	Intel	8080,8085
8	Fairchild	F-8
8	Motorola	6800,6809
8	National	IMP-8
8	RCA	Cosmac
8	Mos Technology	6502
8	Signetics	2650
8	Zilog	Z-80
16	Texas Instruments	9900
16	Motorola	68000
16	Intel	8086
16	Zilog	Z-8000

Examples of fourth generation computers are the TI-99/4 and TRS-80 and computers like them.

Continual improvements in technology have tremendously increased the number of components and connections that can be placed on an IC chip.

The microprocessor and computer-on-a-chip were made possible by the development and refinement of the techniques that were used for the first integrated circuit and by newly developed techniques to increase circuit density. Circuit density refers to how many components and interconnections can be put on a chip. The maximum density is limited by manufacturing techniques since the spacing is fantastically small, by the type of circuit, and by how much electrical power it must handle. Circuit density in IC's is normally referred to by "level of integration" which uses a common, simple gate circuit as the basis of comparison. The progressive increase in the level of integration is shown in *Table 1-3*:

**Table 1-3.
Level of Integration.**

LEVEL OF INTEGRATION	NUMBER OF GATES PER CHIP	PERIOD
Small Scale Integration (SSI)	12	Early 1960s
Medium Scale Integration (MSI)	100	Late 1960s
Large Scale Integration (LSI)	1,000	Early 1970s
Very Large Scale Integration (VLSI)	50,000	Late 1970s

As circuit density has
risen, costs have dropped.

You can see that the level of integration increased 4,000 times from SSI to VLSI in a period of less than 20 years. But this is not the complete picture, because the area of the chip used *per gate* was being decreased at the same time, so that the total chip size did not increase in proportion to the total number of gates. In fact the chip size only increased by 25 times. Since the size of the IC chip did not increase much, and since improvements in the manufacturing process held down processing costs, the cost of each IC chip increased only slightly. But, because of the increase in gates per chip, the cost *per gate* had been reduced tremendously by a factor of 1000. This has provided a very low-cost CPU with outstanding computational capability for use in computer systems that are small size, use low power and are highly reliable.

IC's have also provided another benefit to computer systems. In addition to low cost microprocessors and microcomputers, VLSI has allowed large semiconductor memories to be placed on a single chip. A 65,536 bit memory on a chip, as shown in *Figure 1-19*, is now commonly available. This size memory is generally referred to as a 64K memory. (K means 1024 or 2^{10} when used in reference to computer words, bytes, and bits because the binary number system and powers of two are used in computers. You probably already know that K means 1000 or 10^3 in the decimal number system which we use in our everyday life. Number systems will be discussed in Chapter 2.) From these two developments, along with advances in the software that is used to program computer systems, even smaller, more efficient, more capable computer systems will evolve.

**Figure 1-19.
64K Memory Chip.**

DEVELOPMENT OF COMPUTER SOFTWARE

We mentioned earlier in this chapter that software is the general term used to refer to computer programs and their documentation. The term was coined from "soft" and "ware" because the paper on which the programs were written was "soft" as opposed to the hard metal and plastic of the hardware of the physical computer.

THE PROGRAM

A computer, that is, the hardware, is completely dumb and useless without a program. In some special purpose computers, particulary those using a microprocessor, the program may be "built-in" to the hardware during manufacture using a type of memory called a read-only-memory (ROM). As the name suggests, the memory contents cannot be changed; therefore, the program cannot be changed. In fact, as shown in *Figure 1-20* preprogrammed software in ROM is contained in modules that are packaged to just plug-in to the system. (This ROM software is sometimes referred to as "firmware".) However, in most computers, the program is read in or loaded to the computer memory from storage media such as punched cards, paper tape, magnetic tape, or magnetic disk. When that program is finished and the task is complete, the computer memory is cleared and a new program is loaded to do a different task. As you recall from our earlier discussion, this stored program concept was a major contribution to the success of the commercial computer.

The first uses of the mass-produced computer were for sorting and tabulating large volumes of data, for solving difficult scientific and mathematical calculations, or for performing obvious repetitive and time consuming chores. Most people did not know how to use a computer, and even many who did, did not recognize its true potential. It was a time of learning.

Some specialized computer programs may be permanently stored in ROM (Read-Only Memory). In most cases, however, programs are read into RAM (Random-Access Memory) and stored for the duration of a task. Afterwards, the memory can be cleared for a new task.

**Figure 1-20.
Software Plug-In Module
for Home Computer.**

Because of this, almost all early computer programs were written by a person with very narrow vision, by a person looking only for a solution to his immediate problem. That is, the programs were written for one application without considering that a slight modification in the program would also allow it to solve someone else's problem. Fortunately, someone woke up to the fact that they were using many of the same steps, or even whole blocks of steps, in many different one-application programs. This led to the development of programs and procedures that were more general and could be used in other applications. You'll learn more about these later in this book.

COMPUTER LANGUAGES

Computers execute their instructions in machine language, which consists of binary 1's and 0's. Computers interact with their human operators in higher-level languages such as FORTRAN and COBOL.

A computer program is written in a special computer language. Humans can communicate with each other in our most simple and universal language which is the sign language. However, we normally communicate or talk in a higher-level language called English. We could also communicate in other languages such as Spanish or German if we both studied and learned these languages. We communicate with computers by using their language, which we also have to learn. Computers, too, can be made to use different languages, but they can handle only the one they were designed for. The most simple and universal computer language is called *machine language* which consists of binary digits. You remember we said that there are only two binary digits, 0 and 1, and that the short name for binary digit is *bit*. The machine language is what the computer uses to talk to itself; that is, within the machine. However, the machine language is much too tedious and time consuming for us to use to talk to the computer. Because of this, higher level programming languages were developed for us to use. These languages allow us to make one short simple statement using our alphabet and decimal system to instruct the computer to perform an operation that may take many steps of machine language within the computer. Let's review some of these higher-level language developments.

**Table 1-4.
High-Level Computer
Languages**

LANGUAGE NAME	FEATURE
FORTRAN	Scientific Applications
COBOL	Business Applications
PL/I	Combines best of FORTRAN and COBOL
PASCAL	Proper Programming Techniques
BASIC	Ideal for personal computers

Different computer languages have been developed for different applications.

As shown in *Table 1-4*, two of the commonly used high level languages are FORTRAN for scientific applications and COBOL for business applications. These have been further developed and refined since their introduction to make them more versatile and useful. These were, and still are powerful languages; however, many other languages have also been developed. One of these, PL/I, was developed by IBM by taking the best features of FORTRAN and the best features of COBOL and putting them together. That description is an oversimplification, of course, but you get the idea.

One of the reasons PL/I was developed was to enhance the concept of compatible software. You recall that we talked about the upward compatibility of the IBM System/360 family of computers. This concept applied to all software so that it could be compatible, transportable, maintainable, and more efficient.

The Pascal programming language was developed as a tool for teaching good programming techniques. Remember we mentioned that as programmers moved along the learning curve of their technology, they discovered that program steps could be grouped as procedures or routines and used in different programs. Structured programming was a product of that continuing evolution. Structured programming incorporates a number of ideas. "Top down" program design is the first. This means dividing the program development into parts at levels from the top. Each level is a more detailed description of the program step above it. Structuring the program into basic functions is the second idea. "If-Then-Else", "Do-While", "Do-Test" structures and sequential control with the program segment being developed are examples. With these principles, a program segment written for one application may be more easily used again in another program for another application. This makes for more efficient use of the dollars paid for the cost of preparing software.

Another programming language called BASIC was developed to simplify programming so that many more people could use computers. Instruction statements in BASIC look very similar to an ordinary mathematical statement in the English language. BASIC received widespread usage when the personal computer came on the market. BASIC is appropriate for these computers because it is easier to learn and it can be used as an interactive language; that is, the computer responds directly to input instructions by displaying the results as the program is executed.

SOFTWARE SUPPORT

The proliferation of small computers has heightened the demand for good pre-programmed software.

The widespread use of minicomputers and microcomputers brought on the requirement for much more compatible and reusable software which could be used on other machines that use the same language. Programs that do payroll, business accounting, inventory, etc. written by original developers were now being offered for sale to be used by other persons with compatible systems. In fact, some of the older lanuages were revised or redesigned to meet the new requirements.

Out of all of this, the term "software engineering" has been coined to describe the process of breaking down a problem into smaller parts and designing the software structure to meet these compatibility requirements. As high-level languages were developed to make it easier for humans to get their ideas into a form so that a computer could be used to solve their problem or perform a task, more software was required to translate the higher level languages into machine language that the computer could understand. In general, this software has been given the name compiler.

Therefore, as each high-level language was developed, compilers (the software to interpret and translate the high-level language to machine language) had to be developed so that the high-level lanuage program could run on a system. Manufacturers of systems were required to have the compilers developed for the various languages for their system as an incentive to use their systems.

As the personal computers came on the market, the demand for this same support software requirement became even greater. Because more and more people with less and less programming and computer usage experience are beginning to use computers, the need for good preprogrammed software is essential. Therefore, many programming hours will be required to fulfill this growing need for preprogrammed software for the future.

So, we find computer software has been evolving right along with the computer hardware; and just as surely, software will continue to change to accommodate new hardware developments and new programming techniques.

WHAT HAVE WE LEARNED?

In this first chapter, we looked at how the computer affects our daily lives, reviewed the development of the computer hardware from the abacus to the microcomputer and reviewed the development of computer software. We defined computer science and we learned that the major functional blocks of an electronic digital computer are input/output, memory, and CPU. We became acquainted with some of the terms used in discussing computer systems such as: peripheral equipment, programs, computational power, bit, program execution, hardware, software, down time, upward compatibility, and structured programming. We saw that computers are classified by physical size and computational power, and that cost comparisons are often made on the basis of bits-per-second-per-dollar. We learned that the microprocessor has brought the power of a computer to each of us on a personal basis at a relatively low price with devices like the hand-held calculators and single-chip microcomputers. We learned that the microprocessor was made possible by the integrated circuit and we saw that the level of integration has advanced from SSI to VLSI in just a few years. We learned that software developed right along with hardware and that it has changed to meet the requirements of more and more people using computers.

WHAT'S NEXT?

In the next chapter, we will explain the physical computer and peripheral equipment, and how they can be fit together to form a computer system. Future chapters explain programming and other facets of the study of computer science. Take some time to answer the quiz that follows to check your understanding of this chapter before going on.

Quiz for Chapter 1

1. Relate the following men to the
   appropriate technological advances.
   4 **a.** Babbage   **1.** Stored Program
   5 **b.** Hollerith   **2.** Integrated Circuit
   3 **c.** Aiken   **3.** Mark I
   1 **d.** Von   **4.** Analytical Engine
       Neumann   **5.** Punched Card
   2 **e.** Kilby   **6.** ENIAC
   6 **f.** Eckert

2. Relate the following terms.
   5 **a.** TI-99/4   **1.** Second
   4 **b.** System/360   Generation
   1 **c.** 1604   Machine
   2 **d.** 650   **2.** First Generation
   3 **e.** 8085   Machine
              3. Microprocessor
              4. Third Generation
                  Machine
              5. Personal
                  Computer

3. Answer the following questions
   true or false.
   a. The abacus is still useful for
   adding numbers.   T
   b. The first electronic computer
   used transistors.   F
   c. Microprocessor technology was
   responsible for the personal
   computer.   T

4. Answer the following true or false.
   a. Most microcomputers are as
   powerful as the first and some of
   the second generation
   computers.   T
   b. Current computers operate in a
   manner similar to the abacus.   F
   c. Serial transfer of data is usually
   faster than parallel transfer.   F
   d. The vacuum tube is rarely used
   in today's computers.   T
   e. The fourth generation of
   computers was initiated by the
   introduction of the transistor.   F

5. When one gives the size of memory
   as 64K, this typically means:
   a. 64,000 bits
   b. 65,536 bits
   c. 64,000 words

6. Match the following pairs.
   3 **a.** TI-9900   **1.** 4-bit
   2 **b.** INTEL 8080   **2.** 8-bit
   1 **c.** INTEL 4004   **3.** 16-bit

7. Relate the following terms:
   3 **a.** BASIC   **1.** Scientific
   1 **b.** FORTRAN   **2.** Business
   2 **c.** COBOL   **3.** Personal
   1 **d.** IBM 1620
   3 **e.** TI-99/4

8. Answer the following questions
   true or false.
   a. Down time is the time a
   computer cannot function
   properly.   T
   b. Firmware means that the
   program is listed on hard paper.   F
   c. A compiler is a machine.   F
   d. The concept of storing a
   computer program in the
   machine's memory was of little
   significance in computer
   development.   F

9. Structured programming was
   developed
   a. To decrease computer hardware
   cost
   b. To decrease memory
   requirements
   c. To develop more transportable
   and useable software
   d. None of the above

10. Relate the following terms:
    4 **a.** Software   **1.** Structured
    3 **b.** CPU,   Programming
         Memory,   **2.** Binary Digit
         Input/   **3.** Main Divisions
         Output   of Computer
    1 **c.** Software   **4.** Computer
         Engineering   Program
    7 **d.** ROM   **5.** Magnetic Tape
    2 **e.** Bit   **6.** Peripheral
    5 **f.** Auxiliary   Equipment
         Storage   **7.** Unchangeable
         Medium   Memory
    6 **g.** Magnetic
         Disk Unit

(Answers in back of book.)

Computer Architecture and Hardware

ABOUT THIS CHAPTER

Recall that in the previous chapter we said that a set of instructions arranged in a sequence is called a program. The program is used to tell the computer how to perform a selected task. After the program is entered into the computer, the computer executes operations called for by the instructions and accomplishes the specified task. The computer programs and their descriptions are referred to as software. The actual computer and the equipment that works with it are referred to as the hardware. In this chapter we are going to look at the computer hardware, how the units function, and how they fit together. In the next chapter we will look at software and, in particular, how software is developed.

COMPUTER COMPONENTS

CPU, memory, and I/O: the three main elements of a computer system.

Recall that the three main units of a digital computer system are the CPU or central processing unit, memory, and I/O or input-output units (*Figure 2-1*).

**Figure 2-1.
Main Units of a
Computer.**

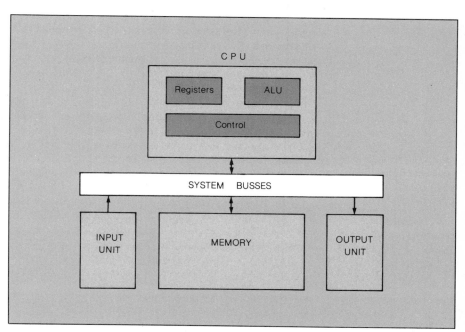

The CPU regulates the activity of the overall computer system.

The central processing unit, or processor, as some call it, is the nerve center of the system. It performs the central control functions. All the computational, logical, and operational decisions are made here. It contains the logic circuitry for performing the various computational activities. It controls the operation of all the functional units. It fetches machine instructions from memory, decodes these instructions and insures that the operations called for by the instructions are executed correctly. In order to do all this, it communicates or interfaces with the input and output units and the memory.

The memory stores instructions and data inputs for computer operations, as well as data generated by computer operations.

The memory unit is used to store instructions and data. Instructions in the form of digital codes are stored in a step-by-step sequence so the computer system knows what to do. While it is doing a particular operation it needs data to use or operate on. This data is usually brought in through an input unit and stored in memory. After the computer system has completed an operation it stores the results of the operation in memory. This also is data. Data may be words, letters, characters, numbers, symbols, etc.

The input/output units transfer information from the outside world to the computer, or to the outside world from the computer.

The input units, as the name implies, pass input information to the computer. The input information may be programs or program related, or it may be data.

Output units send the information from inside the computer to the outside so we can use it. The output from the computer may appear on a video display (a TV-like screen), be printed out on a printer, be displayed on an LED (light emitting diode) display, be sent to another digital system over a transmission line, or be stored in auxiliary storage such as magnetic tape or magnetic disks.

How the System Units Work Together

When the system units are working together, results of computations are periodically being saved in memory for read-out at a later time or new data is being written into the memory and saved for use at a later time. The data may be communicated into the system from the outside by the input units, used internally in the system, or fed outside the system by the output units.

The central processing unit controls what happens. It tells the input when to bring information into the system, or the output to write information. It sends signals to the output to turn on a motor or form a letter or number on a display. It controls when and at what time each operation is to be accomplished. The CPU does this by following instructions stored in memory in a step-by-step sequence called the program.

Inside the computer, the information is not recognizable as written letters or numbers because it is all converted to electrical signals of digital codes so that it may be handled easily inside the computer system. Let's see how these signals are handled.

The digital codes carrying the information inside the computer system must be coupled from one unit to another. The multiple wires which do this are called busses. There are three principles busses in a computer system as shown in *Figure 2-2.*

**Figure 2-2.
Three Principal Busses
of a Computer.**

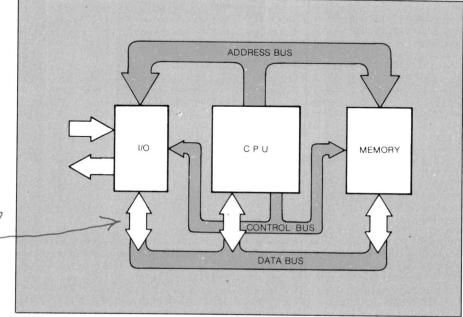

This bus carries data in both directions.

Address, Control and Data Busses

Digitally coded information travels among the CPU, memory, and I/O units on electrical connections called busses.

When mail comes to your home it must be addressed correctly in order for the post office to locate you. So it is with the computer. Each I/O unit of the computer system is given an address and each information location in memory is given an address. To locate specific information in memory, a digital code — the address of the information — is sent on the address bus to memory by the CPU. At the same time, other digital codes representing control signals are sent on the control bus (*Figure 2-2*) to tell the memory what to do — either to read or to write information from the memory location designated by the address on the address bus. The information coming to the CPU from the memory when the memory is read, or going to the memory from the CPU to be written into memory, is also in digital codes and travels along the data bus. The description just presented for memory also applies to any I/O unit.

This is necessarily a simplified description of the signals on the busses because many functions are involved and each requires a separate signal that is synchronized to occur at a specific time. But basically, the address signals, the control signals, and the data signals (which may be either data or instructions in the program) flowing at set times control all the operations of the computer system.

For more efficiency, some computer systems use a supplementary processor to control the interaction between the CPU and external devices.

**Figure 2-3.
Computer With an I/O
Processor.**

As shown in *Figure 2-3*, sometimes an additional special processor is used to provide more efficient system operations by relieving some of the control requirements of the central processor unit. When used as such, the I/O processor is referred to as a data channel, direct memory access channel, or peripheral processor.

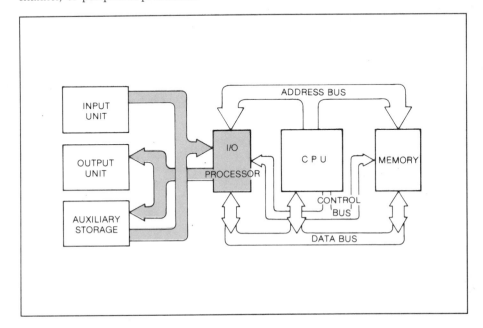

Figure 2-4 shows a common type of input medium which was shown previously. It is a punched card, often called an "IBM card". It has holes located in coded patterns with a unique code for each number or letter. The original cards are punched by a key-punch machine in response to an operator's input on a typewriter-like keyboard.

**Figure 2-4.
Punched Card.**

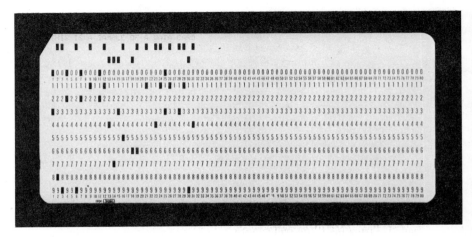

A typical sequence of events: the program and data are encoded and read into computer memory, the CPU executes the program, and the final results are output to a printer.

Figure 2-5 summarizes the information flow that has been discussed. The punched cards containing the instructions that make up the computer program and the data to be used in the program are read into the system by a card reader and stored in memory. Each instruction is then read from memory (fetched) by the CPU in the order directed by the program. The CPU interprets (decodes) the instruction and performs (executes) the operation called for in the instruction. The final results are normally outputted to the printer. Intermediate or temporary results are stored in memory for later use.

**Figure 2-5.
Information Flow.**

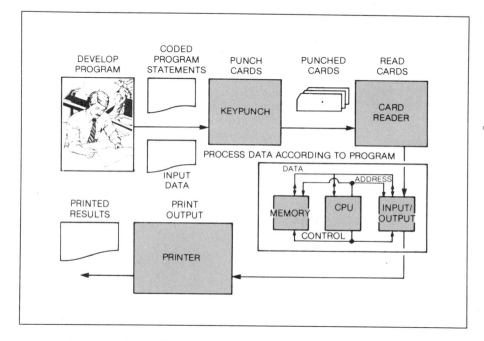

Before we begin discussing the computer system units in more detail we need to understand more about how the digital codes we previously talked about represent information.

LOGIC CIRCUITS AND BINARY BITS

In Chapter 1 you saw how solid-state technology and, in particular, integrated circuits have contributed significantly to the advancement of the use of computers. It was mentioned that large numbers of logic circuits are contained on a single integrated circuit. One of the reasons this is possible is because a large number of the circuits are alike. They are called logic circuits because they make logic decisions electronically. Decisions such as A AND B, A OR B and NOT A or NOT B being a particular value are the types used over and over again in computer systems hardware.

The density of modern IC's is possible in part because of the similarity of the circuitry in them. Logical functions like AND, OR, and NOT form the basis of many different types of digital devices.

Figure 2-6a shows one such circuit represented symbolically. Electronically it operates with a power supply of +5V and electrical signals that vary on the inputs and outputs from +2.4V to 0V.

In *Figure 2-6b* the voltage levels that appear at the inputs and the output for this circuit are plotted against time. During time t_0 input A and input B are at 0V and output C is at 0V. At time t_1, input A has changed to +2.4V, input B is still at 0V and output C is at 0V.

At t_2 input B also changes to +2.4V so that A AND B are at +2.4V. Now output C is at +2.4V.

At t_3 input B has gone down to 0V and so has output C.

At t_4 all signals are at 0V, while at t_5, even though input B has gone up to +2.4V output, C still is at 0V because input A is at 0V.

At t_6, input A goes up to +2.4V while input B also remains at +2.4V and thus output C is at +2.4V.

As input A goes back down to 0V at t_7, output C also goes down to 0V even though input B is still at +2.4V.

At t_8 all levels are again at 0V.

From the time diagram of the levels (*Figure 2-6b*) it is apparent that the signal is only at one of two levels at any time in its operation, either +2.4V or 0V. In order to keep track of the levels easier, in *Figure 2-6c* a 1 has been assigned to the +2.4V level and a 0 has been assigned to the 0V level. The condition of each input and output then can be identified easily at any point in time.

Individual inputs and outputs in digital circuits are always in either of only two possible states: 1 or 0 (high or low).

**Figure 2-6.
AND Gate Operation.**

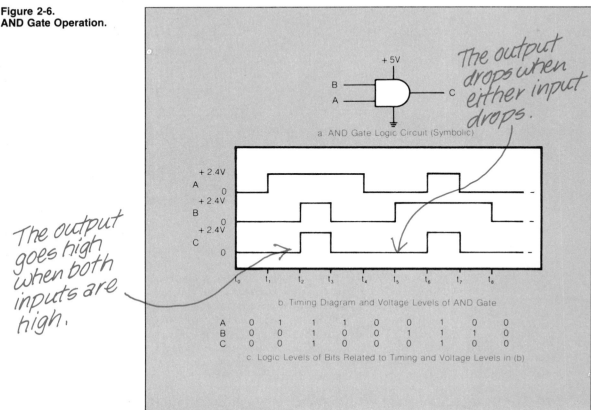

a. AND Gate Logic Circuit (Symbolic)

The output drops when either input drops.

The output goes high when both inputs are high.

b. Timing Diagram and Voltage Levels of AND Gate

	t_0	t_1	t_2	t_3	t_4	t_5	t_6	t_7	t_8
A	0	1	1	1	0	0	1	0	0
B	0	0	1	0	0	1	1	1	0
C	0	0	1	0	0	0	1	0	0

c. Logic Levels of Bits Related to Timing and Voltage Levels in (b)

Examining *Figure 2-6c* reveals that output C is a 1 only when A AND B are both a 1 at the same time. This is how the logic circuit gets its name because electronically it performs the logical AND function.

The signal level can only have one of two states; therefore, it is called a binary circuit and it can only represent one bit of information which can either have a value of 1 or 0.

A "truth table" is used to illustrate the combination of logical or binary input signals which yield a binary output for a specific gate type. The truth tables for the AND, OR and NOT gates are illustrated in *Figure 2-7*. The OR gate is different from the AND gate in that it requires only one of the two input signals to be a one (or 2.4 volts) at any given instant of time in order for the output C to be a logical one. Only when both of the input signals A and B are zero will the ouput signal C be zero.

The NOT gate simply performs an inversion on a signal. When the input signal is a one, the output is a zero and visa versa.

An AND gate's output is 1 if both inputs are 1.

An OR gate's output is 1 if either or both inputs are 1.

A NOT gate inverts its input.

**Figure 2-7.
AND, OR, and NOT Gates
With Truth Tables.**

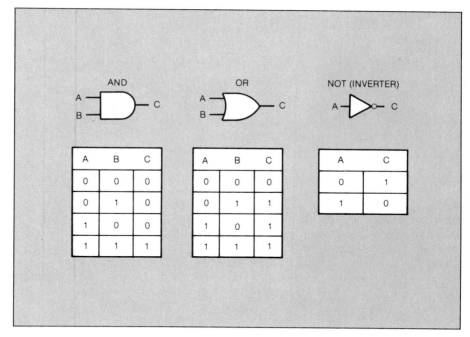

As noted, the computer is made up of thousands and sometimes millions of such circuits. These circuits handle the digital information in digital codes, detect the codes, and execute the operations called for in the codes. Because all of this is being done within the machine in digital code, the codes are called machine language or machine instructions.

Number Systems

For efficiency and simplicity, computers represent information as binary numbers. Binary digits ("bits") have only two possible values, rather than ten.

The machine instructions and data used by these instructions are represented internally as digital codes or numbers consisting of binary digits instead of the usual decimal digits with which we are familar. Numbers represented by binary digits belong to the binary number system. The binary number system is similar to the decimal number system except that a binary digit, referred to as a bit (binary digit), can take on only two values, 0 and 1.

A decimal digit on the other hand, can take on ten values (0 through 9). Number systems have a base or radix. For the decimal system it is ten. When the number equals the radix, it can no longer be represented by one digit so another digit must be added. The amount of weighting for the additional digits depends on its position relative to the decimal point. The weighting is always a power of 10. For example, the digits in the number 567 have the following decimal weights:

$$\text{Coefficient} \times \text{Weight} = \text{Product}$$
$$5 \times 100 \text{ or } 10^2 = 500$$
$$6 \times 10 \text{ or } 10^1 = 60$$
$$7 \times 1 \text{ or } 10^0 = \underline{7}$$
$$\text{Sum of Products} = 567$$

That is, the weights are 10^2, 10^1, and 10^0. We commonly say that the digits have place value. In each digit place the digit value can vary between 0 and 9. The first place is called the units place. If there is a 9 in the units place and 1 is added to it, the units digit is changed to 0 and the next digit (ten's place) is made a 1. By moving the one to the ten's place we have weighted it by a 10^1 power of 10. In general, any decimal integer number can be expressed by the sum of the products of coefficients (the digits 0 thru 9) and the weights (powers of 10).

As in the decimal system, the relative position of a binary digit indicates its weight.

It would be simpler for us to understand machine codes if computers used decimal circuits. They don't, however, primarily because logic circuits can be designed for more efficient operation by using binary circuits. For computers, the thousands of circuits implement numbers by their binary representation. For the binary system, or base 2, the position of each binary digit relative to the binary point determines its weighting. The weights in this case however, are a power of 2 rather than 10 as in the decimal system.

Thus the binary number 1011 (which is read as one zero one one, not one thousand eleven) can be converted to its decimal equivalent, as follows:

$$1 \times 2^3 = 1 \times 8 = 8$$
$$0 \times 2^2 = 0 \times 4 = 0$$
$$1 \times 2^1 = 1 \times 2 = 2$$
$$1 \times 2^0 = 1 \times 1 = \underline{1}$$
$$\text{Sum of Products} = 11$$

Hexadecimal Numbers

The hexadecimal numbering system uses the base 16, with 10 through 15 represented by the letters A through F.

A similar situation exists for numbers to other bases. This is illustrated in *Table 2-1*. For hexadecimal numbers, that is, numbers to the base 16, the hexadecimal digits may take on values 0 to 15. The problem with the hexadecimal number system is that we must have a one digit symbol for the numbers ten through fifteen such as those used for the numbers zero through nine. Thus the alphabetic characters A thru F were selected to represent these values. That is, the letter A is used to represent the number 10, B the number 11, C the number 12, D the number 13, E the number 14, and F the largest number 15. Notice in *Table 2-1* that when 1 is added to F, the 16^0 digit is zero with a carry to the 16^1 digit. This produces the number 10 which is read as one zero, not ten.

**Table 2-1.
Comparison of Numbers in Different Bases.**

BASE 10 DECIMAL	BASE 2 BINARY	BASE 16 HEXADECIMAL
0	00000	0
1	00001	1
2	00010	2
3	00011	3
4	00100	4
5	00101	5
6	00110	6
7	00111	7
8	01000	8
9	01001	9
10	01010	A
11	01011	B
12	01100	C
13	01101	D
14	01110	E
15	01111	F
16	10000	10

Examples:

255 decimal = 11111111 binary = FF hexadecimal
256 decimal = 100000000 binary = 100 hexadecimal

Since the computer is constructed from binary circuits, the digital codes for instructions and data are maintained internally as binary numbers. That is, if we have a register within the CPU (remember that registers are used within the CPU for holding temporary results) which can contain 8 bits of information, then the largest number which may be kept in this 8-bit register will be:

$$1\,1\,1\,1\,1\,1\,1\,1$$

or:

$$1 \times 2^7 + 1 \times 2^6 + 1 \times 2^5 + 1 \times 2^4 + 1 \times 2^3 + 1 \times 2^2 + 1 \times 2^1 + 1 \times 2^0 = 255$$

The largest number a register can contain can be stated by using the number of bits as a power of 2 and subtracting 1 as; $2^8 - 1 = 256 - 1 = 255$ decimal. For a 16-bit register the largest number is $2^{16} - 1 = 65536 - 1 = 65535$ decimal. We see that the greater the number of bits, the larger the number which may be stored and that for an N-bit register the largest number is $2^N - 1$.

Arranging bits in groups of four lets you readily convert binary to hexadecimal numbers or hexadecimal to binary numbers.

Hexadecimal numbers can be converted from binary numbers and **vice-versa** by inspection. The process simply involves grouping bits by four's beginning with the least significant four bits. Then these bits are replaced by their hexadecimal equivalent or:

$$\underset{4}{\underline{0100}} \quad \underset{8}{\underline{1000}} \quad \underset{E}{\underline{1110}} \quad = 48E$$

In converting hexadecimal to binary, the hexadecimal digit is converted to its binary equivalent as illustrated:

$$\underset{1010}{\underline{A}} \quad \underset{1111}{\underline{F}} \quad \underset{0011}{\underline{3}} \quad \underset{0111}{\underline{7}}$$

Hexadecimal notation is much easier to note and record than binary bits because of its simpler form.

Although the computer works well with binary numbers, typically, humans do not. For one thing, it takes too many bits to represent a number. Suppose we wanted to show the contents of a 16-bit register within the CPU. To display contents of each bit within the register would take 16 LED's or lamps as illustrated in *Figure 2-8a*. If we used hexadecimal alpha-numeric displays and decoder circuits which perform the simple conversion just illustrated, we would need only 4 displays as shown in *Figure 2-8b*. Just think, if we had a 32-bit register, then we would need 32 such digits. Just writing the following 32-bit binary number can be exhausting and we are likely to make an error:

1010 1111 0101 0111 0110 0001 0001 1011

It is much easier to write

AF57611B

Therefore, most printouts (sometimes called a "dump") or displays of the machine's internal contents are in hexadecimal rather than binary.

ARITHMETIC OPERATIONS

We have learned that instructions and data are represented internally in the computer in digital codes and that these codes are expressed in the binary number system. A specific code will be used for an add instruction, another code for a subtract, and yet another for a store data into memory instruction. A code will be used to represent the upper case alphabetic character W and another for the lower case w. A code will be used for the number 3.2 and another code for 0.0045. Thus the computer always performs arithmetic and logical operations on numbers.

Figure 2-8.
Binary and Hexadecimal
Display of a 16-Bit
Number.

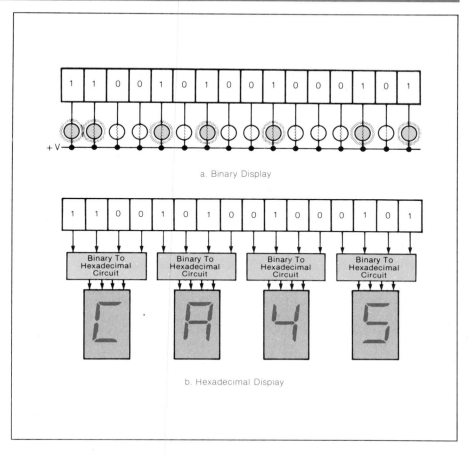

a. Binary Display

b. Hexadecimal Display

Integer Representation

Computers can represent integers (whole numbers) by simply converting decimal integers to their binary equivalents. An eight-bit register can store values of up to 255.

Decimal numbers are usually first converted to the binary equivalent and may be represented in either integer or floating point. First, let's look at integers. If we have an 8-bit register, we may express integer decimal numbers between 0 and $2^8 - 1$ or 255, by converting decimal to its binary equivalent. If we have a 16-bit register, we can store integer decimal numbers between 0 and $2^{16} - 1$ or 65535.

For integer numbers, the decimal or binary point is fixed and is always to the right of the least significant digit, therefore, fractions cannot be represented. The magnitude of the number is always restricted by $2^N - 1$ where N is the number of bits within the registers or memory cell where the number is being stored.

So we have a method to represent positive numbers, but we also need a way to represent negative numbers. An easy way to do this in binary is to take the complement of the number. The complement of a number is the amount necessary to add to a number to make it complete for a given number system. For instance, if we say that 9 is the largest value a digit can have, the complement of 4 is 5 since 4 + 5 is 9. For the binary system, the complement of 1 is 0 and of 0 is 1. The one's complement representation is where each bit is changed or complemented. The one's complement of the 5-bit number 00110 is 11001. The two's complement is obtained by adding one to the one's complement, or, the two's complement of 01001 is 10111 (10110 + 00001 = 10111).

We can let the most significant bit represent the sign bit. Then if the sign bit is one, the number is negative; if the sign bit is zero, the number is positive. In our decimal number system, if we algebraically add the negative of a number to another number, the results are the same as subtracting the absolute value of the negative number from the other number. In binary representation, this also holds; that is, we can subtract by adding. We do this by taking the two's complement of the number to be subtracted and then adding. For example, to subtract decimal 9 from decimal 13, we convert decimal 9 and 13 to binary, take the two's complement of 9, and add it to 13.

Adding a negative number to a positive number is a simple way to subtract. Computers do this by taking the two's complement (one's complement plus one) of the subtrahend (the number to be subtracted) and adding it to another number. •

$$
\begin{array}{ll}
9 = 01001 & 13 = 01101 \\
\text{One's complement} = 10110 & +(-9) = \underline{10111} \\
+ \underline{00001} & 4 = 00100 \\
\text{Two's complement} = 10111 &
\end{array}
$$

Binary numbers are added as follows:

$$
\begin{array}{cccc}
0 & 0 & 1 & 1 \\
\underline{+0} & \underline{+1} & \underline{+0} & \underline{+1} \\
0 & 1 & 1 & 10
\end{array}
$$

Zero plus zero is zero; zero plus one is one; one plus zero is one; and one plus one is zero with a one carried to next place to be added to the next significant bit.

When set to accommodate an equal number of positive and negative values, a 16-bit register can hold values from −32768 to +32767. When the number stored is negative, the most significant bit is always 1; with positive numbers, it is always 0.

Now we see that if we want to accommodate an equal amount of positive and negative numbers, a sixteen bit register can contain numbers from −32768 to +32767 or −2^{15} to 2^{15} − 1. The reason they are not both 2^{15} is because one combination is taken up for the zero value. This is more easily seen if we examine a 2-bit register. The combinations are:

Bit 1	Bit 0	Decimal Value
0	1	+1
0	0	0
1	1	−1
1	0	−2

That is, there are 2^2 or 2^n combinations and one combination is for the number zero. Negative numbers are represented by their two's complement and the most significant bit is the sign bit.

Floating Point Representation

Computers represent fractions and large numbers with a floating-point system similar to scientific notation. Numbers are expressed as decimal values raised to a power.

What we have just discussed is useful for integer numbers. But what if we want to represent a fractional number like 5.724 or a very large number? Such numbers are represented using a system for a floating decimal point which is similar to the scientific notation used by engineers and scientists. For this notation, a number is expressed as a decimal value raised to some power. For instance, the number 32578619518102 could be expressed as 3.26×10^{13} or 0.32579×10^{14}. By rewriting the number in an exponent form, it is often much easier to manipulate but, as noted, we give up the digits that were rounded. As a result, some resolution (the number of digits in the fraction) is usually lost. Floating point notation works in a similar fashion. We are limited by the hardware in the number of bits our registers and memory cells can accommodate. However, we can divide the number of bits into two parts, one for the mantissa or fractional part and one for the sign and exponent as illustrated in *Figure 2-9*.

**Figure 2-9.
Floating Point
Representation.**

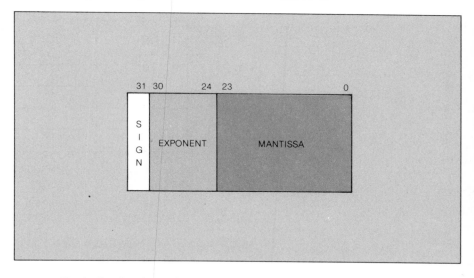

Typically, floating point numbers for the larger computers use a 32-bit number where 24 bits are selected for the mantissa and 8 bits for the sign and exponent. Most such computers also offer what is referred to as double precision which uses a 64-bit number representation, thereby increasing either the size of the mantissa, exponent, or both. This allows better resolution and accuracy, but increases execution time as two 32-bit words must be processed instead of one.

Thus, we see that we can also represent fractional or very large numbers internally within the computer by using the floating point scheme.

Addition

You may be wondering how the computer actually adds these numbers now that they have been converted to machine code. This is done in the Arithmetic and Logic Unit (ALU) which is part of the CPU.

A half-adder circuit can add two inputs and produce a sum and carry, but has no provision for handling a previous carry.

An add operation can be accomplished by use of AND, OR and NOT gates that are arranged to form a half-adder circuit (*Figure 2-10*). This may seem complicated but it's really not. Suppose we want to add the contents of two 1-bit registers. Such a register pair could only hold numbers between 0 and 1. That is, the largest number which could be contained by either register would be 1 and the smallest 0. Let's look at the truth table in *Figure 2-10* for performing this addition.

**Figure 2-10.
Half-Adder Circuit.**

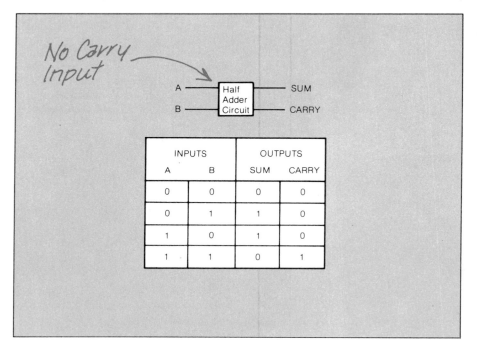

INPUTS		OUTPUTS	
A	B	SUM	CARRY
0	0	0	0
0	1	1	0
1	0	1	0
1	1	0	1

From this table, we can see that a sum of zero is obtained if both A and B are zero; 1 if either A or B is 1 but not both; and zero again, but with the carry of 1, if A and B are both 1. We can write a set of Boolean logic equations for performing this function as follows:

$$\overline{A} \cdot B + A \cdot \overline{B} = SUM$$
$$A \cdot B = CARRY$$

Note that $\overline{A}$ and $\overline{B}$ (read NOT A and NOT B) represent the complements of A and B.

The first equation is read as "NOT A and B or A and NOT B are equal to SUM". The second equation is read as "A and B are equal to CARRY".

Thus, suppose we want to add one plus zero $(1+0=1)$; let A = 1, B = 0 and apply them as inputs to the logical AND circuit. The SUM output will be a 1 and the carry output will be 0 to give the solution to the addition.

Figure 2-11.
Full Adder Circuit.

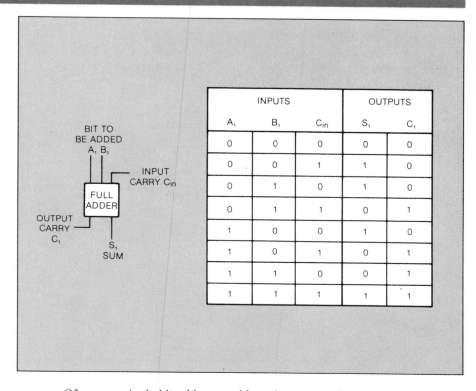

	INPUTS			OUTPUTS	
A_1	B_1	C_{in}	S_1	C_1	
0	0	0	0	0	
0	0	1	1	0	
0	1	0	1	0	
0	1	1	0	1	
1	0	0	1	0	
1	0	1	0	1	
1	1	0	0	1	
1	1	1	1	1	

A full adder circuit not only accepts the input bits to be added to produce a sum and a carry, but accepts a previous carry input as well.

Of course, single bit adders would not be very useful in a computer. N-bit adders, however, can be implemented with a number of 1-bit adders working together in stages. But this requires that a carry input be considered as shown in *Figure 2-11*. Each bit position has its own full adder stage which has its bit inputs and also a carry input from the preceding stage as illustrated in *Figure 2-12a*. Here the least significant bit of A (A_0) is added to the least significant bit of B (B_0), giving a sum (S_0) and carry (C_0) at time t_1 (*Figure 2-12b*). Next the carry out from stage 1 (C_0) is used along with the second bits of A (A_1) and B (B_1) to obtain S_1 and C_1 at t_2. This process then continues through all four stages. The sum outputs go to the accumulator register and the last carry bit goes to a special storage position called the output carry flip-flop. If we assume that each stage takes one second, it takes a minimum of 4 seconds to add two 4-bit numbers in this type of adder.

Subtraction, Multiplication and Division

Multiplication and division, in their most basic form, respectively consist of repeated addition and repeated subtraction.

We can subtract by simply obtaining the two's complement of the subtrahend and adding as was shown previously. We can multiply simply by repetitive addition; that is, $A \times B = A + A + A + A \ldots \ldots + A$, B times. We can divide by repetitive subtraction; that is, $B \div A = B - A - A - A \ldots - A$, until B is zero or smaller than A. Actually, better ways of multiplying and dividing are used but those are not necessary to our discussion at this time.

Figure 2-12.
Multi-bit Adder Circuit.

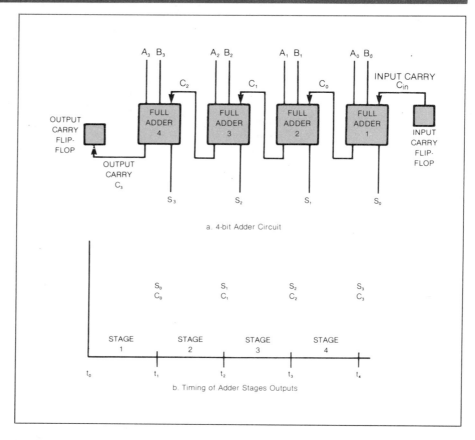

a. 4-bit Adder Circuit

b. Timing of Adder Stages Outputs

Logical Instructions

The logical operations of OR, AND, and NOT are done on a bit-by-bit basis. Each logical operation is performed as if the input were fed into a 2-input gate, each bit position at a time. Refer back to *Figure 2-7*. For the OR operation, the result or output bit is a 1 if either of the input bits is a 1. In the NOT operation, the result bit is a 1 if the input bit is a 0. The NOT operation is useful to product the complement of a number. For the AND operation, the result bit is a 1 only when both input bits are 1. Another logical operation, the exclusive OR (usually abbreviated as XOR), is usually provided. For this operation, the result bit is a 1 only if either input is a 1. If both inputs are 1 or both 0, the output is 0. (Notice that this is different from the normal OR where the output is 1 when either or both inputs are 1).

The OR operation can be used to set certain bits in a binary code to 1 without affecting other bits in a register. For example, if the present contents of register A are as shown in *Figure 2-13*, we can OR them with a binary number 00001001 to change bits 0 and 3 to a 1 without changing the other bits.

Figure 2-13.
Logical OR Operation.

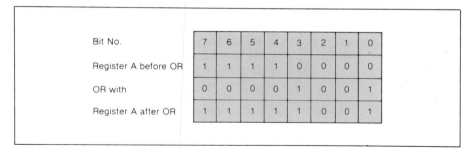

Bit No.	7	6	5	4	3	2	1	0
Register A before OR	1	1	1	1	0	0	0	0
OR with	0	0	0	0	1	0	0	1
Register A after OR	1	1	1	1	1	0	0	1

Logical operations (AND, OR, NOT, and XOR) let you test and manipulate the individual bits in binary numbers, based on logical decisions performed by electronic circuits.

The AND operation can be used to mask out certain bits of a number. For example, in *Figure 2-14*, if bit 0 is the only bit of interest in the register, it can be isolated by masking the other bits with an AND operation as shown.

Figure 2-14.
Logical AND Operation.

Bit No.	7	6	5	4	3	2	1	0
Register A Before AND	1	0	1	0	1	1	0	1
AND with	0	0	0	0	0	0	0	1
Register A After AND	0	0	0	0	0	0	0	1

The XOR operation can be used to compare two binary numbers to see if they are exactly the same. If they are, the output will be all zeros. If they are not the same, a 1 will be output for each bit that is different as shown in *Figure 2-15*.

Figure 2-15.
Logical XOR Operation.

	Numbers Alike	Numbers Not Alike
Number A	1101	1101
Number B	1101	1001
XOR Results	0000	0100

All of these logical operations have more complicated applications in computer systems but they are generally based on variations of the examples given.

We have seen that the ALU is the main processing unit of the CPU and can easily accomplish all forms of arithmetic and logical operations once the data has been coded into binary form and by use of combinations of AND, OR and NOT gates. Even SINE, COSINE and other such functions can easily be accomplished with these gates. This of course is why the digital computer has become so popular.

Let's look next at the CPU in more detail and examine how it executes the various instructions.

CENTRAL PROCESSING UNIT — CPU

The CPU operates by following a continual fetch-decode-execute-increment sequence.

The CPU is responsible for executing instructions and for the overall control of operations in a computer system. Most computers have only one CPU; however, there are some with more than one. Computers with more than one CPU are said to have multi-processing capability. That is, they can have two processors, both operating on different instructions at the same time.

In order to execute a machine instruction, the computer does the following:

(a)   Fetches the instruction from a memory location specified by an internal register called the program counter.

(b)   Decodes the instruction and performs its execution.

(c)   Increments the program counter so as to fetch the next instruction in sequence (unless a jump or transfer of control occurs).

This operation is illustrated in *Figure 2-16*. The address of the next instruction to be fetched is placed on the address bus and the read control signal is activated (1). The next instruction is then sent to the CPU via the data bus and placed in the instruction register (2). The instruction decode circuitry enables the appropriate control signals for executing the instruction (3). The program counter is advanced by one (4) so that the next instruction in sequence can be fetched and the process repeated.

**Figure 2-16.
Instruction Fetch and
Decode.**

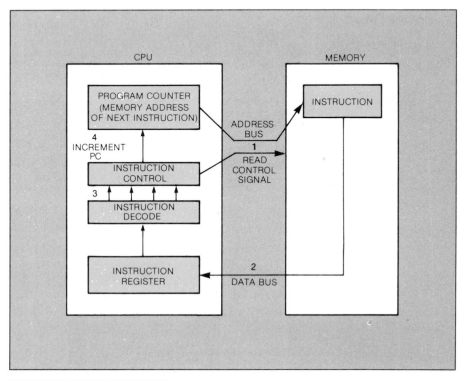

Instructions

Machine instructions can be classified according to function: arithmetic, logical, control transfer, data movement, I/O, and data assignment.

As previously mentioned, machine instructions are somewhat primitive when compared to those used in higher level languages. (High-level languages will be discussed in Chapters 3 and 4.) Machine instructions are usually classified in the following groups:

Arithmetic	(Add, subtract, multiply, divide, and negation)
Logical	(AND, OR, NOT, and EXCLUSIVE OR)
Transfer of Control	(Unconditional Branching, Conditional Branching, Loops, and Subroutines)
Data Movement	(Move, Load, and Store)
Input and Output	
Data Assignment	

Some typical machine instructions are:

LOAD	Register from memory
STORE	Register to memory
MOVE	Register to register
Add, Subtract, Multiply, Divide	Arithmetic operations on register contents with other register or memory contents
AND, OR, NOT	Logical operations on registers or memory contents.

Instructions can cause data to move from one register to another, from a register to a memory location or from a memory location to a register. Instructions can cause contents of one register or memory location to be added to the contents of another register or memory location. They can cause two such data items to be multiplied or divided or subtracted.

The large general purpose machines have these basic instructions and many more in their instruction set, but at the same general level; that is, operating on memory locations and registers.

In general, the lower the price of the CPU, the less sophisticated the instruction set. The instruction sets of microcomputers and minicomputers are usually much more primitive than the larger processors. This doesn't mean they can't do the same processing functions; however, it does mean that usually more instructions and more execution time are required to accomplish the same thing.

Instructions are uniquely identified by an operation code or 'op code'. They may instruct the CPU to fetch operands (data items to be operated on) from memory, transfer data to the I/O processor or I/O devices, or may change the program counter to a different memory location to implement a jump or transfer of control. Machine instructions typically will vary in size (the number of required bits for their representation), depending on type, addressing technique used, and manufacturer.

Addressing

Machine instructions are implemented as "op codes." They usually have an operand (the data to be operated on by the instruction) coupled to them. The addressing technique determines how to obtain the operand.

Addressing is the process of locating specific information (operands) for a given operation. Or, as discussed for a person, it is the process of obtaining his or her address so that information can be sent to them. If for instance, the operand is in memory, the addressing technique determines how to obtain the memory address of the operand and how to use this address to locate the operand and fetch it. If the operand is in one of the CPU's registers, addressing is the means by which the instruction specifies the selected register and the operand is fetched.

**Figure 2-17.
Instruction Formats.**

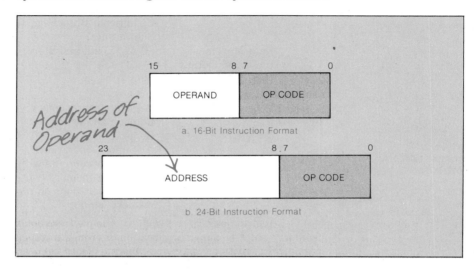

a. 16-Bit Instruction Format

b. 24-Bit Instruction Format

In immediate addressing, the operand is stored with the instruction.

Instructions are contained in one or more memory cells (the number of bits per memory cell will also vary between manufacturers). *Figure 2-17* illustrates two different formats. In the first example, *Figure 2-17a*, a 16-bit format is used to specify an 8-bit op code and an 8-bit operand. The operand is located in the instruction. When operands are part of the instruction it is referred to as immediate addressing; that is, the operand is immediately available once the instruction has been fetched. The op code indicates what is to be done with the operand. For example, it may be used to change the program counter to facilitate a jump or perhaps to add to the contents of another register.

With eight bits, the operand could be any value between 0 to 255 or a number between zero and -128 or $+127$, as one bit is usually used to indicate the sign of the number.

In direct addressing, the operand's memory location is stored with the instruction.

In the second example, *Figure 2-17b*, 24 bits are used. Here, the first eight bits are used to specify the operation or op code as before. However, the next 16 bits are used to specify the memory address of the operand. Addresses obtained by instructions such as these are said to be obtained directly from the instructions or direct addressing. In this example, the operand may be uniquely selected from any one of a possible 64K (2^{16} or 65536) memory locations.

Registers

Registers shorten processing time by providing temporary CPU storage for fast-changing data and by continuously monitoring CPU status.

One major variation between different CPU's is in the number and types of registers. These registers, as mentioned previously, are used for holding temporary results and data for CPU operations. With registers located within the CPU, fetches to memory or external storage are not necessary as often, thus speeding up the computational process. That is, contents of registers within the CPU can be obtained much faster than from memory and much faster than going outside to one of the other system units. A special register is also included for the program counter. The program counter keeps track of where the next instruction is located in memory. Other special registers are kept within the CPU to keep track of the status of the operations of the computer as it executes a program. The status register holds the status of the individual flags which are one-bit flip-flops. Most processors have at least these four flags: (1) zero (Is the result equal to zero?), (2) sign (Is number + or − ?), (3) carry (Did a carry occur?), and (4) parity (Check whether total number of bits are even or odd). Most processors have other status flags but we'll not attempt to cover them all since their functions vary considerably.

Figure 2-18. Control Circuitry Interface.

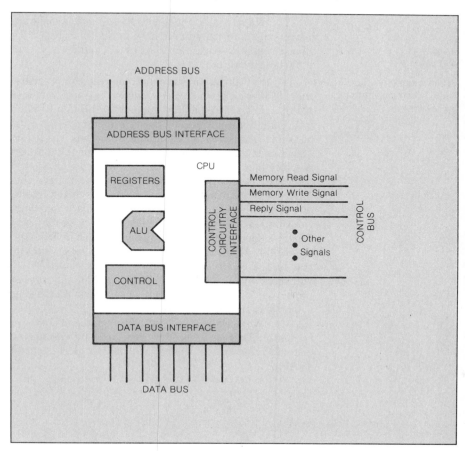

Control

Control circuitry carries signals that coordinate the interaction between the various elements of the computer system.

The control circuitry insures that the various signals or communication needs with other components are provided so that the instructions are performed. The CPU and its interface with the control, data, and address busses are illustrated in *Figure 2-18*. As discussed, the address bus is used to carry the memory addresses and input/output device addresses so that the appropriate operand is selected. The operand is sent on the data bus. The control bus is used to send the various control signals for executing the instructions. One control signal, for instance, is used for directing the appropriate memory unit to send the contents of the memory cell specified on the address bus to the CPU. This signal is the memory read signal. A second signal is used by memory to tell the CPU that it has placed the selected memory cell contents on the data bus. This signal is illustrated in *Figure 2-18* as the reply signal. Other such control signals exist for controlling memory writes, input/output operations, and so forth.

Next let's look at the way data consisting of information in the form of strings of letter and numbers (alphanumeric) may be coded so the CPU can work with this type of information.

Coded Representation of Alphabetic and Other Characters

We have discussed how the computer maintains data operands and instructions internally in memory as digital codes. We also have said that all such items are maintained as binary numbers that are strictly integers or floating point numbers.

Alphanumeric characters, not used in computations, are represented in industry-standard digital codes such as ASCII and EBCDIC.

For alphanumeric characters the computer uses a special digital code. That is, a special coded number has been developed for the character A through Z, as well as the numbers 0 through 9. These coded numbers for 0 through 9 are not usually used for arithmetic operations. When a 5 is to be printed, the program communicating with the I/O device or printer knows that this is a special coded value for the number 5 and not an absolute numerical value to be used in a computation. Such procedures have been used for many years in computer technology. There are a number of different codes available for representing alphanumeric characters, but two of the more widely used codes are the American Standard Code for Information Interchange (ASCII) (pronounced like "as-key") and Extended Binary Coded Decimal Interchange Code (EBCDIC) (pronounced like "eb-see-dick"). ASCII was one of the first codes developed and accepted as a standard. EBCDIC, an 8-bit code, was developed by IBM and introduced with their System/360 line. ASCII is a 7-bit code and in addition to the upper and lower case alphabetic characters, it also permits many special symbols as shown in *Figure 2-19*.

We already discussed how an integer number is maintained in the computer. That is, suppose we have a 16-bit register and this register contains number 262 decimal or 0106 hexadecimal ($0 \times 16^3 + 1 \times 16^2 + 0 \times 16^1 + 6 \times 16^0$).

**Figure 2-19.
ASCII — American
Standard Code for
Information Interchange.**

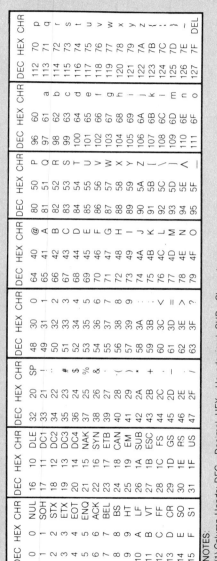

DEC	HEX	CHR	DEC	HEX	CHR	DEC	HEX	CHR	DEC	HEX	CHR	DEC	HEX	CHR	DEC	HEX	CHR	DEC	HEX	CHR	DEC	HEX	CHR
0	0	NUL	16	10	DLE	32	20	SP	48	30	0	64	40	@	80	50	P	96	60	`	112	70	p
1	1	SOH	17	11	DC1	33	21	!	49	31	1	65	41	A	81	51	Q	97	61	a	113	71	q
2	2	STX	18	12	DC2	34	22	"	50	32	2	66	42	B	82	52	R	98	62	b	114	72	r
3	3	ETX	19	13	DC3	35	23	#	51	33	3	67	43	C	83	53	S	99	63	c	115	73	s
4	4	EOT	20	14	DC4	36	24	$	52	34	4	68	44	D	84	54	T	100	64	d	116	74	t
5	5	ENQ	21	15	NAK	37	25	%	53	35	5	69	45	E	85	55	U	101	65	e	117	75	u
6	6	ACK	22	16	SYN	38	26	&	54	36	6	70	46	F	86	56	V	102	66	f	118	76	v
7	7	BEL	23	17	ETB	39	27	'	55	37	7	71	47	G	87	57	W	103	67	g	119	77	w
8	8	BS	24	18	CAN	40	28	(	56	38	8	72	48	H	88	58	X	104	68	h	120	78	x
9	9	HT	25	19	EM	41	29	)	57	39	9	73	49	I	89	59	Y	105	69	i	121	79	y
10	A	LF	26	1A	SUB	42	2A	*	58	3A	:	74	4A	J	90	5A	Z	106	6A	j	122	7A	z
11	B	VT	27	1B	ESC	43	2B	+	59	3B	;	75	4B	K	91	5B	[	107	6B	k	123	7B	{
12	C	FF	28	1C	FS	44	2C	,	60	3C	<	76	4C	L	92	5C	\	108	6C	l	124	7C	|
13	D	CR	29	1D	GS	45	2D	-	61	3D	=	77	4D	M	93	5D	]	109	6D	m	125	7D	}
14	E	SO	30	1E	RS	46	2E	.	62	3E	>	78	4E	N	94	5E	^	110	6E	n	126	7E	~
15	F	SI	31	1F	US	47	2F	/	63	3F	?	79	4F	O	95	5F	_	111	6F	o	127	7F	DEL

NOTES:
(1) Column Heads: DEC = Decimal; HEX = Hexadecimal; CHR = Character.
(2) Characters For HEX 0 through 1F are control functions.

Since alphanumeric characters and binary numbers are coded in entirely different ways, software must be able to distinguish one coding system from another.

The binary number is illustrated below.

0 0 0 0 0 0 0 1 0 0 0 0 0 1 1 0

This register could hold a number in this form as large as $2^{15} - 1$ or 32767 when the most significant bit is used for the sign. To code the number 106 in the ASCII code, 21 bits would be required, 7 for each character. That is, looking at *Figure 2-19* and converting the hex number to the special code for each character, we see that:

the character 1 is represented as   0110001,
the character 0 as   0110000,
and the character 6 as   0110110.

Since word sizes are typically multiples of 8, it becomes more expedient to just use 8 bits (a byte) for each ASCII character so the 24 bits for 106 are:

00110001   00110000   00110110

We can see that with this and other such codes the computer's memory could contain various alpha-numeric strings of information. However, we must remember that when we write programs to work with such coded data, we need to structure the program to distinguish between the various types of digital codes. Remember that the binary code for integer numbers 0 through 9 is entirely different from the ASCII code for numeric characters 0 through 9. Some example integer data, floating point data, and ASCII data codes are characterized in *Figure 2-20*.

Figure 2-20.
Coded Data Examples.

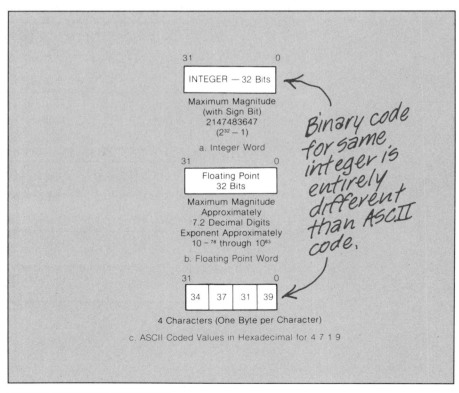

31   0

INTEGER — 32 Bits

Maximum Magnitude
(with Sign Bit)
2147483647
$(2^{32} - 1)$

a. Integer Word

31   0

Floating Point
32 Bits

Maximum Magnitude
Approximately
7.2 Decimal Digits
Exponent Approximately
10^{-78} through 10^{63}

b. Floating Point Word

31   0

| 34 | 37 | 31 | 39 |

4 Characters (One Byte per Character)

c. ASCII Coded Values in Hexadecimal for 4 7 1 9

Binary code for same integer is entirely different than ASCII code.

MEMORY

The memory units of a computer system are used for storing programs, data or operands. The first computers used little memory since it was very expensive. 16K and 32K memory cells were considered large. Now, even most microcomputers can easily interface with up to 64K memory cells. The larger computer systems can interface with several million memory cells.

The smallest addressable unit in most memories is a byte, eight bits in length. One byte can hold one ASCII or EBCDIC character.

Memory cells are composed of a number of bits. Because the two most common digital codes for representing alphanumeric characters (ASCII and EBCDIC) are easily maintained in 8 bits, most computers are structured so that the smallest addressable cell consists of eight bits. Eight bits are referred to as a *byte*. By addressable, we mean a cell has a unique address which locates all the bits in its contents. If there are N cells (e.g. N = 1000), and each cell contains a byte, then the addressable units consists of 0 to N – 1 bytes (0-999). If an address consists of K (e.g. K = 12) bits, then the addressing capability or the largest number of cells which can be uniquely selected is 2^K ($2^{12} = 4096$). This range is called the address space of the computer and it doesn't need to have actual memory cells for all of these locations. For instance, most small microcomputers have an address space of 64K bytes; however, if the application only calls for, say 4K bytes, only 4K of memory need be included and the other 60K of address space is unused.

Memory cells are also often specified in terms of words. A word may consist of one byte or several bytes. Typically, the word size relates to the CPU and is usually the size of the arithmetic and logic unit registers in bits. Addressable cell units can be less than this word size. However, a word is usually some multiple of the cell size. For instance, a word may be 32 bits and the memory addressable by four bytes of 8 bits each.

Memory Organization

Memories are generally organized in banks containing rows and columns of equal length. An address designates the intersection of a specific row and column in a given bank of memory.

Memories are typically organized in square form (*Figure 2-21a*) so that they have an equal number of rows and columns. Each intersection of a row and column comprises a memory cell which may be one or more bits. A specific address of six bits is divided into two parts as illustrated in *Figure 2-21a*. The least significant three bits are decoded to specify one of the eight rows. The most significant three bits are decoded to yield one of the eight columns. The specific cell selected, then, is at the intersection of the selected row and column.

There may be one or more of these memory blocks or banks. If so, the specific bank is likewise selected from the 2^{K-N} possibilities as illustrated in *Figure 2-21b* where K is the total number of bits and K – N is used for addressing the specific bank. As shown in *Figure 2-21b*, the two most significant bits of the 8-bit address are decoded to select one of the four memory banks. Then the remaining six bits are decoded to select a specific cell in that bank as just explained in *Figure 2-21a*.

Figure 2-21.
Memory Organization
and Addressing.

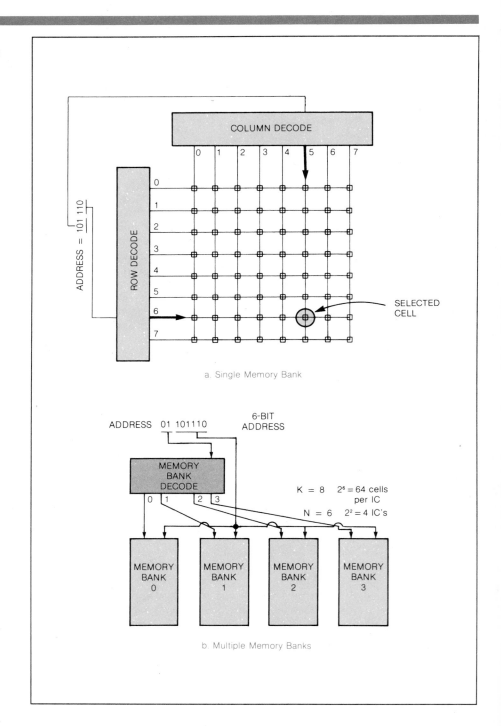

a. Single Memory Bank

b. Multiple Memory Banks

Volatile Memory

Volatile memories lose
their contents when you
turn the computer off or
when power is lost.

Memory units are of two types, volatile and nonvolatile. Volatile memories are those which lose their contents when the power is turned off. You probably are familiar with one of the small calculators that has a memory which can store one or more results. If so, you know that when the power is turned off, you lose the information because the semiconductor memory used is volatile. Most small computer systems use semiconductor memories.

Figure 2-22 illustrates a circuit commonly used for semiconductor memory. It shows how two inverters can be 'cross-coupled' to hold a bit. (This circuit is called a flip-flop.) If the input S_1 to the first inverter is 0, then its output S_2 is 1. If S_2 is 1, then the output of the second inverter is 0 and, since this is S_1, it holds the first inverter in a stable state. If S_1 is 1, then S_2 is 0 and the output of the second inverter would be a 1 to match S_1. The states S_1 and S_2 remain at 0 or 1 as set until intentionally changed or until the power is turned off.

**Figure 2-22.
Cross Coupling of Two
Inverters.**

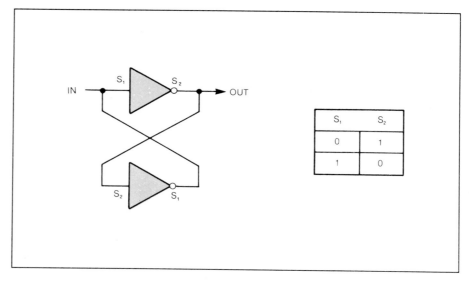

Nonvolatile Memory

Nonvolatile memories
(such as the magnetic core
memories used in earlier
computers) retain their
contents when you turn
the computer off, or even
when power is lost.

Nonvolatile memories do not lose their contents when power is removed. Core memory is an example of nonvolatile memory (*Figure 2-23*). Core memory consists of many small ferromagnetic doughnut shaped rings called cores. Each ring holds one bit. The ring is magnetized with one polarity for logic 0 and the opposite polarity for logic 1. Core memory is relatively low cost but information cannot be stored as fast in core memory or accessed as fast as with semiconductor memory. Also, the physical size of core memory is much larger than semiconductor memory for the same number of bits stored. Each ferromagnetic ring is only about the size of a pinhead, but one 8-bit byte requires 8 such rings. A 64K-byte (65,536) memory would thus require 524,288 of these rings.

**Figure 2-23.
Magnetic Core Memory.**

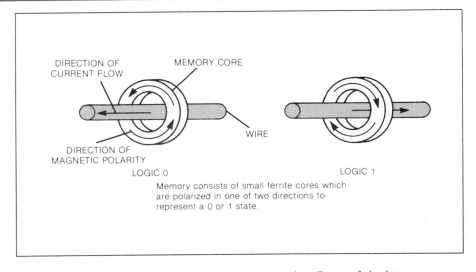

DIRECTION OF
CURRENT FLOW

MEMORY CORE

WIRE

DIRECTION OF
MAGNETIC POLARITY

LOGIC 0

LOGIC 1

Memory consists of small ferrite cores which
are polarized in one of two directions to
represent a 0 or 1 state.

Semiconductor memories
have generally supplanted
core memories due to their
faster access times and
smaller dimensions.

Most computers no longer use core memories. Some of the late
models of computers that used core memories used the fast semiconductor
memories along with core memories. The faster access memories are used
to contain the more likely used instructions and data to speed up the access
time (*Figure 2-24*). Such memories are called cache or buffer memories and
operate transparent to the user. That is, a particular section or bank of
core memory which is needed is copied into the faster semiconductor
memory. Future accesses to this bank then are made to the semiconductor
memory rather than core until an address outside of this bank occurs. Then
another group of core memory cells are copied.

**Figure 2-24.
High Speed Memory
Techniques.**

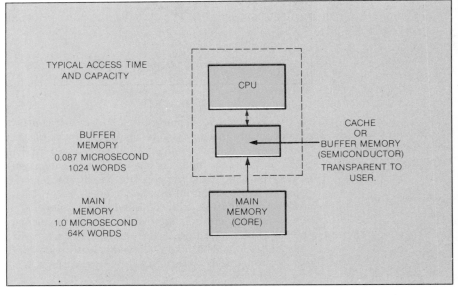

TYPICAL ACCESS TIME
AND CAPACITY

CPU

BUFFER
MEMORY
0.087 MICROSECOND
1024 WORDS

CACHE
OR
BUFFER MEMORY
(SEMICONDUCTOR)
TRANSPARENT TO
USER.

MAIN
MEMORY
1.0 MICROSECOND
64K WORDS

MAIN
MEMORY
(CORE)

There are other types of memories which are not in widespread use today, but may be in the future. Notable among these is the bubble memory (*Figure 2-25*) which is non-volatile and requires less power and less space than core memory. It is about the physical size of an IC and uses tiny magnetized areas called bubbles in specially manufactured crystalline material. The complete structure is operated in a magnetic field. It currently is much slower than semiconductor memory and core memory. Its major impact, however, probably will be in replacing some auxiliary storage devices. Auxiliary storage typically has longer access time but can contain much more information at less cost than the main memory.

**Figure 2-25.
Bubble Memory.**

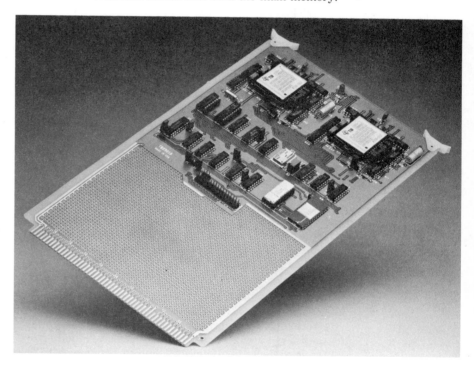

I/O PROCESSOR

Before discussing auxiliary storage devices, we need to briefly mention the I/O processor illustrated earlier in *Figure 2-3*. Recall that this digital component interfaces between the I/O devices (such as disks, tapes, and printers) and the memory and CPU. The function of this component is to control the transfer of data between the devices connected to it and memory. Typically, the CPU will direct the I/O processor to initiate a particular operation. A channel block or block of data words are structured in memory, listing the specific device the I/O processor is to control; the number of words to transfer; where these words are to come from or go to in memory; and what is to be done after the operation is complete. When the CPU instructs the I/O processor to begin the I/O operation (as directed by the computer program), the CPU specifies the address of this channel block. The I/O processor is also often referred to as a data channel, a direct memory access channel, or a peripheral processor.

The I/O processor acts as a direct "data channel" between the external device and computer memory.

The term data channel came about because it provides a channel for the data to flow between the I/O device and memory. If direct memory accessing (DMA) is used, the data channel provides direct access to memory by the I/O device without going through the CPU. The term peripheral processor was introduced by Control Data Corporation in their 6600 computer systems which had programmable I/O processors. CDC called them peripheral processors. Besides handling data transfers, these processors could also do a small amount of computation on this data, such as code conversions, etc.

The I/O processor is necessary to free the CPU from actually reading or writing each word and to meet the data transfer speed requirements necessary for some of the higher speed devices. Auxiliary storage devices use these I/O processors for interfacing with the other system components.

AUXILIARY STORAGE DEVICES

Although main memory is used for programs and data, it is still relatively expensive when compared to several other devices which can store data and/or programs. These other devices, which are referred to as auxiliary storage or mass storage devices, require more time for obtaining their contents than semiconductor or core memory. The amount of time required to obtain a particular byte or word is referred to as the access time. This time includes when the address is sent to the device until the device responds with the information.

Access Techniques

There are three general classes of storage devices, depending on their access technique. These are; random access, direct access, and sequential access.

Memory access can be either random, direct, or sequential.

For random access, the time required for obtaining a specific operand or data item is identical, regardless of its address. That is, the contents of location 5000 can be obtained as fast as the contents of location 2. In direct access, a specific item can be directly reached or obtained without having to search through a number of other data items to get to the item desired. The access time to obtain one specific item as opposed to another specific item; however, can be different, depending on the two addresses. In sequential access as shown in *Figure 2-26*, all data items in a record occurring before the one desired must be accessed before obtaining the desired item.

**Figure 2-26.
Sequential Access of
Data.**

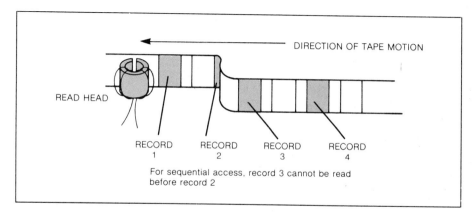

DIRECTION OF TAPE MOTION

READ HEAD

RECORD 1   RECORD 2   RECORD 3   RECORD 4

For sequential access, record 3 cannot be read before record 2

Data is usually stored in blocks of related information called logical records.

Data to be accessed from an auxiliary storage unit is typically for a specific data item which may encompass a number of bytes or words. The data item may be some attribute, such as a person's name or address or an object type and its size and weight. The data items are usually grouped according to a specific relationship where each group is referred to as a logical record. This is shown in *Figure 2-27*. Records can have various fields of fixed and variable lengths as illustrated in *Figure 2-28*. If the record length is not fixed, then the length must be indicated by an end of record symbol to know how much to read or write.

**Figure 2-27.
Logical Record.**

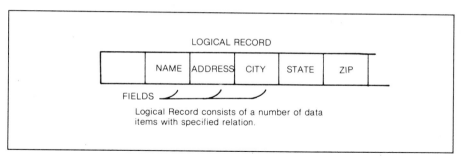

LOGICAL RECORD

NAME | ADDRESS | CITY | STATE | ZIP

FIELDS

Logical Record consists of a number of data items with specified relation.

**Figure 2-28.
Variable Length Records.**

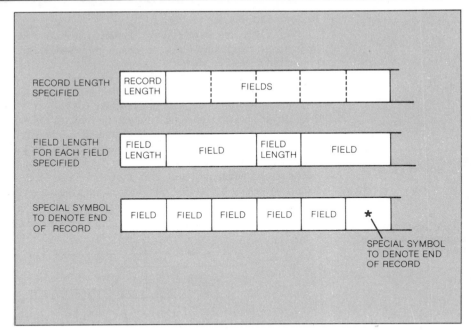

Magnetic tape systems
store data in "frames"
seven or nine tracks in
width. Each bit of an
ASCII or EBCDIC char-
acter code occupies one
track in a frame.

There are different types of auxiliary storage devices. We will
investigate only the two more popular ones, magnetic tapes and magnetic
disks.

Magnetic Tape Storage Systems

One of the first widely used mass storage devices was the
magnetic tape. For such devices, data is stored on one or more tracks.
There are usually 7 or 9 tracks for large computer systems. Initially 7 track
tapes were the most common, but with the third generation of computers,
the 9 track tape units shown in *Figure 2-29* became more popular since they
could accommodate EBCDIC or ASCII coded characters. In operation, the
magnetic tape is moved from one reel to another similarly to a conventional
home tape recorder. The tape passes underneath a read and write head
which can sense (read) or magnetize (write) a specific polarity on each
track. There is both a read head and a write head for each track. This
allows read-after-write to check for errors.

Figure 2-29.
Magnetic Tape Format.

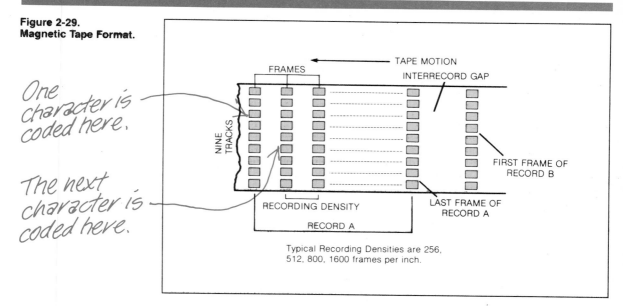

One character is coded here.

The next character is coded here.

Parity

The last track (7th or 9th) is usually used for a parity bit. Parity checking is a way of detecting errors by determining the number of ones or zeros for a particular frame (see *Figure 2-30*). Parity may be either odd or even. For odd parity, if there is an even number of ones in the first eight bits of a frame, a one is written in the parity bit so that the total number of ones for the frame is odd. Conversely, if the number of ones is odd, the parity bit is zero. For even parity, the total number of ones in the frame must be even and the parity bit is set accordingly. To detect a parity error, each frame is read and the number of ones are counted. If one, three, five,

Figure 2-30.
Parity.

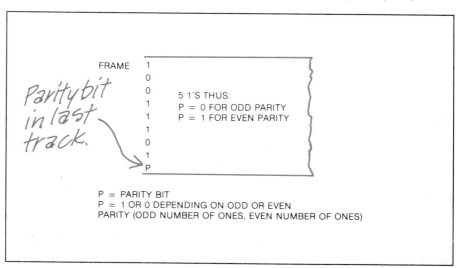

Parity bit in last track.

or seven of the original bits have changed so that the number of ones is not odd, or even depending on the parity scheme used, an error is indicated. Of course, parity does not guarantee 100% error detection since two, four, or six bits can change and parity is still correct. Therefore, parity only aids in detecting errors, other techniques must be used to completely eliminate errors.

Recording Density and Access

The amount of information which can be stored on a tape is a function of the recording density. Modern tapes usually record at 800 or 1600 bits per inch (bpi) (*Figure 2-29*). This also may be stated as 800 or 1600 frames per inch. Transfer rates are a function of tape speed. A single 2400 foot reel of tape can hold millions of bits and typically cost less than $15.00. The tape drive units, on the other hand, can cost over $50,000.

Accessing data or records from tape is typically referred to as sequential access. Records stored toward the back of the tape cannot be accessed as quickly as records at the front. Thus, if tape is used, the more frequently used records should probably be toward the front of the tape to minimize access time.

The data structure for tape is divided into records and files. Records can be of any length. They are separated by inter-record gaps as shown in *Figure 2-29*. This is the physical length of tape allowed for speed-up when starting and slow-down when stopping. The data between gaps are referred to as a physical record. Files are one word records with a special code used to separate a group of records. In addition to access time, tapes have the problem that records can be added only at the end.

> Data on tape is typically recorded at densities of 800 or 1600 frames per inch, structured in records separated by gaps, and accessed sequentially.

Physical and Logical Records

A punched data card such as described earlier can have a maximum of 80 characters. We can then say for the 80 column card that the physical record size is 80 characters (or bytes if we use EBCDIC or ASCII for internally representing our characters). That is, the physical record size is the smallest amount of information which can be accessed and it is related to the hardware's characteristics whereas logical records are groups of data items related by some particular attribute as discussed previously. Physical records may thus consist of one or more logical records. Blocking is the process of writing a number of logical records within each physical record. If the blocking factor is five, for instance, a block of data consists of five logical records. Eighty column card data can be read and placed in memory as eighty byte records. Then it can be written on tape where each physical record (data separated by the inter-record gap) consists of 640 bytes. The blocking factor is eight.

Cassette Tapes

Cassette tapes are an economical means of data storage for small computer systems.

Microcomputers and small minicomputer systems often use small single-track tapes. For such devices, the data can be stored in a digital recording scheme as above, or can be stored as an analog tone where one frequency is used for logic one and a second frequency for a logic zero. The analog tones can be recorded on a simple, inexpensive home type cassette recorder. The large tape units used for the more expensive general purpose computer systems can be quite reliable in recording and reproducing the data, but the tape cassettes (*Figure 2-31*) used on micro and some small minicomputer systems, even though very inexpensive and quite useful, don't have high reliablity of data reproduction.

Figure 2-31.
Audio Tape Cassette and
Cassette Recorder.
(Courtesy of Radio Shack Corporation)

Magnetic Disk Storage Systems

Hard Disks

Hard disks provide expensive but fast, reliable, and high-capacity storage for both small and large computer systems.

The magnetic disk has become one of the more popular mass storage devices for the modern computer system. Large computer systems use very expensive disk systems with the capability of storing millions of bytes of data. Disks are direct access storage devices; therefore, the access time for a particular record is much faster than it is for tape. A disk is a circular, flat object which resembles a phonograph record without grooves and with one or both surfaces coated with a magnetic material. It may range from 1½ to 3 feet in diameter for the large expensive disk system, or it can be much smaller (5 to 12 inches) for the micro and mini systems. For the larger systems, several hard disks are usually attached to a shaft (*Figure 2-32*). The disk rotates very rapidly and the disk drive unit has one or more read-write heads which move from one track to another. Data is stored on the circular tracks. Typically, there is a read-write head for each surface. All heads are attached to a common support and move together. Some older units have fixed heads, one for each track.

Figure 2-32.
Multiple Disk System.

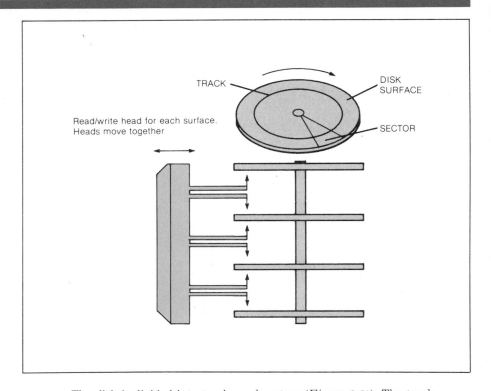

The disk surface is organized into tracks and sectors. Within a sector, the track is a physical record. There may be one read/write head per disk surface, or one head per track. Multiple heads shorten access time.

The disk is divided into tracks and sectors (*Figure 2-34*). The track of each sector constitutes a physical record. The recording density is greater for the inner tracks than the outer tracks so that records are the same length. A particular data block is addressed according to head or surface, track, and sector. All sectors which can be read for a particular track is called a cylinder. That is, it includes all sectors for a given track for each surface.

As noted, there may be one head per surface, or there may be a head for each track which decreases access time. The disks may be fixed or removable. Removable disk packs provide a means of transferrring data from one location to another or for filing the disk pack on a shelf. Large capacity disk systems can store 800 to 1600 million bytes with data transfer rates (read and writes) of up to 806,000 bytes per second. Such systems cost many thousands of dollars.

Most small personal computers can interface with the smaller and much less expensive flexible disks called the floppy disk or diskette. The floppy disk will be described in detail in the section that follows.

Floppy Disks

Floppy disk systems, used extensively with micro-computers, offer fast storage and retrieval, excellent reliability, and high data capacity.

Just as in large computer systems, much more storage is required for maintaining programs and/or data than is available in memory for mini and microcomputers. Bulk storage devices such as floppy disks and cassette tapes provide a relative inexpensive storage media for satisfying these needs. Floppy disk systems are more expensive than cassette tape systems but they offer faster data transfer rates, easier data modification or update, and large data capacity in a small package.

**Figure 2-33.
Floppy Diskette.**

The floppy disk, also called a diskette, is somewhat similar to a 45 RPM phonograph record in size (*Figure 2-33*). The floppy disks, which are made from thin plastic and coated with a magnetic material, are flexible and bend easily. The disk is permanently contained within a sleeve which protects it from dust and handling. A slot in the sleeve allows head access. Currently, two sizes of floppy disks are available — the regular floppy which is 8 inches in diameter and the smaller, mini-floppy which is 5¼ inches in diameter. Information is read or written by a magnetic read/write head which is physically moved to one of the invisible concentric tracks as illustrated in *Figure 2-34*. For the standard 8 inch floppy there are typically 77 tracks.

**Figure 2-34.
Floppy Disk Format.**

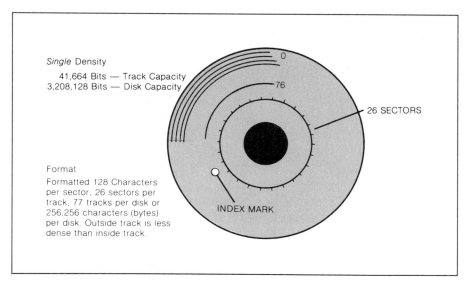

Single Density

41,664 Bits — Track Capacity
3,208,128 Bits — Disk Capacity

0
76
26 SECTORS

Format
Formatted 128 Characters per sector, 26 sectors per track, 77 tracks per disk or 256,256 characters (bytes) per disk. Outside track is less dense than inside track.

INDEX MARK

The disk surface is organized into tracks and sectors. A typical eight-inch floppy disk has 77 tracks with 26 sectors per track. Single density holds 128 characters per sector; double density holds 256. Double-sided disks double the storage.

The disk surface is divided into sectors which are designed to hold a specified number of bytes. The number of sectors per track and the number of bytes per sector is the same for all tracks. Although disks can be organized in many different ways; the single-density, 8-inch floppy typically has 77 tracks with 26 sectors per track and 128 characters per sector. Thus, 256,256 ($128 \times 77 \times 26$) 8-bit bytes can be stored on a surface.

The double density disks can record 256 characters in approximately the same physical sector size. Thus, these disks hold twice as much, or about one-half million bytes. Some disks can only be written on one side, others on both sides. In order for data recorded on the disk to be accessed, information such as sector and track identification must be provided. IBM established a format that provides this information for the 8 inch floppy. Many other manufacturers also have adopted this format. This soft-sector format is illustrated in *Figure 2-35*. The term 'soft-sectored' is used to describe disks which have only one physical hole or index mark per disk. The index mark is used to establish the beginning of each track. Specific sectors within each track can then be located only by reading each sector along the track until the appropriate one is found. A specially written code called an index mark is associated with each sector. Hard sectored formats are disks which have a physical hole for each sector to fix the exact physical location of each record.

**Figure 2-35.
Soft-Sector Format.**

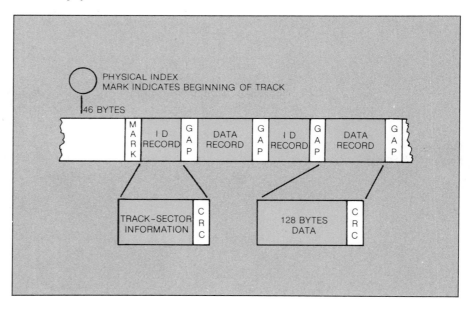

Blank disks must be formatted before use.

Before a new or blank disk can be used, a preliminary formatting step must be accomplished. In this step the various index marks, track and sector identification, etc. are written on the disk. This typically is an operation performed by the disk controller which may be a microprocessor itself.

Data is recorded serially on the diskette. This data is written one byte at a time where the most significant bit is written as the first bit, 0, and the least significant bit as the last bit, 7. During reading, bit 0 is always the first bit read, followed by bit 1, etc. until bit 7 is reached.

Data is written in fixed length sectors or records where each record is separated by record gaps or spaces. Such spaces are necessary for record up-dating because of the minor variations which can occur in recording speed.

As noted in *Figure 2-35*, each field written includes two cyclic redundancy check (CRC) bytes. These bytes provide an error checking procedure much better than the parity scheme discussed earlier.

The CRC is computed by the disk controller with the received data and compared to the CRC sent with the data. If they are not identical, an error is detected.

The floppy disk system consists of two principal components called the disk drive and the disk controller. *Figure 2-36* illustrates a block diagram of a disk system. The drive contains the motor and other mechanical and electro-mechanical components that spin the disk and move the head. The controller typically combines the functions of an I/O processor. That is, it provides the necessary interface between the microcomputer system busses and the floppy drive, and controls the block data transfers between memory and the drive. In addition, it also controls disk seeks, (moving the recording head to a specified track) and formats new disks. Microprocessors are often used to perform the various controller functions.

Disk systems have two main parts: the drive (to read and write data) and the controller (to interface between the drive and the computer). The time needed for data access depends on how far the read/write head has to move.

**Figure 2-36.
Floppy Disk System.**

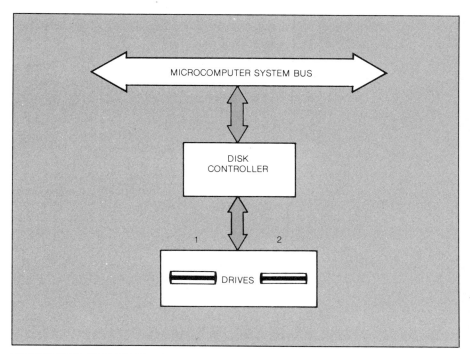

The diskette drive performs the actual recording functions; that is, it moves the read/write head to a selected track and performs the reading or writing of the data. Some typical performance specifications for an 8-inch, single-density floppy are given in *Table 2-2*.

**Table 2-2.
Diskette Drive
Performance
Specifications.**

Capacity:	Per Disk	256,256 Bytes (Formatted)
	Per Track	3,328 Bytes (Formatted)
Data Transfer Rate:	250 Kilobits/Second	
Access Time:	Track to Track — 10 ms	
	Settling Time — 10 ms	
Rotational Speed:	360 Revolutions per Minute	

The access time is a function of how far the read/write head has to travel. For the example in *Table 2-2*, it takes 10 milliseconds to move to each adjacent track and another 10 milliseconds once the head has arrived to a specific track for the mechanical system to settle. That is, if the head is moved over three tracks, it would take 30 milliseconds to move plus 10 milliseconds to settle before the track sectors could be read. Access time and data transfer rate for the floppy disk system are much slower than the more expensive hard disk system discussed earlier.

5 1/4-inch mini-floppy disks are gaining in popularity. A typical 5 1/4-inch disk has 35 tracks with 13 sectors per track, and holds 256 characters per sector.

The mini-floppys are less expensive than the 8-inch floppys and are used with many of the personal computer systems sold today. The track and sector allocation for the 5¼-inch mini floppy disk are a little different than those used on the 8-inch floppy disk. As you would expect, there are fewer tracks. One formatting scheme allocates 35 tracks and each track contains 13 sectors of 256 bytes.

The floppy disks are small and removable. There are other small, fixed disk systems also available which can store much more information than the floppy. Such systems have a somewhat similar track sector organization and cost about 5 to 10 times more than the floppy system.

There are other I/O devices used with computer systems such as printers, card readers, etc. We have primarily been concerned with those used for auxiliary storage; however, we will discuss these other units in more detail in later chapters.

WHAT HAVE WE LEARNED?

In this chapter, the various hardware components of the digital computer system have been examined. We discussed the three busses used for transferring address, data and control signals. Digital signals within the computer are coded to represent numbers, alpha-numeric character strings, and instructions. The computer performs operations on these signals by using thousands and thousands of AND, OR and NOT gates. These gates are used for constructing the CPU as well as the other system components.

The CPU or central processing unit performs the actual processing functions. It obtains instructions from memory and executes these instructions. The CPU sends and decodes control signals during the execution of each instruction. It performs the central control functions of the computer system. It contains the arithmetic and logic unit, registers, and control circuitry.

Numbers are represented within the computer as binary signals. N-bit registers can contain integer or fixed point values of magnitudes up to 2^{N-1} where one bit is used for the sign bit. To represent fractional numbers or very large numbers in floating point, the binary word is divided into two parts, one for the fractional part or mantissa and one for the exponent.

Data and instructions are stored in memory. Space in the internal main memory is limited, so auxilary storage devices outside the computer are used for providing additional and more economical storage. Information contained in such storage, however, cannot be accessed as quickly as from main memory. Magnetic tape and magnetic disk systems are currently the most popular mass storage devices. Tapes were developed first but data can be accessed from disk systems faster than from tape systems. Micro and minicomputers utilize floppy disks which are inexpensive and reliable.

In later chapters, we will review many of the things we have discussed in this chapter and see how they fit into overall computer system operations.

WHAT'S NEXT?

In the next chapter, we will see how to develop a program for a computer system so that the most efficient and most maintainable software can be developed to solve specific computational problems.

Now sit back for a moment and see if you can work the quiz at the end of this chapter.

Quiz for Chapter 2

1. The three main components of a
computer system are:
  a. CPU, memory, auxiliary storage
  b. CPU, memory, I/O
  c. CPU, auxiliary storage, floppy
    disk
  d. Tape, CPU, printer
  e. None of the above

2. Addressing is the process of
selecting the proper module or
referencing the desired memory
location.
  True or False

3. Which of the following are typical
machine instructions groups?
  a. Arithmetic operations
  b. Transfer of control
  c. Data movement
  d. All are typical machine
    instruction groups

4. The ASCII code for the number 5
can be used in an addition
operation.
  True or False

5. The following binary number,
10011101, is equal to which
hexadecimal number?
  a. 5A
  b. FF
  c. 9D
  d. 9E
  e. 9F

6. The number in problem 5 is equal
to which decimal number?
  a. 27
  b. 157
  c. 13
  d. 144
  e. 125

7. Which of the following is not a
typical machine instruction?
  a. Load register
  b. Store register
  c. Add
  d. Raise X to the 10th power
  e. AND operation

8. The op code is that portion of an
instruction used to determine the
exponent of a data item.
  True or False

9. Given a 32 bit word CPU, which
technique would be best to
represent 0.025?
  a. Integer
  b. Two's complement
  c. One's complement
  d. Floating Point
  e. None of the above

10. The two's complement is useful for
expressing negative numbers.
  True or False

11. The ASCII code in hexadecimal for
the number 5 is:
  a. 5
  b. 65
  c. 35
  d. 105
  e. None of the above

12. If the address space of a computer
system is from 0 to 32767, how
many address bits are necessary
for addressing?
  a. 10
  b. 2
  c. 16
  d. 15
  e. 12

13. Which of the following storage is
volatile?
  a. Floppy disk
  b. Semiconductor memory
  c. Bubble memory
  d. Core memory

14. Which access method is used for
obtaining a record from a cassette
tape?
  a. Direct
  b. Sequential
  c. Random

15. Parity *will always* detect a
transmission error.
  True or False

(Answers in back of book.)

How to Tell a Computer What to Do — Programming

ABOUT THIS CHAPTER

In previous chapters you have learned how the various hardware components of a computer system relate to each other. You have also learned that all this hardware is virtually useless unless it has instructions that tell it what to do. The list of instructions that direct the computer to perform a specific task is called the computer program.

In this chapter, you will find out what is involved in designing a computer program. Programs can be designed many ways to accomplish the desired end results; however, some programs have definite advantages over others. For instance, of two programs that yield identical results; one may use more instructions, require more memory space, and take more time to execute than the other.

HOW TO DEVELOP A COMPUTER PROGRAM

To start with, let's clear up one common misconception. Programming does *not* consist only of writing program statements or instructions in one of the many different high-level languages. That is only a part of programming and it certainly isn't the first part. So let's back up and define what programming is. Programming consists of five steps:

1) Understanding the problem
2) Designing the program
3) Coding the program
4) Translating the program
5) Testing the program

We'll investigate each of these in detail in the next few pages.

The first step in developing a program is to understand exactly what the program is to do. Formal specifications, narrative descriptions, lists of statements, flowcharts, and tables are helpful in defining the task.

Understanding the Problem

This first step in program development can often trip up a programmer. If you jump into design without understanding the problem that your program is to solve, then your program is doomed from the beginning. You must have a clear and complete description of inputs and outputs and of what is expected of your program, whether it is for your own use or to be used by someone else. There are a number of ways to define the problem. A written narrative description, and/or a list of statements or paragraphs, and/or a flow chart should be sufficient for a relatively simple problem; although tables may also be used if they help to understand the problem better.

For complex problems, particularly when someone else wants you to design a program for them, a formal written specification may be necessary to insure that everybody involved understands and agrees on what the problem is and what the results of the program should be.

Let's try a very simple problem for illustration. We'll use a narrative description, a list, and a flowchart.

PROBLEM: A teacher wants a program that will determine a student's grade by calculating an average grade from six grades the student received over a grading period. The teacher will supply the six grades to the program as input. Only the average grade is needed as an output.

Now we can make an orderly list of what the program has to do.

LIST:
(1) Input the individual grades
(2) Add the grade values together to find their sum.
(3) Divide the sum by the number of grades to find the average grade.
(4) Print out the average grade.

We can also prepare a flowchart of the problem as shown in *Figure 3-1*.

About Flowcharts

Flowcharts help to grasp the relationships among different parts of a problem, and preliminary ones should use narrative descriptions.

Flowcharts graphically present the details of the structure of a complex program so that the relation between parts can be easily understood. When the flow of control is complicated by many different paths that result from many decisions, a good flow chart can help the programmer sort things out. The flowchart is often useful as a "thinking-out" tool to understand the problem and to aid in program design. At this stage, then, the flowchart symbols should have English narrative descriptions inside rather than programming language statements since we want to describe *what* is to be done, not *how* it is to be accomplished. At a later stage, if formal flowcharts are required for documentation, the flow chart may contain statements in a program language. These flowcharts can be most helpful to another person who at some future time may need to understand your program.

Preparing a formal flowchart is time consuming and modifying a flowchart to incorporate changes is often difficult. Because of this, you may have heard some programmers express their dislike for flowcharts, but most likely they still use them as a development tool.

**Figure 3-1.
Initial Flowchart for
Grade Averaging
Program.**

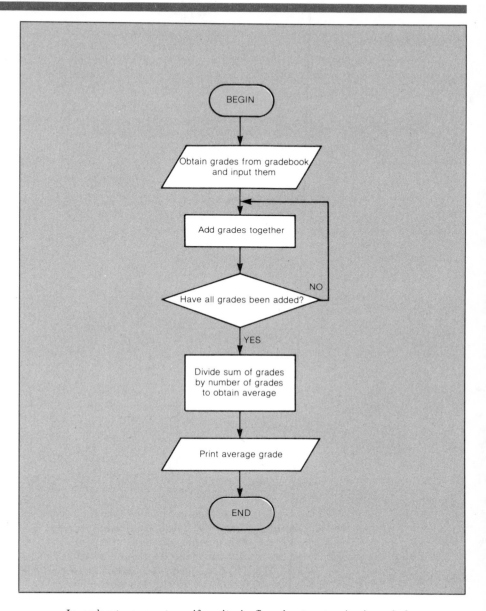

Program flow is normally
top-to-bottom and left-to-
right.

In order to promote uniformity in flowcharts, standard symbols
have been adopted by several organizations. The symbols of the United
States of America Institute (USASI) are widely accepted, and some of their
most commonly used symbols are shown and defined in *Figure 3-2*. The
normal direction of flow in a flowchart is from top to bottom and from left
to right. Arrowheads on flow lines are used to indicate flow direction, but
they are sometimes left off if the flow is in the normal direction.

Figure 3-2.
Flowchart Symbols.

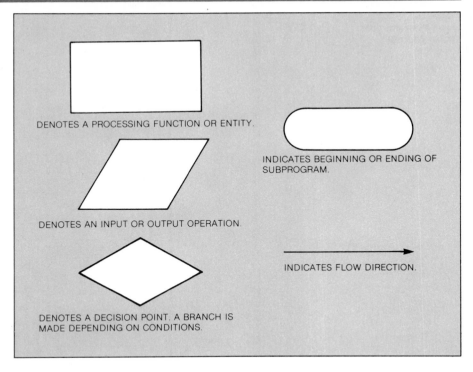

DENOTES A PROCESSING FUNCTION OR ENTITY.

DENOTES AN INPUT OR OUTPUT OPERATION.

DENOTES A DECISION POINT. A BRANCH IS
MADE DEPENDING ON CONDITIONS.

INDICATES BEGINNING OR ENDING OF
SUBPROGRAM.

INDICATES FLOW DIRECTION.

Designing the Program

Programs can be designed in different ways to accomplish the same end result. Some of the objectives that influence the design of a program are:

Minimum Cost	Maximum Flexibility
Minimum Program Size	Maximum Reliability
Minimum Data Storage Size	Maximum Ease of Maintenance
Minimum Execution Time	Maximum Modularity

As you might expect, some objectives can be accomplished only by eliminating others, or compromising between them. Therefore, the final program design is a result of modifications in objectives, modifications in design, and modifications in expected end result.

There are two basic approaches to program design: (1) bottom-up design and (2) top-down design. Bottom-up design means that you define all of the details first and then put them together to make the whole program. This is the method that has been taught in many schools, but it has lost favor because of inherent disadvantages. When you begin at a very low level of detail, it is easy to lose sight of the big picture. Then, when you try to put the pieces together to form the whole program, you may find that they will not fit together or interface properly. Or you may discover to your dismay that you've overlooked a requirement and then have to restructure part or all of the program.

In "bottom-up" program design (no longer in general favor), you begin with detailed solutions for separate parts of a problem and build to the total program.

**Figure 3-3.
Top-Down Design
Concept.**

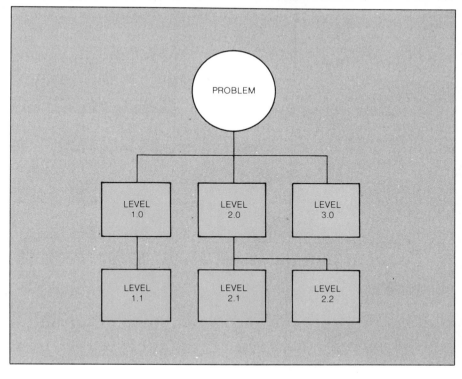

Top-Down Design

The top-down design method is preferred today. The concepts of top-down design and structured programming were introduced in the early 1970's by E.W. Dykstra[1] and others in an attempt to reduce program development cost and maintenance.

Essentially, the concept of top-down design is a systematic procedure for problem solving and can be used in many fields other than programming. The top-down design process simply consists of first specifying a solution to a problem in rather general terms. This solution makes up the top level. Next, each top level statement is broken down into a finer solution to make up the second level. Each succeeding level involves a more detailed solution until no more detail is necessary. The last level then is the bottom level. The process is illustrated symbolically in *Figure 3-3*.

Implied in the concept of top-down design is modular or structured programming and each block in *Figure 3-3* represents a program module. Each module should be structured somewhat independently of the others to permit each module to be developed and tested separately. All communication between modules should be in a predefined manner. Modules are implemented in higher level languages by means of subprograms called subroutines or procedures.

"Top-down" design progresses from a general solution of a problem to specific solutions of its various parts, with levels of detail added as necessary.

[1]E.W. Dykstra, "GO TO Statement Considered Harmful," *ACM Communications* Vol. 11 No. 3 (March 1968): 147-148

Let's consider the problem we used earlier in the flowchart example where we wanted to determine the average grade of a student. First, we begin with the problem.

Problem — Determine the average of a set of N numbers, where the variable N equals 6.

We begin by deciding what the inputs are, what the outputs are, and the numerical algorithm or formula that will be used. This is illustrated in *Figure 3-4*. Thus, the first level of problem solution can be defined as follows:

The first level of program design is a general statement of the inputs, outputs, and algorithm. When these main tasks are identified, you can add levels of detail as they become necessary.

1.0 Read Numbers
2.0 Compute Average
3.0 Print Answer

The next levels are then:

1.1 Read N number of values to be averaged,
2.1 SUM = SUM + V

and the last levels are

1.1.1 Read each value of N numbers, V
2.1.1. AVERAGE = SUM/N

**Figure 3-4.
Top-Down Design
Example.**

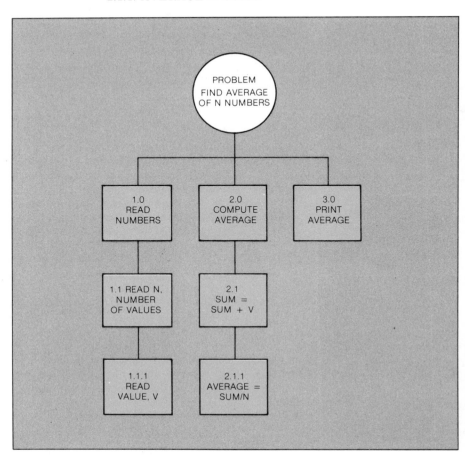

This is a fairly simple example, but does illustrate how the problem can be divided into levels to make the solution simpler. It's much easier to write programs for small modules and verify their correctness, rather than large complicated modules which include a number of different or unrelated operations.

A flowchart lets you visualize the program's flow within each level of the structure.

The flowchart in *Figure 3-5* shows the flowchart relation to the level structures that we defined. (Complex programs will not always be so easy to relate.) This flowchart is similar to *Figure 3-1* except that this one has psuedo-program language statements in the blocks.

Figure 3-5. Flowchart Using Pseudo-Program Statements.

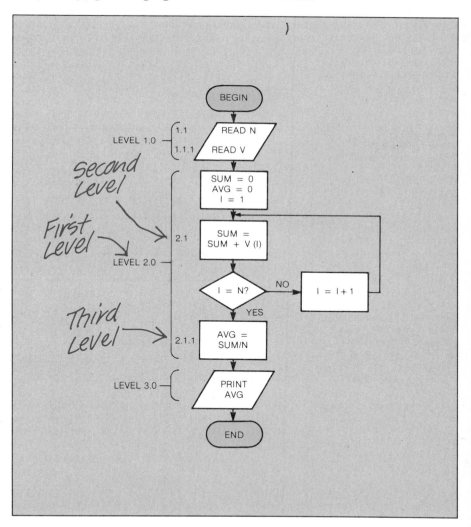

Program Execution

Let's leave our discussion of program design for a moment and take a look at how the program represented by the flowchart in *Figure 3-5* might be executed. Executing the instructions is called processing instructions. We'll not include every little detail of what's going on in the computer, but we'll see enough to get the idea.

The first thing that has to be done is to tell the computer to start working on our problem, which we do with the BEGIN instruction. (We'll assume that we have already prepared punched cards to contain the quantity (N) of how many numbers (grades) we have and the value of each grade. We'll further assume that a punched card reader is connected to the computer.) The next instructions tell the computer to read in the quantity of grades (N = 6) and store the value in a memory location named N, then read in the individual grades and store them in memory locations named V_1 through V_6 as shown in *Figure 3-6a*. (Note that in *Figure 3-6* we are using decimal numbers instead of binary numbers which would be in the machine.)

The sample program first reads in the number of grades to be averaged and the value of each grade. After the variables for the sum, average grade, and number of addition loops are initialized, the program begins to add the grades, testing loop variable I each time. When I equals N, the average is computed.

Figure 3-6.
Memory Map and
Addition Loop Variables.

MEMORY ADDRESS (1)	001	002	003	004	005	006	007	008	009	010
VARIABLE NAME (1)	N	V_1	V_2	V_3	V_4	V_5	V_6	SUM	I	AVG
INITIAL VALUES (1)	6	95	92	86	90	100	89	0	1	0
FINAL VALUES(1)	6	95	92	86	90	100	89	552	6	92

(1) All Numbers are in Decimal rather than Binary

a. Memory Allocation and Values Stored.

These values are fetched from memory for each addition.

		I = 1	I = 2	I = 3	I = 4	I = 5	I = 6
ACCUMULATOR REGISTER	SUM	0	95	187	273	363	463
REGISTER B	V_I	95	92	86	90	100	89
SUM LOCATION IN MEMORY	SUM	95	187	273	363	463	552

b. Addition Loop Repetition to Obtain Final Sum.

"SUM" is updated after each addition.

We also need storage locations in memory for the variables that we have named SUM, I and AVG. (*Figure 3-6a*). The computer must be told the name of each variable used in the program so that memory space can be allocated and addressed. The SUM location will store the sum of the grades. We want to be sure that the sum location is empty; that is, contains the value zero before we start, so we have the instruction to store zero there.

Then we have an instruction to do the same for the AVG location. This is called initializing variables. The value of I must also be initialized to the value of 1, so we have that instruction. The variable I is used to count the iterations or number of times that the addition loop is performed which identifies the successive values of V in memory.

Now the computer is ready to enter the add loop. Remember that the computer is a simple device, but extremely fast. It adds a column of numbers, such as we have, by adding them one at a time to the previous sum. That's why we have an instruction loop; that is, so that the add instruction is repeated as many times (N) as we have numbers (grades) to add. The computer executes our add instruction, SUM = SUM + V(I), by fetching the value from the SUM location and placing it in the accumulator register in the CPU (*Figure 3-6b*). Then the value V_1 is fetched from memory and added to SUM. The new sum is then placed in the SUM location.

Now it's decision time — does the value of I equal the value of N? If it does (YES path), the computer does one thing. If it does not (NO path), the computer does another thing. On the first iteration of the loop, the value of I is 1 and the value of N is 6, so the NO path is followed where I is incremented or increased by 1 for each pass through the loop. You can easily see that I will be 6 for our problem after all numbers (grades) have been added together and their final sum is stored in the SUM location.

When I is equal to N, the computer gets out of or exits the loop through the YES path. (It is important that you always provide an exit or escape path from any loop. If the computer gets hung-up in a loop, it will never reach the end of your program.) The next instruction tells the computer to divide the value in SUM by the value in N and store the result in the AVG location.

We want the average grade to be output on a printer (which we assume is connected to the computer), so we have the instruction that tells the computer to fetch the value from AVG and send it to the printer for print out. Now everything that we wanted has been accomplished, so we tell the computer to stop working on our program and release it for another job with the instruction END.

There are two things you should notice from this description:
1) We gave the computer the power to make a decision.
2) The program has flexibility since we used the variable names N and V for our inputs. This allows the program to process any number of grades, not just six as we used, and many different values for the grades.

Another Example of Using Top-down Design

The top-down approach is even more useful in the design of more complex programs, like this football strategy aid.

Let's get back to program design by applying the top-down design method to a more complex example. Suppose you were talking one day to your school's football coach. The coach was having a problem summarizing scouting information on the forthcoming opponents. The coach went on to explain that typically, each opponent's team is scouted for three games prior to the weekend the team is played. The scouting information consists of noting each offensive formation used, the ball carrier, the yard line, the yards gained, the play used, etc. Each Sunday following the last game scouted, the reports are summarized by one of the assistant coaches and statistics are computed. These statistics include, for instance, which offensive play the opponents team usually runs from a given formation and field position or hash mark, (*Figure 3-7*) (left side of field — left hash, center of field — center hash, and right side of field — right hash), and the average yards gained for each situation. Other useful information for the same field positioning includes plays run for a given down and yard line position, pass versus run statistics, pass routes, ball carriers, etc. The defensive coach then takes this information and uses it for planning his defense against the opponent team.

**Figure 3-7.
Field Positions for
Football Problem.**

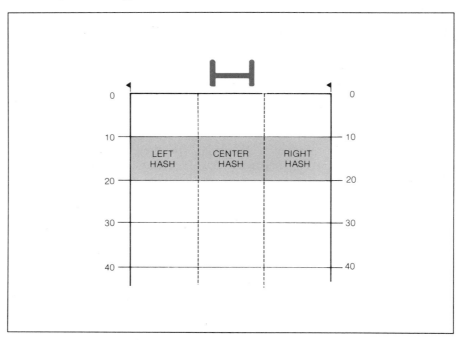

The coach went on to explain that he was short-handed this year and was having a problem summarizing the scouting reports to adequately provide these desired statistics. He has heard that you have your own personal computer and was wondering if you could write a program which would read this scouting information on a play by play basis and compute and print out the game statistics.

Your computer system is one of the popular personal computers (such as the Texas Instruments, Radio Shack or Apple computer) and consists of the computer with 16K bytes of storage, a keyboard, a printer, a video display, and a dual drive mini floppy disk (See *Figure 3-8*).

**Figure 3-8.
Personal Computer
System.**

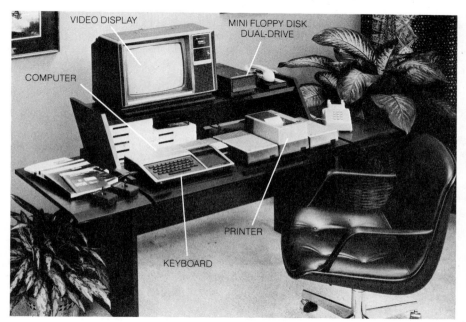

As in the previous example, the first level of program design is a general statement of the inputs, outputs, and algorithm.

In order to use the top down design, the problem is defined: design a program which will read in play-by-play information; perform summations and averages for each formation, field location (hash), direction of play, and yards gained; and print reports. The first level is illustrated in *Figure 3-9* and consists of:

1.0 Read in plays for all formations
2.0 Compute game statistics
3.0 Print out game statistics

The input data available for each game is illustrated in *Table 3-1*. One desired output report is shown in *Table 3-2*.

**Figure 3-9.
Top-Down Design of
Football Problem.**

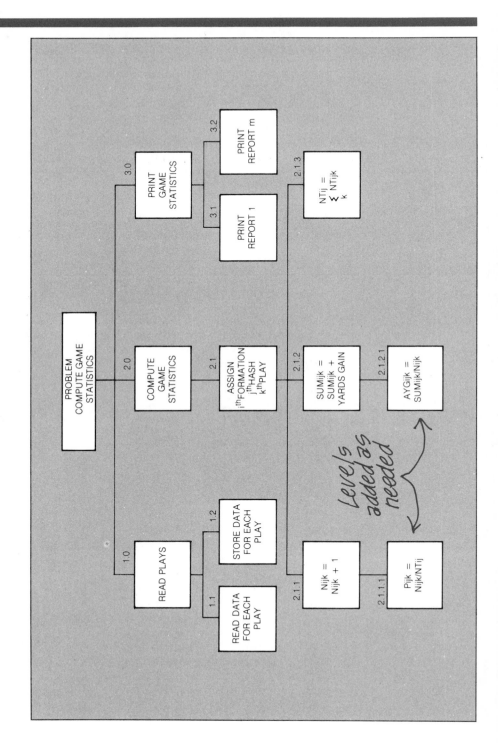

The input data should summarize the opposing team's recent performance.

The input data illustrated in *Table 3-1* defines the characteristics of the variables that are assigned to this information. This assignment process will be discussed in a later chapter. The input data will also be stored in a file so that it can be used again; next year, for example, for comparison purposes.

**Table 3-1.
Input Data**

PLAY NO.	HASH (R,C,L)	FORMATION	PLAY	YARDS GAINED	CARRIER	DOWN	YARD LINE
1	R	I	R	6	FB	1	20
2	R	Wishbone	C	3	FB	2	26
3	C	Shot Gun	C	16	QB	1	29
.	.	.	.	.	.	.	.

Notes:
FB = Full back, QB = Quarter back, etc. The play would be the play number your team would typically assign, depending on which route the ball carrier would take. For this example, we will use wide left (WL) to indicate it was run around the left end, left (L) to indicate between the center and the left end, center (C) for over the center, and right (R) and wide right (WR) defined similarly.

In the output data, the team's game statistics should be organized for easy evaluation.

Let's look at *Table 3-2*, the final result we expect from our program. We can see that there are three variables that are descriptive rather than numerical: formation, hash position, and direction of play. In order to easily use these in equation construction, let's assign each of these variables a letter as follows:

Formation = i   Hash Position = j   Direction of Play = k

**Table 3-2.
Output Report 1**

FORMATION
'I'

HASH — LEFT

PLAY	NUMBER OF TIMES	PERCENT	AVG. YARDS GAINED
WIDE LEFT	0	0	0
LEFT	25	45	18.9
CENTER	15	28	5.1
RIGHT	5	9	2.1
WIDE RIGHT	10	18	0.8

HASH — CENTER

PLAY	NUMBER OF TIMES	PERCENT	AVG. YARDS GAINED
.	.	.	.

HASH — RIGHT

PLAY	NUMBER OF TIMES	PERCENT	AVG. YARDS GAINED
.	.	.	.

FORMATION
'SHOT GUN'
.
.
.

Since we don't know how many formations the scouted team may use, our program must assign a number for the value of i to each unique formation. It will do this by keeping a list of the formation names and their assigned number. As each data item is read in, the formation name will be compared to the list and assigned the appropriate number. Refer to level 2.1 in *Figure 3-9*.

We have defined three hash positions and five directions of play so we can assign them integer values as follows:

Hash Position	Value of j	Direction of Play	Value of k
Left	1	Wide Left	1
Center	2	Left	2
Right	3	Center	3
		Right	4
		Wide Right	5

To compute game statistics, the program must keep track of the number of occurrences of various formation, hash-position, and direction-of-play combinations, and the yardage gained with each combination.

We can also see that in order to generate the outputs shown in *Table 3-2* we must have summations or accumulations of the following: (1) number of times a particular combination of formation, hash position, and direction of play occurred and, (2) total yards gained for all the times that a particular combination occurred. From these, the percent and average yards gained can be calculated. Again, for equation purposes, let's assign each of our two accumulators a designation using our previously assigned letters for input variables:

$$\text{Number of times} = N_{ijk}$$
$$\text{Total yards gained} = SUM_{ijk}$$

For example, $SUM_{1,3,2}$ is the accumulation of the total yards gained using the first formation in our list, from the right hash position, with the direction of play being left. These accumulations are represented at levels 2.1.1 and 2.1.2 of *Figure 3-9*. Therefore, we now have the following program modules:

Level 2.1   Check formation read in against list F_i. If not in list, add name to list and assign i value of $F_{\text{last } i+1}$. If in list, assign appropriate i value.

Level 2.1.1 $N_{ijk} = N_{ijk} + 1$

Level 2.1.2 $SUM_{ijk} = SUM_{ijk} + (\text{yards gained this time})_{ijk}$

After all plays have been read and processed accordingly, the Percent and Average Yards Gained for each i,j,k combination can be obtained. The total number of times a play (k) is run for each hash (j) in a particular formation (i) is the summation of N_{ij} for each value of k, which we will denote as NT_{ij} in level 2.1.3 of *Figure 3-9*. Thus, the Percent, P_{ijk}, and Average Yards Gained, AYG_{ijk}, variables can be computed accordingly as illustrated in levels 2.1.1.1 and 2.1.2.1 or:

Level 2.1.1.1 $P_{ijk} = N_{ijk}/NT_{ij}$

Level 2.1.2.1 $AYG_{ijk} = SUM_{ijk}/N_{ijk}$

Report 1 can now be printed for each formation as illustrated in level 3.1 of *Figure 3-9*. Other reports desired would be considered accordingly in levels 3.2, 3.3, etc.

As you can see, the top-down approach provides a step-by-step systematic problem solving procedure. It insures that all inputs and outputs are defined and that the necessary computations identified for the desired outputs are performed. From the various levels or modules, the program can then be written.

Structured Programming

As discussed earlier, computer programs should be developed and implemented (run as a final program) in a well-disciplined modular (sub-program) fashion. Error free instructions, maintainable code (computer ease for program listings), and portable code (modules which can easily be used with other programs) are major design objectives. We looked at the various levels of structured program development using the top-down approach for an example problem. In preparing the final program using this method, program modules are devised to solve small, well-defined portions of the final calculated statistics that are needed (*Figure 3-10*). The main control module calls for each of the modules directly below it, for example:

Top-down design produces a set of versatile, easily maintained program modules that are "called" by a main control module when needed.

```
/*Main Control Module*/
CALL MODULE 1.0
CALL MODULE 2.0
CALL MODULE 3.0
```

**Figure 3-10.
Processing Modules
Relationships.**

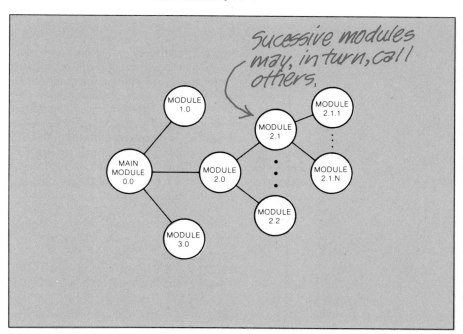

The main program may contain numerous CALL statements that temporarily pass control to specified program modules.

The CALL statement is an instruction to the computer to leave the program instruction list (calling program) that it is currently in and begin processing instructions in the module or subprogram that is named in the CALL statement. The called module has a RETURN instruction at its end to tell the computer to return to the calling program. As shown in this example, the main program may consist primarily of CALL statements to lower level modules. These modules, in turn, may use the CALL statement to call still lower level modules, as follows:

```
/*Module 1.0*/
CALL MODULE 1.1
CALL MODULE 1.2
         .
         .
         .

/*Module 2.0*.
CALL MODULE 2.1
CALL MODULE 2.2
         .
         .
         .

/*Module 3.0*/
CALL MODULE 3.1
CALL MODULE 3.2
         .
         .
         .
```

In structured programming, processing within each module follows a somewhat similar pattern. Processing should be essentially in sequence or in a particular order in its flow with as few jumps as possible. Both a simple sequential program and a more complicated processing sequence are illustrated in *Figure 3-11*. For the simple sequential flow, processing is as just described with a series of CALL or other processing statements. In the second example, control is transferred to different parts in the program depending on various conditions. Programs structured similarly to this second example are difficult to follow and thus difficult to maintain and/or debug. Sometimes even the person who writes such complicated programs often forgets what the various alternatives are that **affect** program transfers.

Structured programming calls for the usage of three principal structures to help simplify the program. These are:

```
1) Sequential Control
2) IF - THEN - ELSE Control
3) Replication - DO WHILE or DO AND TEST
```

Figure 3-11.
Processing Sequence.

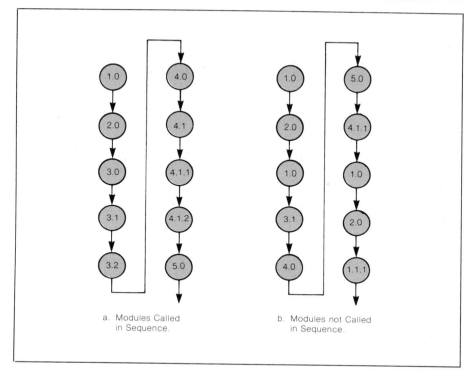

a. Modules Called
   in Sequence.

b. Modules not Called
   in Sequence.

These structures are illustrated in *Figure 3-12a* through *3-12d.*

The first, *Figure 3-12a*, is the conventional sequential flow in a given order. That is, Module A is called, followed by Module B, etc. Examples:

1) Data is read, data is processed, and data is printed.

2) You sit at the table to eat dinner; you eat dinner; you get up from the table.

The second structure, *Figure 3-12b*, is used for processing if a specific condition is true. Examples:

In IF-THEN-ELSE control, the program tests for a specified condition. Control passes to one module if the condition exists, to another if the condition does not exist.

1) IF the condition is true, THEN Module A is processed, ELSE the condition is not true and Module B is processed.

2) IF all data items have not been read, THEN read a new one and sum; ELSE compute the average and print.

3) IF dinner is ready, THEN sit at the table to eat; ELSE continue reading this book.

The processing modules can be single statements or a block of statements, For example:

```
IF I > J THEN
     CALL A
         ELSE
     CALL B
```

Figure 3-12.
Principal Structures.

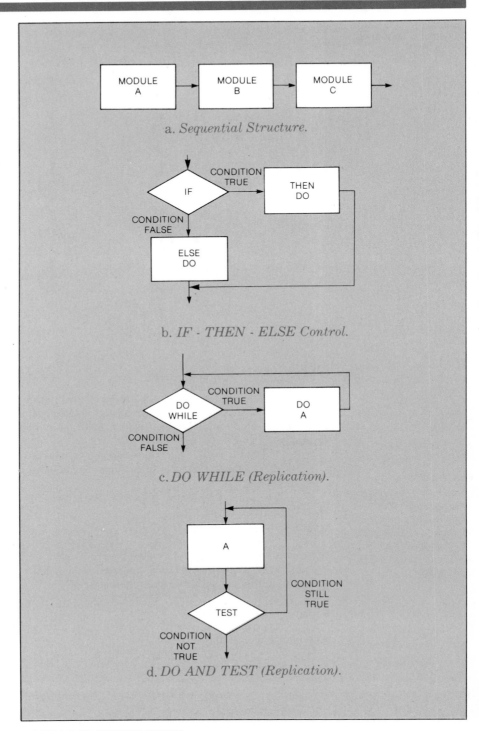

a. *Sequential Structure.*

b. *IF - THEN - ELSE Control.*

c. *DO WHILE (Replication).*

d. *DO AND TEST (Replication).*

In replication, the program repeats a given process as long as a specified condition exists. When the condition no longer exists, the program goes on to the next operation.

The third structure, *Figure 3-12c* and *Figure 3-12d*, is used for repeated operations.

Examples:

1) Do the following sequence of instructions WHILE the condition is true.

2) Read data items WHILE the count I is equal to or less than N.

The DO AND TEST (sometimes referred to as the DO UNTIL) is similar to the DO WHILE with the difference being primarily in when the condition is checked. That is, in the DO WHILE, the condition for executing Module A is first checked and if not true, Module A is not executed. In the DO AND TEST, Module A is first processed, then the condition tested. This is an important difference. Some languages implement only the DO AND TEST condition, while others provide both.

```
WHILE I>J
   DO

      CALL A

   END DO
   .

   .
DO AND TEST I > J
   CALL A
END DO
   .

   .
```

Programs are constructed of combinations of these various structures. The newer languages directly provide these three control structures, but with the other languages, it may be difficult to implement these control structures.

Coding the Program

With the program design complete, your next step is to write the program in the computer language you intend to use.

Coding a program is what most beginners think of as programming, but as you have seen, much programming work must be done before coding of the program begins. Coding is the act of putting your program design into a language that can be used by a computer. This could be machine language or an assembly language, although that is very unlikely. You will probably use a high-level language such as FORTRAN, COBOL or BASIC. These and other high-level languages are discussed in Chapter 4 of this book.

Instructions that implement arithmetic, logical, control transfer, data movement, data assignment, and I/O functions are common to all computer languages.

Regardless of which language you use, there are some fundamental instruction types that are common to all. These are listed here and explained in the following text.

Data Movement (move, load, and store)

Data Assignment

Arithmetic (add, subtract, multiply, divide, absolute value and negation)

Logical (AND, OR, NOT, and EXCLUSIVE OR)

Transfer of Control (Unconditional Branching, Conditional Branching, Loops and Subroutines)

Input and Output Instructions

Program Instructions

Data movement and assignment instructions are used for transferring values between storage locations. Storage locations are used to hold data values and are assigned variable names. The contents of a location can be changed with such instructions.

Arithmetic instructions are typically provided for performing exponentiation, multiplication, division, addition and subtraction. Other numerical capabilities such as matrix multiplication are provided by some special languages. In these special languages, preprogrammed subprograms are usually available and can be called from a main program to perform various popular functions such as obtaining the sine or consine of an angle, etc.

The transfer of control instructions permit the unconditional or conditional transfer of control to begin processing instructions from selected subprograms. The direct transfer or GO TO type instruction (unconditional transfer) is usually frowned on in structured programming methods because it can overly complicate a program.

Looping instructions are used to provide the repeated execution of a certain number of instructions or even a certain number of subprograms.

Input instructions control the reading of data into the computer so it can be processed. Output instructions control the printing out or displaying of results for use or the transfer of output data to auxiliary storage devices. Associated with these input/output instructions may be other instructions which are used to specify the location of the printer where the information is to be written, whether the memory contents are in binary form or ASCII coded form, etc. That is, they provide additional information concerning the input/output operation, but are not executed by the computer, per se, as a multiplication or addition instruction would be executed.

Some computer languages are better suited than others to structured programming techniques.

In the next chapter, we'll examine the more common programming languages and find that some are better suited for structured programming than others. For example, the newer languages such as Pascal and PL/I are much better than FORTRAN, one of the most widely used languages. However, because there are so many programs written in FORTRAN, and because there are so many programmers experienced in using them, it is doubtful that FORTRAN will be totally replaced in the near future. Newer versions of FORTRAN have been updated to permit easier implementation of structured programs.

BASIC is an interactive language that was developed before the advent of structured programming, but has been updated to better accommodate structured program development.

One of the most widely used interactive languages for small computer systems is BASIC. BASIC was one of the earlier languages, so it was developed before structured programming concepts were emphasized. It was developed to provide quick processing capability in a direct interaction or dialog with the computer. It is referred to as an interpretive language. Such languages are different in that the translator (called an interpreter) translates each high-level language instruction and executes it before proceeding to the next instruction. In languages that are compiled, all instructions are first converted to machine instructions, then the instructions are executed. These two types of processing will be discussed in more detail later.

BASIC has been modified by some manufacturers to permit more structured features. For instance, in some personal computers, the IF statement was changed to permit an IF-THEN capability, where a block of statements following the THEN, and not attached to another line number, are executed if the condition is met. (In BASIC, when line numbers are attached to statements, the computer is instructed to execute each line number in sequence in ascending (smaller to larger) order unless a transfer of control occurs. If a transfer of control is encountered, the computer moves to the instruction identified in the transfer of control and again executes instructions in an ascending order sequence.) Consider the following example of the IF-THEN statement:

```
10 IF A>B THEN
      PRINT "A>B":
      PRINT "IT REALLY IS"
20 PRINT "CONTINUE"
```

The two BASIC statements with line numbers 10 and 20 will execute as follows:

IF A is greater than B, then print
```
A > B
IT REALLY IS
```
on the screen of the computer terminal followed by:
```
CONTINUE
```
otherwise (A not greater than B) only
```
CONTINUE
```
will be printed.

Some computer sytems, such as the DEC 20, provide a BASIC which implements the IF-THEN-ELSE structure. In the next chapter, BASIC will be examined in more detail.

Translating the Program

The computer translates programs written in high-level languages (source code) into machine language (object code).

This step in programming is not required if you have coded your program directly in machine language, but that will happen rarely, if ever. Therefore, your coded program must be translated to machine language (*Figure 3-13*). Fortunately, the translation is performed by other computer programs, called assemblers and compilers, so there is little effort on your part. Your coded program that is fed into the translator is called the source program or source code, and the output of the translator is called the object program or object code.

**Figure 3-13.
Conversions of High-Level Language and Assembly Language Programs into Machine Language Programs the Computer Can Understand.**

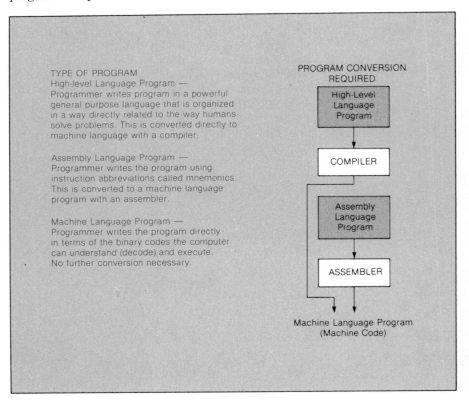

TYPE OF PROGRAM
High-level Language Program —
Programmer writes program in a powerful general purpose language that is organized in a way directly related to the way humans solve problems. This is converted directly to machine language with a compiler.

Assembly Language Program —
Programmer writes the program using instruction abbreviations called mnemonics. This is converted to a machine language program with an assembler.

Machine Language Program —
Programmer writes the program directly in terms of the binary codes the computer can understand (decode) and execute. No further conversion necessary.

PROGRAM CONVERSION REQUIRED

High-Level Language Program

COMPILER

Assembly Language Program

ASSEMBLER

Machine Language Program (Machine Code)

Assembly-language programs, written in mnemonic codes, are translated into machine language by "assembler" programs.

As you recall, computers only understand the digital code which is in binary 1's and 0's and we call this machine language. We humans have a lot of trouble writing programs in machine language because it is tedious and time consuming and we are likely to make mistakes. A higher level language than machine language is called assembly language. In it, we use an alpha-numeric system to write code in abbreviated forms called mnemonics. This is a tremendous improvement over machine language for coding. A program written in assembly language is translated to machine code by an assembler. Assemblers and the corresponding assembly language mnemonics are generally limited to use with one particular machine, which limits their transportability, or use on other machines.

High-level programming languages, written in statements that resemble everyday words, are either "compiled" or "interpreted" into machine language.

The mnemonic codes are still not human language, so even higher-level languages have been developed so that we can code programs in instructions that are similar to our everyday language. Some high-level languages come closer to this ideal than others. A program written in a high-level language may be translated to machine code by a compiler. As you would expect, the compiler program is usually much more complicated than the assembler program. Another type of translator for high-level languages is called an interpreter.

As mentioned, in an interpreter, each statement line is translated *and executed* immediately. This is the type of translator used in interactive applications where the computer "talks back" or prompts you, as is normally done with personal computers. This differs from the compiler where all instruction statements are translated and stored in machine code, then the whole program is executed at once. Thus, the compiled program may be saved in object code on a storage media such as magnetic tape, then used over and over without retranslation. Any high-level language may be either interpreted or compiled, but because of their applications, certain languages are usually interpreted and others are usually compiled. For instance, COBOL is usually compiled while APL is usually interpreted. BASIC can be used both ways.

Testing the Program

After all that work of defining the problem and designing, coding, and translating the program, the program is ready to run. Test runs with the program for the first time should use carefully selected data inputs so that the results can be predicted and easily compared with the computer output. If the program runs to completion the first time, the programmer should be given a big pat on the back. Even the most careful programmer can let an error or two slip in. If it is your first program and it doesn't run, remember that the computer is dumb, so it doesn't know you intended that 0 (zero) to be a letter O. However, if you did a good job through the first steps of program development that we have discussed in this chapter, your program will most likely be running smoothly after a few test runs.

Just remember that testing is to verify that you did a good job. Finalizing the design is not the intent of testing. If you depend on testing for final design, your program will probably be so patched-up that no one else can understand it. Also, be aware that runs with artificial test data may not reveal an error that actually exists, and someday it may occur at the most inopportune time when a particular combination of events exist.

Errors in programs are usually called "bugs" and the testing and removal of the errors is commonly called "debugging."

PROGRAM CLASSIFICATIONS

Programs are typically written for one of four application areas — Scientific, Business, Systems and Personal (*Figure 3-14*). The advent of the personal computer recently ushered in the fourth category.

Programs for scientific applications typically solve complex mathematical equations.

Scientific: Scientific applications involve the uses of the computer to solve various engineering and scientific problems. In such problems, mathematical equations or algebraic formulas are solved by assigning digital values to the variables. An example might be to identify the electrical current and voltages at various locations within an electrical circuit, or suppose we want to determine the average of a set of readings from an instrument such as a voltmeter.

**Figure 3-14.
Computer Applications.**

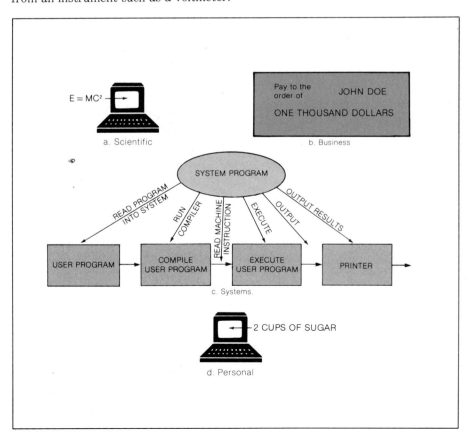

The space program would never have been successful without the electronic digital computer. Scientific programs were written and run to determine the trajectory for the Saturn and Apollo space vehicles. Necessary decisions for operational changes during the ill fated Apollo 13 flight could not have been so successfully made without rapid executions of scientific programs, thus preventing a possible disaster and serious set back for our nation's space program. Even the development of the integrated circuit, which has played such a major role in the computer revolution, could not have been as easily accomplished without data obtained from mathematical equations solved by the use of the computer. Scientific programs usually are written for solving mathematical equations; therefore, computer languages used in these programs are structured for such problem types.

Business: Probably every large business in the United States uses a digital computer. Each time that the payroll program is run, a digital computer searches its files on auxiliary storage for each employee and determines the amount of money that the employee receives. After the appropriate deductions are made, a check is automatically printed by the computer.

Business programs perform such tasks as generating payrolls, maintaining inventories, printing reports, and graphing trends, while system programs (compilers, assemblers, operating systems, monitors, etc.) create and control the operating environment within a computer.

In addition to programs for generating payrolls, other business programs are written for generating invoices for products sold or rented, maintaining a file on each customer, and keeping track of when payments are made, maintaining inventories, printing summary reports, and plotting graphs of trends. Languages such as COBOL and another called RPG (Report Generator), are used most frequently for business applications.

Systems: System programs are not used to solve mathematical or business problems but make possible the solution of such problems. Systems programs are programs written to use the computer system efficiently. The language translators or compilers and assemblers are systems programs. These programs, as discussed earlier, translate a high-level instruction to the appropriate machine instructions. When a program is submitted to the computer for processing, a system program called an operating system is used for insuring that the task or application program is executed. Special directions are interpreted by this program to set up the proper environment for executing the program at hand. The operating system program loads in the appropriate language translator; for example, a FORTRAN compiler. The operating system program then passes control to the compiler program. When the compiler finishes, the system program or operating system then directs the computer to execute the machine instructions generated by the compiler for the application program. The system programs category also includes programs for hardware systems which include computers. For example, in a manufacturing system, control programs for monitoring various instruments and performing desired operations, such as turning on a valve or switch, etc., are system programs. As the book continues, other tasks performed by these system programs will be discussed in a later chapter.

Personal computer programs are written for applications such as entertainment, education, and household budget management.

Personal: Personal computer programs are a new class and made possible by the new personal computers. Such programs might include a bank statement and budget routine to keep track of current expenditures for a family or a filing system for keeping cooking recipes. Home entertainment programs such as pinball, computer chess, space wars and other such games are programs included in this class. The football statistics program discussed earlier would probably fall within this class.

The four classifications presented above are rather broad areas and were chosen to describe the various program types in general terms. There could be applications consisting of combinations of these categories. We've already discussed how the various high-level languages were developed to make programming easier in these various categories.

WHAT HAVE WE LEARNED?

In this chapter we have learned the five basic steps in developing a computer program; understanding the problem, designing the program, coding the program, translating the program, and testing the program. We saw how flowcharts are useful in understanding a problem and designing a program. We learned that differently constructed programs with different design objectives can produce the same solution to a problem. We contrasted the bottom-up and top-down design methods and used the top-down method with example problems. We learned that the top-down design concept can be successfully used regardless of the program language used in coding. We discussed structured programming and the inherent portability of its modular construction. We discussed coding and the types of instructions common to all codes. We learned about the three different types of translators; assembler, compiler, and interpreter. We discussed testing of the completed program and learned that testing is often referred to as debugging.

WHAT'S NEXT?

In the next chapter, we'll investigate the high-level languages in detail and find out why some are better suited than others for certain applications.

Quiz for Chapter 3

1. Two programs can both yield the same results, yet one takes much more time to execute than the other.
   True or False

2. Programs written in a high-level language are generally easier to write than those in assembly language.
   True or False

3. Top-down program design is where the computer executes instructions from the top down.
   True or False

4. Top-down program design can be used only with BASIC.
   True or False

5. There are many different high-level languages.
   True or False

6. A compiler is more complex than an assembler.
   True or False

7. 'Debugging' a program is finding and correcting errors so that it will run as designed.
   True or False

8. Proper program design can reduce testing costs.
   True or False

9. A flowchart is always required for proper program development.
   True or False

10. Program development cost is usually reduced by using structured programming.
    True or False

11. Which flow diagram more closely describes the following statements?
    ```
    WHILE A < B DO
         SUM = SUM + A
         END DO
    ```

a.

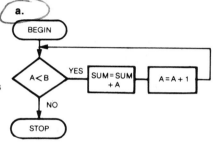

b.

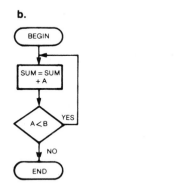

12. Which of the following flow diagrams
more closely describes the following
level description?

1.0 READ DATA VALUES
    1.1 READ N
       1.1.1 READ N VALUES OF X
       1.1.2 READ N VALUES OF Y
2.0 COMPUTE AREA
    2.1 AREA (I) = X(I)*Y(I), I = 1
        TO N
3.0 PRINT AREA
    3.1 PRINT AREA (I), I = 1 TO N

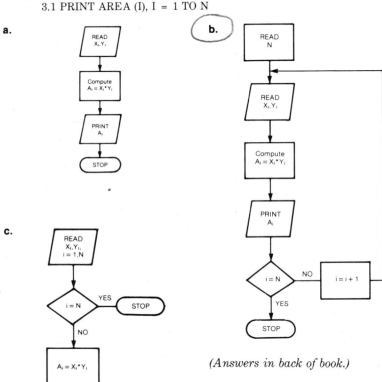

(Answers in back of book.)

Languages

ABOUT THIS CHAPTER

In the last chapter we discussed programming, and in particular, the five steps in program development. We learned that coding or actually writing the instructions in program language is only one step and, although important, is not any more so than, say, program testing or verification in the overall task. That is, programming requires all five steps. Coding cannot be done properly without a working knowledge of the program language that is to be used. In this chapter, we will investigate program languages and find out why there are so many. We will spend a little more time discussing the program language, BASIC, than on the other languages, so that in a later chapter we can discuss algorithms for data structures using BASIC statements. Let's begin our discussion of programming languages with the BASIC language.

BASIC

BASIC is a popular programming language for small, interactive computer systems that allows direct interaction between a single user and the program.

As discussed in previous chapters, BASIC is a very popular high level language. Although designed primarily as an interactive language (and one which usually requires an interpreter), there are some BASIC compilers. (Recall our discussion in Chapter 3 regarding interpreters and compilers.) BASIC is popular because it is easy to learn and use. Most all interactive computer systems (systems which allow direct interaction between the user and the user's program) support BASIC. This includes almost all personal computers such as the TI-99/4, Radio Shack TRS-80, APPLE II; microcomputers; and minicomputers, such as the DEC PDP 11 series. BASIC is an acronym for Beginner's All-Purpose Symbolic Instruction Code. It was developed to provide an easy to use and easy to learn interactive language for time-sharing computer systems.

As noted, interactive systems are those which permit direct interaction between the user and the user's program while it is being executed. Time-sharing systems are those which provide·the hardware and systems software that allow two or more users to directly interact with their programs at essentially the same time. Thus, although there may be many users, the system treats each one as if he or she were the only one using the system. The computer can do this because the execution speeds of the computer are so much faster than the response time of humans. In the time it takes you to punch a character on a keyboard, the computer can execute millions of instructions. *Figure 4-1* illustrates the time-sharing concept.

Figure 4-1.
Time-Sharing Computer
System.

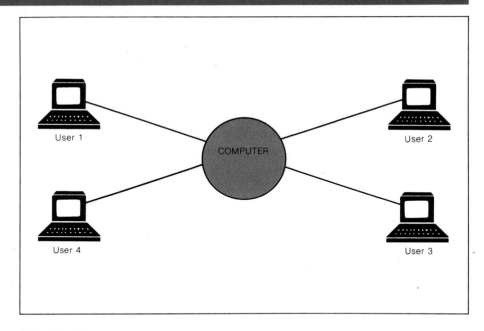

User 1

User 2

COMPUTER

User 4

User 3

BASIC Statements

BASIC statements tell the
computer what to do.

BASIC statements tell the computer the type of operations that
are to be performed. That is, if you want to multiply two numbers and set
the result to the variable A, you say;

    LET A = 3 * 4

Simple, isn't it?

When this instruction is typed into a computer terminal, or CRT
keyboard, the computer multiplies 3 times 4 and sets the variable A
(memory storage location assigned to A) to the number 12. Twelve is stored
at location A in floating point representation. Floating point is used
because you may want to execute a statement like;

    LET A = 3∧32

or set $A = 3^{32}$, which is 1.8530202E + 15. (This is scientific exponentiation
and means 1.8530202×10^{15}.) The caret or upward arrow (∧) is used to
indicate exponentiation. Some BASICS also permit a double asterisk or **
for exponentiation. This statement will generate a number much bigger
than can be represented by a 16-bit word or even a 32-bit word, unless
floating point is used.

We can subtract or divide with similar types of BASIC statements.
Most BASIC translators will permit you to leave out the "LET" so you
simply say;

    A = 3 − 4

or

    A = 16/9

To see the value of A stored in memory you simply type PRINT A. See
Figure 4-2.

**Figure 4-2.
Examples of BASIC
Statements on a CRT
Screen.**

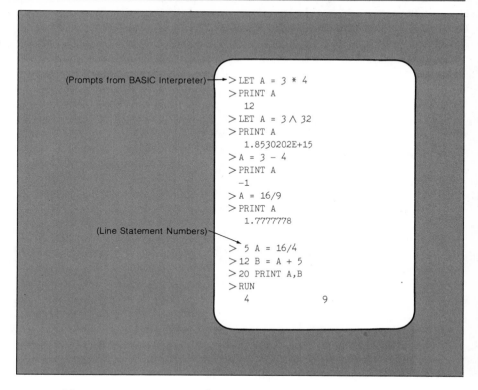

(Prompts from BASIC Interpreter)

```
> LET A = 3 * 4
> PRINT A
   12
> LET A = 3 ∧ 32
> PRINT A
   1.8530202E+15
> A = 3 - 4
> PRINT A
  -1
> A = 16/9
> PRINT A
   1.7777778
```

(Line Statement Numbers)

```
>  5 A = 16/4
> 12 B = A + 5
> 20 PRINT A,B
> RUN
    4              9
```

When used in a program BASIC statements are numbered, and are normally processed in ascending order. They execute when given the command RUN.

Now suppose we want to first assign A a value and then later on in the program assign B to equal A + 5. To do this, these BASIC statements must begin with a line number nnnnn; that is, it can be any number from 1 to the limit of memory or the limit of the digit values, such as, 99999. A program can then be written where the instruction execution order will be determined by the line number and, of course, any transfer instruction will designate to which line number to transfer. That is, when directed by a RUN command, the computer will first execute the line with the smallest line number. If this statement does not specifically direct the computer to go to a different line number, then the instruction with the next higher line number will be executed. Thus, we can write a two statement program:

```
 5 A = 16/4
12 B = A + 5
```

We then type;

```
RUN
```

and the computer executes first the statement with line number 5 which sets A = 4, and then executes line 12 which sets B = 9. To print A and B add the statement (*Figure 4-2*).

```
20 PRINT A,B
```

Statements are executed immediately if no line numbers are provided. With a line number, they are deferred for later execution when directed by the RUN command. For deferred execution, all statements must be numbered and each line must have a unique line number. If you attach a new statement to a previously used line number, the new statement will replace the former statement.

The symbol = is used to assign a variable to an expression. An expression is some combination of operators and variables and constants. The following arithmetic operators may be used:

+ addition

− subtraction

* multiplication

/ division

∧ , ↑ or ** exponentiation

Variables are used for assigning specific memory locations for values which can change. The current value is maintained in memory, but the memory contents for that variable may be changed with a new assignment as demonstrated in *Figure 4-2* for the variable A. Variable names may be one or more alphanumeric symbols, however, the first digit in the name must be alphabetic.

Variables can be integers, real numbers, or alphanumeric strings.

Variables are locations which may be assigned integer or real numbers or they may be assigned coded alphanumeric characters. To identify the second case from the first, a $ symbol is attached to the end of the variable name for alphanumeric assignments. For example:

```
10 A$ = "THIS IS A GOOD BOOK"
```

This statement will tell the computer to assign the necessary storage locations to contain the digital codes, such as ASCII codes, for the symbols or characters that follow beginning at a memory location specified by A. The quotation marks around the character string are used to tell the computer to assign digital codes for this alphanumeric data. Note that blank spaces are treated as characters and there is a code for space. Now a statement, 60 PRINT A$, will cause THIS IS A GOOD BOOK to be printed. Numeric constants are directly specified without quotation marks.

Now let's recall the problem we discussed in the last chapter, that is, to obtain a student's average grade for 6 grades.

Let's look once again at the levels defined in Chapter 3, *Figure 3-4* or:

```
1.0   Read numbers
1.1   Read the number of values to be averaged, N
1.1.1 Read N values of numbers, V
2.0   Compute average
2.1   SUM = SUM + V
2.1.1 Average = SUM/N
3.0   Print answer
```

We have seen that it's easy in the BASIC language to set SUM = 0, or SUM = SUM + V, or AVERAGE = SUM/N. These operations can be indicated by simple commands or statements. But, how do we read N or V and how do we print AVERAGE?

Input to and output from the computer terminal is done by an INPUT statement and a PRINT statement. That is, to input the number N, we simply say:

```
10 INPUT N
```

The INPUT and PRINT statements respectively cause the computer to receive information at its input and to display or print information at its output.

This statement, when executed prompts you with a question mark and waits until you press in a number for N from the keyboard, followed by a carriage return (press the RETURN or ENTER key). Remember, BASIC is designed for interacting directly with your program, so you don't want to punch your program on the IBM cards discussed in Chapter 1. You enter it on a keyboard that looks very similar to a typewriter (*Figure 4-3*) and is connected directly to the computer. When a key is pressed, the corresponding character or symbol is displayed on a CRT or television-like screen.

Figure 4-3.
Typical CRT Terminal.

Now, let's see how we display or output something on the CRT. To do this, we use the PRINT statement, or:

```
60 PRINT AVERAGE
```

This statement, when executed, will cause the value assigned to the variable AVERAGE to be printed without any identification. If we want it to be identified, we can print THE AVERAGE IS, followed by the value. Recall that alphanumeric data may be specified by use of quotation marks.

You can enclose a remark in quotes to have it displayed with the input or output data.

Thus we can change line 60 to be, 60 PRINT "THE ANSWER IS   "; AVERAGE. The semicolon is used to tell the interpreter not to leave any designated spaces between the last character in quotations and the most significant digit of the answer.

Your choice of a comma or semicolon to separate the items in the PRINT statement determines the spacing of output data.

Recall in *Figure 4-2*, we used a comma between A and B; that is, the statement 20 PRINT A, B. The 4 (for A) was printed in the second character position and the 9 (for B) in character position 16. If the statement, 20 PRINT A;B had been used, the result would have been 4 in the second character position and 9 in the fifth character position, since the semicolon spaces the printout differently from the comma. By using commas or semicolons, the programmer can vary the positioning of the information as it prints out on the screen. Although the print positions given in this example are true for a particular machine, print positions can vary depending on the computer make and model.

Now, let's see if we have introduced enough BASIC statements to write or code our program.

A Program in BASIC

```
10 REM THIS PROGRAM COMPUTES AVERAGE OF N
   NUMBERS
20 PRINT "ENTER NUMBER OF ITEMS"
30 INPUT N
40 SUM = 0
50 I = 1
60 PRINT "ENTER GRADE"
70 INPUT V
80 SUM = SUM + V
90 IF I = N THEN 120
100 I = I + 1
110 GO TO 60
120 AVERAG = SUM/N
130 PRINT "THE AVERAGE IS  "; AVERAG
140 STOP
```

REM identifies this line as comments.

Prompt asks for grades.

Hold it! There are some statements we haven't discussed. Specifically, what is statement number 10?

```
10 REM THIS PROGRAM COMPUTES AVERAGE OF N NUMBERS
```

This is a remark or comment statement. It allows you to make comments about (document) your program. The word REM tells the interpreter to simply ignore this statement, that is, no execution will occur once the REM has been identified. However, remark statements are printed if a program listing is printed.

OK, next we see that statement 20 will tell us to enter the number of grades for our example. Statement 30 tells the computer to wait for N, the number of grades, in our case 6, to be entered on the keyboard and assigns the number of grades to the variable N. Statement 40 zeros SUM as discussed in Chapter 3, and in statement 50, the computer sets I to 1. Statement 60 prompts us to enter the grade. Statement 70, as statement 30, tells the computer to wait for input and assigns the grade entered to the variable V. Statement 80 accumulates the grades. Now, how about 90.

Recall from Chapter 3 that we need some way of testing to get out of a loop. Statement 90, provides this ability. The IF statement takes on the general form;

```
nnnnn IF relational expression THEN statement
number
```

The "relational expression" is an expression consisting of variables and relational operators rather then arithmetic operators. These operators are as follows:

= Equal to
> Greater than
< Less than
> = Greater than or equal to
< = Less than or equal to
> < or< >Not equal to

The IF-THEN statement is used to signify that all grades have been received and to transfer control to compute the average grade.

In the IF statement, the computer will transfer control to the statement number following the word THEN if the expression is true. If it is not true, then the next statement following the IF statement will be executed. That is, if the value assigned to I is equal to the value assigned to N, then statement number 120 will be executed. If not, statement number 100, which follows 90, will be executed.

For the first five values read, I will be less than N and statement 100 will be executed. Statement 110 is a direct or unconditional transfer of control instruction. That is, when the "nnnnn GO TO statement number" instruction is executed, control passes directly to the specified statement number, regardless. When I is less than 6, one will be added to I at statement 100 and statement 110 will direct the computer to loop back and execute the program again starting at statement 60. As a result the six values for the grades get entered.

This is what we want until I = 6, in which case all grades have been summed and we are ready to compute the average. When I = N, statement 90 directs the computer to execute statement 120. Here, the variable AVERAG is assigned to the accumulated grades in the location SUM divided by the number of grades N.

Why did we leave off the E in average? Well, some BASIC interpreters only permit variable names to be a maximum of 6 characters. In fact, some only permit a maximum of 2 unique characters. Recall that the first character must be alphabetic. You may also be wondering why we didn't use statement line numbers beginning at 1 and continuing 2, 3, 4, etc. Using larger numbers leaves gaps in case we want to insert another statement later on. That way we don't have to renumber all the other statement lines and change the line numbers in statements such as the 120 in statement line number 90.

Statement 130 prints the result we want from our program. Statement 140 directs the computer to stop.

With the commands just described, we could write or code programs for a number of different applications. There are however, some additional features of BASIC which make it easier to write other program types.

We will examine some of these additional BASIC capabilities next.

Additional BASIC Features

The READ and DATA statements enable you to keep data with the program rather than reading it in separately each time.

Suppose we want to preset our grades rather than reading them in from the terminal, one by one. This can be done with the DATA statement. This statement is of the form;

```
nnnnn DATA data-list
```

To set values to the data-list a READ statement is used. The READ statement is of the form;

```
nnnnn READ variable-list
```

Let's assume the grades we want to average are 82, 47, 95, 100, 68, 91. We can rewrite our program as follows

```
10 REM THIS PROGRAM COMPUTES AVERAGE OF N NUMBERS
30 READ V1, V2, V3, V4, V5, V6
80 SUM = V1 + V2 + V3 + V4 + V5 + V6
120 AVERAG = SUM/6
130 PRINT "THE AVERAGE IS "; AVERAG
140 STOP
150 DATA 82, 47, 95, 100, 68, 91
```

Statement number 30 reads the values of the data items specified in statement 150. The variable V1 is assigned 82, V2 assigned 47 and so forth.

The DATA statement and corresponding READ statement is useful for presetting variables. Notice that to change the six values to six other grades, only the DATA statement of line 150 need be changed. We could of course, have used direct assignments for the variables V1 to V6 or;

```
12 V1 = 82
14 V2 = 47
16 V3 = 95
```

and so forth instead of using the data statement, but then to make a change, we would need to change the value in each statement.

The method is still not as flexible as the first, in that in order to change the number of grades to be averaged, we would have to add or take away one or more V's.

Another way to solve this problem is to define a table or array of variables. An array is a collection of variables arranged in a way that allows them to be used easily in a computer program. The dimension statement is used to declare such a table or array:

```
DIM V(50)
```

Setting up an "array" is an efficient way to assign variable names to a group of related data items. Subscripts following the variable name identify individual data items in the array.

This statement directs the computer to set aside 50 memory locations for the one dimensional array, V. This one dimensional array is the same as having items listed in sequence. A particular data item in this array is obtained by a value in parenthesis (a subscript) following the V which identifies the array. The subscript can be any positive value from 1 to 50. Or the subscript may be another variable constant or expression which can assume any positive value from 1 to 50. The Ith item in this array for example, can be assigned to the variable A by any one of the following statements where the value within the parentheses is the value of I;

<u>Comments</u>

```
 5 A = V(20)              for the 20th item
10 A = V(J + 3 * 5)       variable, dependent on value of J
15 A = V(20 - J + X * 2)  variable, dependent on J and X
```

If the value within the parentheses exceeds 50, then an error will occur and will be denoted on the CRT screen.

To read all values from the array V one can use statements as follows:

```
20 FOR T=1 TO 50
21 READ V(T)
22 NEXT T
```

and all values that are in the array can be used. Of course, a data statement is required to give values to the array items. (The language structure of statements 20, 21 and 22 is explained a little later in the section on subroutines.)

Expression Evaluation

BASIC evaluates arithmetic expressions from left to right, and in a particular order of priority.

When combining arithmetic operators with variables and constants in an expression, the results depend on how the expression is evaluated. For instance, consider the following expression:

```
A + B/C * D
```

This expression should be evaluated as

$$A + \frac{B*D}{C}$$

However, it could be interpreted as

$$\frac{A + B}{CD} \text{ or } A + \frac{B}{CD} \text{ or } \frac{A + B}{C} * D$$

To ensure expressions are evaluated properly, a hierarchal structure was established. For this structure, the following rules apply.

(1) Expressions within parentheses are evaluated first.

(2) When the expression is evaluated, first exponentiation is performed, then multiplication and division and lastly, addition and subtraction.

(3) If there are two operators at the same level, evaluation occurs from left to right.

Let's look at our example again,

$$A + B/C * D$$

According to our rules, first B/C is computed, then this result is multiplied by D, yielding

$$\frac{BD}{C}$$

Finally, the A is added, yielding

$$A + \frac{BD}{C}$$

Now let's look at an expression with parentheses. Consider the algebraic relation,

$$A + \frac{B + CD + E}{F} + G$$

We can write this as,

$$A + B/F + C*D/F + E/F + G$$

or

$$A + (B + C * D + E)/F + G$$

In the first example, B is divided by F, then C is multiplied by D and the product divided by F. E is divided by F. Finally, all terms are added together.

In the second example, the expression within the parentheses is first evaluated. First the product of C and D is obtained. Next, B is added to this product. E is then added and the sum divided by F. Finally, A and G are added to this term.

Subroutines

Subroutines can be called repeatedly from the main program. You can use subroutines as modules in structured programming.

BASIC, as well as all other languages, provides a means for implementing subroutines.

Although there is no set rule for their usage, subroutines, which were discussed earlier, are typically used when a section of code is to be referenced two or more times. That is, subroutines define a means by which the same set of code can be executed a number of times. Subroutines are also used in structured programming for defining the various modules even if the module is only called once.

Recall that a subroutine is called for from a main program by a statement in the main program. After the statements in the subroutine are completed, the execution is returned to the main program. For this reason, subroutines must end with a RETURN statement. The RETURN statement transfers control back to the calling routine.

Subroutines are called for use by the following form of instruction:

```
GO SUB    nnnnn
```

a command where nnnnn is the beginning statement number of the subroutine. *Figure 4-4* illustrates the general usage of the subroutine. In this figure two subroutines beginning at line numbers 1000 and 2000 respectively are shown. Each returns control to the calling routine.

**Figure 4-4.
General Usage of
Subroutines.**

	BASIC	GENERAL FORM
	REM BEGIN	(* BEGIN *)
	.	.
	100 GO SUB 1000	CALL SUB A
	.	.
	200 GO SUB 2000	CALL SUB B
	.	.
	300 GO SUB 1000	CALL SUB A
	.	.
	400 GO SUB 2000	CALL SUB B
	.	.
	500 STOP	END
	1000 REM SUBROUTINE A	SUBROUTINE A
	.	.
	1099 RETURN	RETURN
	2000 REM SUBROUTINE B	SUBROUTINE B
	.	.
	2099 RETURN	RETURN

For instance, we could have had the program read in the grades as a subroutine. Consider the program,

```
10 PRINT "ENTER NUMBER OF GRADES"
20 INPUT N
30 GO SUB 60
40 REM OTHER PROGRAM STATMENTS
50 STOP
60 FOR I = 1 TO N
70 PRINT "ENTER V"
80 INPUT V
90 NEXT I
100 RETURN
```

In this example, once the total number of (how many) grades has been read in statement number 20, the subroutine at statement number 60 is called to read in the individual grades. It does this N times to record all the grades, returns to statement 40, then 50 and stops. The remaining averaging statements would need to be added to get the average.

You have just seen another feature of BASIC in lines 60, 70, 80, and 90. It provides the capability to process a group of statements over and over again. This is called a loop. BASIC provides the two statements, FOR and NEXT, for implementing a loop. The general syntax or proper form for these statements is as follows;

> The FOR-TO-NEXT sequence is a straight-forward way to imple-ment loops in BASIC.

```
nnnnn FOR variable =
        expression 1 TO expression 2
        STEP expression 3
              .
              .
              .
              .
              .
        NEXT variable
```

That is, in our earlier example, we could write this program as follows;

```
 10 DIM V(100)
 20 PRINT "ENTER NUMBER OF GRADES"
 30 INPUT N
 40 SUM = 0
 50 FOR I = 1 TO N
 60 PRINT "ENTER GRADE"
 70 INPUT V(I)
 80 SUM = SUM + V(I)
 90 NEXT I
100 PRINT "THE AVERAGE IS"; SUM/N
120 STOP
```

Notice that this program is similar to the ones before, except that we have added statements 50 and 90. Statement 50 is used to direct the computer to process all those statements down through statement 90, N times. Each time statement 90 is reached, I will be incremented by 1 and if the result is not greater than N, the loop will be repeated beginning with statement 50. Once I is greater than N, statement 100 will be executed. Notice that in statement 100 that the division for SUM/N is performed in the PRINT statement. This saves a separate line of code and saves one memory location that in previous programs we have named AVERAG.

As noted the increment which is added to I each time statement 90 is reached is one. We could change this increment or step size by specifying it in the FOR statement. If it is left off, it will always be one. A step size of 2 would be:

```
50 FOR I = 1 TO N STEP 2
```

For this case statements 50 to 90 would be executed N/2 times.

There are other features of BASIC which will not be discussed in this book, but which you can find in one of the many books describing the language. Some BASIC interpreters provide the "IF THEN ELSE" feature. This control structure, as discussed in the preceding chapter, helps to implement structured programming. Unfortunately, however, this feature alone is not enough for good structured programs and BASIC is not one of the languages typically recommended for implementing good software engineering or structured programming techniques. However, BASIC is still a very popular language because it is easy to learn and apply.

Notice that we examined several programs which accomplish the same functions. This is typical for programming. That is, there will usually be several ways to write a program to obtain the same results. Later however, we will see that different programs may have different resource requirements. Resources are things such as memory, auxiliary storage, or computer CPU time. A person with good programming skills will select a programming method which will minimize these resource requirements and also make the program easy to write and maintain. If consistent with other objectives, an attempt should be made to make a program easy to run on other equipment (transportable) so it may be used in other systems.

One language which was developed in the late 1960's and early 1970's for teaching good programming skills is Pascal. Pascal has become a very popular language and has features which will permit structured programming. Let's look at this language next.

PASCAL

Pascal was introduced by Professor Niklaus Wirth in the early 1970's to teach good programming style to computer science students. It was named for Blaise Pascal, a French mathematician. Since it is a name, not an acronym, only the first letter is capitalized. One of the major advantages of Pascal is that it does not use a lot of different language constructs or statement types. Even though it was initially used in academics, it has rapidly become one of the more popular languages. Although most Pascal compilers do not employ some of the more useful characteristics like data statement etc., it still is an extremely useful language for scientific, personal and systems programming. Because of its lack of many varied statement types, Pascal has been implemented on many small mini and microcomputer systems.

Pascal differs from BASIC. Variables must be defined with a VAR statement at the start of the program.

The first noticeable difference between Pascal and BASIC is that in Pascal, all variables used must be defined at the beginning of the program. This assignment is accomplished by a VAR statement. Variables can be specified as integer or real (floating point). For example, considering once again our problem of computing the average of N values, we have to define not only the variable V, but also I and N.

We do this with the following statements:

```
VAR I, N : INTEGER ;
SUM, AVERAGE , V : REAL ;
```

That is, variable I and N are integer, SUM, AVERAGE, and V are real. Also, notice we used the seven character word, AVERAGE. This is another feature of Pascal. Variable names may be as many as eight characters in length. If they are longer, usually the first eight must be unique and the remainder are ignored.

Now let's look at the Pascal program for computing the average of a set of N numbers and compare it with our BASIC program doing the same.

```
1.  PROGRAM AVERAGE (INPUT, OUTPUT);
2.    (* THIS PROGRAM COMPUTES THE AVERAGE OF N
      GRADES *)
3.    (* N = NUMBER OF GRADES *)
4.    (* V = CURRENT VARIABLE OR GRADE READ *)
5.  VAR I , N : INTEGER ;
6.    SUM, V, AVERAGE : REAL;
7.  BEGIN
8.  READ (N) ;
9.  I := 1 ;
10.   SUM := 0 ;
11. FOR I := 1 TO N DO
12.   BEGIN
13.     READ (V) ;
14.     SUM := SUM + V ;
15.   END ;
16. AVERAGE := SUM/N ;
17. WRITELN ('THE AVERAGE IS ' , AVERAGE) ;
18. END.
```

In Pascal, program lines are usually unnumbered, variable names can be up to eight characters in length, and program statements end with a semicolon.

The above program lists line numbers that will be used only for reference in describing the program. They are not required or used as the statement numbers are in BASIC. If the program is typed on cards, a separate IBM or data card is used for each line-numbered statement.

The program begins with the statement

PROGRAM AVERAGE (INPUT, OUTPUT);

This statement may vary between systems but, essentially, it specifies the name of the program, its beginning, and that it will use both input and output in its execution. Statements are terminated by a semicolon.

Lines 2 thru 4 are comments. Comments are denoted by an opening or closing parenthesis with the asterisk as shown. Comments can be placed anywhere on any line or card. They are not considered anywhere as statements and thus, do not require the semicolon.

The main program body starts with the BEGIN statement and finishes with the END. statement.

Line numbers 5 and 6 contain the statements for declaring variables. As discussed above, the variables I, N, SUM, V and AVERAGE must be declared. Following variable declarations is the main program body. This set of statements is initiated by the BEGIN statement and is terminated by the END. statement. This last END differs from the others (like in the loop) in that the last END has a period following it.

Line number 8 is used to read the number of grades to be averaged, N. Statements at lines 9 and 10 are used to assign values to the variables I and SUM. Notice that assignments are made with the colon and equal sign as,

```
9 I := 1 ;
10 SUM := 0 ;
```

The general form of the assignment statement is as follows:

```
identifier : = expression ;
```

As mentioned, on the left hand side of the : = symbols is a single word variable identifier and this variable must have previously been declared. The right hand side represents an expression.

Expressions are evaluated much in the same fashion as those in BASIC. Logical expressions are assigned to logical variables; arithmetic expressions to real or integer variables. The arithmetic and logical operators used in BASIC are the same for Pascal. The order of evaluation is also similar.

Pascal provides a number of constructs or control statements for controlling program flow. Recall that with BASIC we had essentially three control statements;

```
IF expression THEN nnnnn
GO TO nnnnn
FOR variable = expression TO expression
NEXT variable
```

The FOR-DO loop construction in Pascal is similar to FOR-NEXT in BASIC.

In Pascal, we have the equivalent of these and several more. In place of the FOR - NEXT instruction sequence (construct) of BASIC, we have:

```
11 FOR I := 1 TO N DO
12    BEGIN
13       READ (V) ;
14       SUM := SUM + V;
15    END ;
```

The group or block of statements initiated by the BEGIN and END keywords will be executed N times as in the BASIC program. The variable I is incremented as before when the END keyword is reached, signifying the end of the block. Once incremented, it is tested and if the result exceeds N, the next statement (line 16) following this block is executed.

Another construct which permits looping is the WHILE. The statements reading and summing the V values could have been executed in the following way.

```
WHILE I < = N DO
   BEGIN
      READ (V) ;
      SUM := SUM + V ;
      I := I + 1 ;
   END ;
```

The WHILE statement is one recommended for use in structured programming. The block of statements are executed while I is equal to or less than N. I is tested first and if the condition in the expression is not satisfied, then the block of statements is not executed. Notice that this is different from the FOR loop where the block will always be executed at least once since testing is not done until the block has been processed.

Returning to our full program, the average is computed and printed in the statements at line number 16 and 17.

Additional Pascal Statements

A Pascal program consists of blocks of statements enclosed by BEGIN and END. The program treats each block collectively as a statement.

As previously stated, Pascal does not provide as many statement types as some of the other languages. However, the ones it does provide can be used to write well-structured programs. We have already seen the uses of blocks. Blocks are one or more statements contained within a BEGIN and END keyword. The entire block is treated as a *single* statement. Blocks may have other blocks nested within. A third control structure, useful for decision making processes, is the IF, THEN, ELSE structure. The general form is:

```
IF expression THEN
(statement or block)
ELSE
(statement or block)
```

For this structure, IF the expression is true THEN the first block is executed. If the condition fails, the second block which follows the ELSE is executed. Recall from our discussions on structured programming that these three constructs,

```
FOR,
WHILE, and
IF THEN ELSE,
```

and subroutines are all that are needed for structured programming.

Procedures in Pascal correspond to subroutines in BASIC.

In Pascal, subroutines are referred to as procedures. Procedures in Pascal provide a means not only of reducing total code requirements, but they provide a means of defining independent modules so as to implement modular programming. Pascal procedures are treated similarly to subroutines in BASIC except for a few important differences. The most important is the ability to declare local variables.

"Local" variables are defined and used within a given procedure. "Global" variables are defined in the main program and can be used anywhere.

This simply means that new variables can be declared within a procedure and they are completely independent of those outside the procedure.

On the other hand, global variables are variables defined before procedures are called and which may be referenced directly within each procedure or module.

We could redefine our program as follows:

```
PROGRAM AVERAGE (INPUT, OUTPUT) ;
  (* COMMENTS SAME AS BEFORE *)
VAR N : INTEGER ;
  AVERAGE : REAL ;
BEGIN
  READN ;
  READANDSUM ;
  PRINTAVERAGE ;
END ;
```

Each of these lines references a procedure. →

A procedure for each READN, READANDSUM and PRINTAVERAGE could then be written. These would be as follows:

```
PROCEDURE READN ;
BEGIN
  READ(N) ;
END ;

PROCEDURE READANDSUM ;
VAR V, SUM : REAL ;
  I : INTEGER ;
BEGIN
  SUM := 0 ;
  FOR I := 1 TO N DO
    BEGIN
      READ (V) ;
      SUM := SUM + V ;
    END ;
  AVERAGE = SUM/N
END ;

PROCEDURE PRINTAVERAGE ;
BEGIN
  WRITELN ('THE AVERAGE IS ', AVERAGE);
END ;
```

First of all, notice how this program closely resembles the first level statements discussed earlier, describing the problem, i.e.:

1.0 Read Numbers
2.0 Compute Average
3.0 Print Answer

We could have made it exact by reading the grades into an array as will be discussed shortly. Notice that the variables N and AVERAGE are global variables. That is, they are defined at the beginning and all procedures called following their declaration may reference these variables. On the other hand variables declared within the procedure, such as SUM and I are only available to procedures called within this procedure.

Another feature of Pascal is the declaration of arrays. Recall that arrays are defined in BASIC by use of the dimension statement.

DIM V(50)

Arrays in Pascal are defined in advance, like other variables.

In Pascal, arrays are declared at the same time as variables. We can now make our program very similar to the top down, first level statements except that procedures, like variables, must be defined before reference by other statements.

```
PROGRAM AVERAGE (INPUT, OUTPUT).
  (* COMMENTS SAME AS BEFORE *)
  VAR N,I : INTEGER ;
    AVERAGE : REAL ;
    V : ARRAY [1..50] OF REAL ;
  PROCEDURE READNUMBERS ;
    BEGIN
      READ (N);
      FOR I := 1 TO N DO
      READ (V[I]) ;
    END ;
  PROCEDURE COMPUTEAVERAGE ;
    VAR SUM : REAL ;
    BEGIN
      FOR I := 1 to N DO
        BEGIN
          SUM := SUM + V[I];
        END ;
      AVERAGE := SUM/N ;
    END ;
  PROCEDURE PRINTANSWER ;
    BEGIN
      WRITELN ('THE AVERAGE IS ', AVERAGE) ;
    END ;
  BEGIN
    READNUMBERS ;
    COMPUTEAVERAGE ;
    PRINTANSWER ;
  END.
```

Procedures are defined before the program calls them

The main difference in this program and the previous one is the use of the array V declared for 50 values. The declaration,

```
V : ARRAY [1..50] OF REAL ;
```

is used for making this declaration. The grades are then read in the first procedure, READNUMBERS; the average computed in the second, COMPUTEAVERAGE; and the answer printed in the third, PRINTANSWER. The array declaration also defines the range for the index (I) values with the [1..50].

We could have a range of indexes, 6 to 15 with,

```
VAR V : ARRAY [6..15] OF REAL.
```

and use them instead, so it is easy to pick out particular values.

As you can see, Pascal has many features which permit top-down design and structured programming. But, of course, it was designed for such programming. Additional characteristics for this new popular language can be found by reading one of the many books on Pascal.

Before proceeding to the next language type, let's discuss two ways in which Pascal programs are executed. First, Pascal is typically compiled. (We discussed compilers in Chapter 3.) *Figure 4-5a* illustrates this compilation process. First, the Pascal compiler is loaded into the system. The compiler program reads in the Pascal statements and generates the appropriate machine instructions for execution on the target machine. Next, these machine instructions are loaded and executed.

In the second commonly used method, the compiler generates pseudo code instructions called 'P code' (*Figure 4-5b*). Then a simulator is executed which translates each P code instruction into the appropriate set of machine instructions. The simulator works like an interpreter where each P code instruction is executed before proceeding to the next instruction.

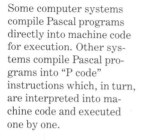

Some computer systems compile Pascal programs directly into machine code for execution. Other systems compile Pascal programs into "P code" instructions which, in turn, are interpreted into machine code and executed one by one.

Figure 4-5.
Pascal Program
Execution.

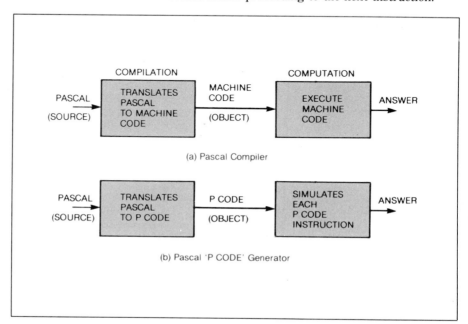

(a) Pascal Compiler

(b) Pascal 'P CODE' Generator

The P code could even be completely assembled to generate all machine instructions before execution. This second method makes Pascal quite transportable as only the P code simulator need be written for a given machine. This is much easier to write than a complete Pascal compiler.

Let's next look at yet another high-level language, FORTRAN. FORTRAN was one of the first high-level languages developed and is still the most commonly used.

FORTRAN

The FORTRAN programming language was developed originally for scientific applications. Recent enhancements have made it more suitable for structured programming.

FORTRAN, an acronym for FORMULA TRANSLATOR, was one of the first high-level languages developed. FORTRAN and COBOL accounted for most all programs written during the 1950's and 1960's. FORTRAN was developed primarily for scientific applications whereas COBOL was developed for business applications. Because of their popularity, the American Standards Institute (ANSI) developed standards for both FORTRAN and COBOL. Most computer companies provided compilers which not only met these standards but included many other additional features. Because it was hard to keep programmers from using the additional features or adhering to the ANSI standards, programs written in FORTRAN still weren't very transportable. That is, they could not be run on a different computer without modification. This tended to lock users to one particular computer manufacturer (which may have been the intent) and caused problems in developing good transportable code. FORTRAN, being developed in the 50's and used in the 60's and 70's, was not well suited for structured programming. The last standard specification derived for FORTRAN by ANSI, FORTRAN 77, provided features to make it more suitable for structured programming.

There are literally millions of programs written in FORTRAN, and FORTRAN programmers have been reluctant to change to a new language such as Pascal or PL/I for scientific programming. So, while FORTRAN is not necessarily the best language, it certainly has enough good features, as well as followers, to keep it popular for years to come.

To introduce FORTRAN, let's once again go back to our simple example, computing the average of N grades. Here is the FORTRAN version of this problem:

```
 1      C        FORTRAN PROGRAM TO COMPUTE
 2      C        AVERAGE OF N GRADES
 3               READ (5, 10) N
 4      10       FORMAT (I2)
 5               SUM = 0
 6               DO 20 I = 1,N
 7               READ (5, 15) V
 8      15       FORMAT (F5.0)
 9      20       SUM = SUM + V
10               AVERAG = SUM/N
11               WRITE (6, 30) AVERAG
12      30       FORMAT (16H THE AVERAGE IS , F6.2)
13               END
```

FORTRAN programs are compiled for execution. Program lines have a maximum length of 80 columns.

Upon reviewing this program, note once again that we use line numbers for reference purposes. The numbers are not required as they were for BASIC. However, the statement numbers on lines 4, 8, 9 and 12 are required . The FORTRAN program must be compiled to generate machine object code for execution. If source code input is via a CRT terminal, then each line is limited to 80 columns.

First note lines 1 and 2. FORTRAN permits the use of comment cards or statements. Unlike Pascal, however, comments are denoted by the letter C in column one of the data card. In fact, we will see that FORTRAN statements must follow specific guidelines as to where they may begin on a data card. Once a C has been placed in column 1, the remainder of the card is treated as a comment by the machine.

Line 3 is the first executable statement. It is a READ statement much like those in other languages. The READ references a statement number, 10, and a logical input unit 5. The statement number 10, line 4, will tell the computer the form or 'FORMAT' of the data value to be read in — specifically, that it is to be an integer number (the I means integer) found in the first 2 columns of the first data card. The two column specification, I2, is to allow for any integer number from 1 to 99. If it is always 9 or less, we could have used the format descripter, I1.

The logical unit number 5 tells the computer which I/O device (a card reader in this case) has this data card. Five usually signifies that the card is on the same card reader which reads the program. This may seem confusing at first but, it's better than saying, READ (from same device that read this program, under the direction of the format statement 10); Or is it? Anyway, that's what it means (see *Figure 4-6*).

We will discuss the logical unit to physical unit assignment in detail in the chapter describing operating systems. In fact, as you will see later, it's the operating system which insures that you read from the right card reader. There may be more than one!

The statement numbers, by the way, must be located in columns 1 through 5. The statement must not begin until column 7. Recall that in BASIC and Pascal, nothing was said about where statements must begin. That's because it didn't matter. It does in FORTRAN.

In line 5, the assignment of SUM to zero is in the same form as before except we don't need the := as in Pascal, just the = as in BASIC.

The statement at line 6,

```
DO 20 I = 1, N
```

is used for looping and is similar to the FOR statements of BASIC and Pascal. That is, it directs the computer to execute all statements which follow, down to and including the statement with the number 20, N times. This type of loop is appropriately named the "do loop".

Figure 4-6.
Input Specification.

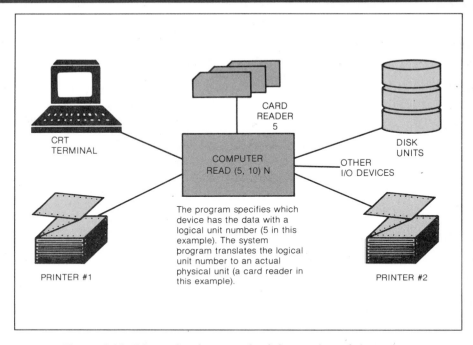

CRT
TERMINAL

CARD
READER
5

DISK
UNITS

COMPUTER
READ (5, 10) N

OTHER
I/O DEVICES

The program specifies which
device has the data with a
logical unit number (5 in this
example). The system
program translates the logical
unit number to an actual
physical unit (a card reader in
this example).

PRINTER #1

PRINTER #2

The variable I is used to keep track of the number of times the loop has been executed as in BASIC and Pascal. After statement 20, (line 9) has been executed, I will be increased by 1 and if greater than N, the statement at line 10 will be executed. Otherwise, control returns to the statement following the DO at line 7.

The statement at line 7 is another read but this time using format F5.0. This format directs the system to read the grade from the first 5 columns and that it is to have a decimal point assigned. The grades are summed with line 9. The statement at line 10,

    AVERAG = SUM/N

is used to compute the average. Note, that the variable name is limited to six characters as it is in BASIC.

Our answer is finally printed at line 11. This time, logical unit 6 is used. You're right if you guessed 6 means the printer. The format of the output is specified by the statement at line 12. Specifically, it says to print, beginnning at the first column of the output page on the printer,

    THE AVERAGE IS XXX.XX

The answer is to be given as a decimal number with the decimal fraction to two places. The total number of digits plus the decimal point is not to be greater than 6.

The END statement ends the program.

4

Other FORTRAN Features

Variables whose names begin with characters I through N are assumed to be integers.

Variables used in FORTRAN, as in BASIC or Pascal, may be integer, real or logical. They can handle complex numbers or direct the computer to double the word size for greater precision by declaring double precision. Variables are assumed integer if the variable name begins with the characters I thru N. Otherwise, they are assumed to be in floating point form. Any variation from this requires a TYPE statement for declaration. Recall that in Pascal all variables had to be declared.

Expressions are evaluated as in BASIC or Pascal, where the same arithmetic operators apply. Logical operators however, must be of the form:

```
.EQ.    for equal to
.NE.    for not equal to
.GT.    for greater than
.GE.    for greater than or equal to
.LT.    for less than
.LE.    for less than or equal to
```

FORTRAN uses the following control statements for directing program execution:

```
GO TO S₁
DO nnnnn I = integer 1, integer 2
IF (arithmetic expression) S₁, S₂, S₃
IF (logical expression) statement
```

The first is an unconditional transfer of control as was used in BASIC. The second is the loop statement, as discussed in our example program. The next two are used for conditional transfers. In the first, an arithmetic expression is evaluated and if the results are negative, control is transferred to the statement with the number S_1. If the expression is zero, control is passed to S_2 and if greater than zero, to S_3. An example is;

```
IF (X * 3 + 6/Y) 3, 4, 5.
```

If $X = -6$, and $Y = 1$ control goes to statement number 3. If $X = -2$ and $Y = 1$ control goes to statement 4. If $X = 6$ and $Y = 1$, control goes to statement 5.

The second IF is likewise a conditional transfer, except that a logical expression is evaluated and if true, the statement specified is executed:

```
Examples:
IF (X .GT. Y) GO TO 20
IF (X .LE. Y) Z = X + Y
```

Notice the operator .GT. is used instead of $>$, and .LE. is used in place of $< =$.

As mentioned earlier, recent changes to FORTRAN help in its use in structured programming. However, to date, few computer installations have used these new compilers. Only time will tell if people will use this new structured FORTRAN, or simply go to one of the other languages like Pascal or PL/I.

We have seen that Pascal could be easily used for scientific applications and PL/I, which will be discussed shortly, can likewise be used for such applications. There are yet other features of FORTRAN, but we won't discuss them here. FORTRAN can be studied in detail from one of the many books on this language.

By now you may be getting a little tired of all of these languages, but we still need to talk briefly about two others, COBOL and PL/I. COBOL, like FORTRAN is widely used because it was developed early. PL/I was developed primarily as a replacement for both FORTRAN and COBOL and it permits structured programming. It is being used more and more for this purpose. We will be more brief in our discussion of these two, but tell you enough so that you can get an idea of their capabilities. You cannot become proficient in programming in these languages overnight, or even in a week. In the case of PL/I, it may take a year or more.

COBOL

COBOL was developed for business applications, and is better suited for processing large quantities of data than for performing scientific calculations.

COBOL, an acronym for Common Business Oriented Language, was first developed in 1960 as COBOL-60. As was done for FORTRAN, ANSI established a set of specifications for COBOL. This was done in 1968 and was revised in 1974. The language is implemented in two different levels, a low level which is a somewhat restricted version, and a second level without restrictions.

As noted, it was developed for usage in business type problems. These problems generally involve processing large volumes of data and producing reports on this data. It is generally not used for performing scientific computations which typically involve much less I/O but much greater computational capabilities. A COBOL program, like FORTRAN and Pascal, is first compiled before execution.

Four distinct sections make up a COBOL program: Identification, Environment, Data, and Procedure.

The COBOL program is divided into four specific divisions or sections;

    IDENTIFICATION — program identification
    ENVIRONMENT — equipment description
    DATA — format or form of the data
    PROCEDURE — processing steps

Figure 4-7 illustrates a COBOL program for our problem of determining the average of a set of N grades.

Each of these divisions has a specific form. The Identification division is used for describing the program much as the initial comments were used in our previous examples.

The Environment division is where the particular I/0 requirements are specified. A separate division is provided for this since business problems typically involve inputting and outputting large volumes of data or transactions.

The Environment section of a COBOL program may need modification when the program is run on a different computer system, but the Identification, Data, and Procedure sections are portable.

The Environment division typically has to be rewritten or modified when the program is run on a different computer system, but the Identification division, the Data division, and the Procedure division are machine independent. The Data division is used to describe the format and form of the input and output data much as the format statements were used in FORTRAN. COBOL however provides for much more elaborate data specifications.

**Figure 4-7.
COBOL Program.**

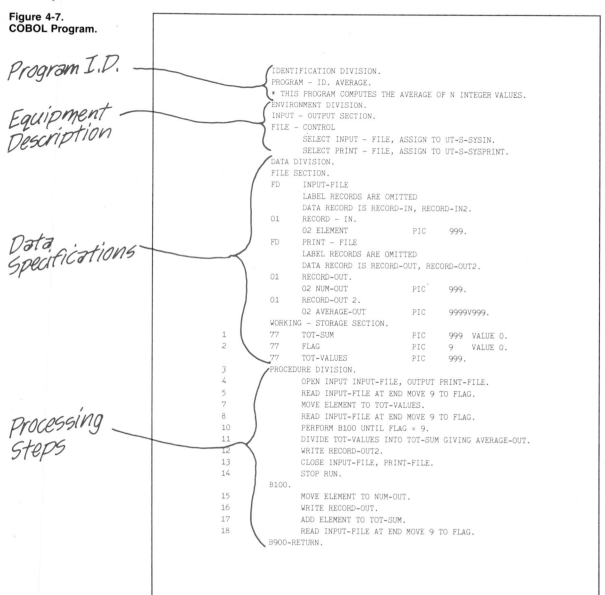

Program I.D.

Equipment Description

Data Specifications

Processing Steps

```
        IDENTIFICATION DIVISION.
        PROGRAM - ID. AVERAGE.
        * THIS PROGRAM COMPUTES THE AVERAGE OF N INTEGER VALUES.
        ENVIRONMENT DIVISION.
        INPUT - OUTPUT SECTION.
        FILE - CONTROL
                SELECT INPUT - FILE, ASSIGN TO UT-S-SYSIN.
                SELECT PRINT - FILE, ASSIGN TO UT-S-SYSPRINT.
        DATA DIVISION.
        FILE SECTION.
        FD      INPUT-FILE
                LABEL RECORDS ARE OMITTED
                DATA RECORD IS RECORD-IN, RECORD-IN2.
        01      RECORD - IN.
                02 ELEMENT              PIC     999.
        FD      PRINT - FILE
                LABEL RECORDS ARE OMITTED
                DATA RECORD IS RECORD-OUT, RECORD-OUT2.
        01      RECORD-OUT.
                02 NUM-OUT              PIC     999.
        01      RECORD-OUT 2.
                02 AVERAGE-OUT          PIC     9999V999.
        WORKING - STORAGE SECTION.
   1    77      TOT-SUM                 PIC     999  VALUE 0.
   2    77      FLAG                    PIC     9    VALUE 0.
        77      TOT-VALUES              PIC     999.
   3    PROCEDURE DIVISION.
   4            OPEN INPUT INPUT-FILE, OUTPUT PRINT-FILE.
   5            READ INPUT-FILE AT END MOVE 9 TO FLAG.
   7            MOVE ELEMENT TO TOT-VALUES.
   8            READ INPUT-FILE AT END MOVE 9 TO FLAG.
  10            PERFORM B100 UNTIL FLAG = 9.
  11            DIVIDE TOT-VALUES INTO TOT-SUM GIVING AVERAGE-OUT.
  12            WRITE RECORD-OUT2.
  13            CLOSE INPUT-FILE, PRINT-FILE.
  14            STOP RUN.
        B100.
  15            MOVE ELEMENT TO NUM-OUT.
  16            WRITE RECORD-OUT.
  17            ADD ELEMENT TO TOT-SUM.
  18            READ INPUT-FILE AT END MOVE 9 TO FLAG.
        B900-RETURN.
```

COBOL resembles English more closely than do most other programming languages.

The Procedure division is where the program steps are actually specified. The statements used in the various divisions are more closely aligned to the English language than statements in some of the other computer languages. For example, statements like OPEN INPUT CARD-FILE, or READ CARD-FILE AT END or STOP RUN, or PERFORM READ-AND-PRINT 20 TIMES, etc. are common.

The COBOL program of *Figure 4-7* can be compared to the previous programs. Note how much longer this program is than the other three that we discussed. However, we could come up with a different example where the reverse case existed, that is, where the COBOL program would take less steps than the Pascal, FORTRAN or BASIC program. For example, one dealing more with generation of various reports after summarizing a large volume of data.

We won't go over all of the program steps as we did before. As you can see, the discussion would get somewhat lengthy. However, there are many books on COBOL to help you if you would like to pursue it further. COBOL or PL/I should probably be used when writing programs for processing various business problems where large amounts of varied types of data are to be read, updated , and/or reported.

Let's briefly examine PL/I as a substitute for FORTRAN and COBOL.

PL/I

PL/I was developed for both business and scientific applications. It is well suited to structured programming.

PL/I was originally defined by IBM personnel and an IBM user's group called SHARE during the 1960's. It was structured as a language which could be efficiently used for processing both business and scientific applications. Like Pascal, it also is structured so that top-down program development and structured programming can be implemented. PL/I can be quickly learned for solving simple problems as in our example for computing the average of N grades. However, it has many features which are not as quickly learned but which make it a very powerful language for solving most any computational requirement.

Once again let's look at our problem of computing the average of N grades. The PL/I program is given in *Figure 4-8*. As may be noted, it is about the same length as the BASIC, Pascal and FORTRAN versions. Note that comments are specified much like those were in Pascal except that the /* and */ symbols are used in PL/I instead of the (* and *) symbols.

Also note that here, too, the variables used are declared. Declaration also specifies the size or number of digits to be used for the variables. Finally, note the use of GET LIST and PUT LIST for input and output. These statements perform the same type of functions as the READ and WRITE or INPUT and PRINT statements discussed before except they have many other options.

Figure 4-8.
PL/I Program.

```
/*THIS PROGRAM COMPUTES THE AVERAGE OF N INTEGER VALUES */
/*N=NUMBER OF VALUES TO BE READ                         */
/*V=VALUE CURRENTLY READ IN                             */
/*I=INCREMENTATION VARIABLE                             */
AVG:PROG OPTIONS (MAIN);
      DECLARE
           (N,I) FIXED (5),
           (AVG,SUM, V) FIXED (7,2),
           SYSIN INPUT STREAM,
           SYSPRINT OUTPUT STREAM;
      GET LIST (N);
      SUM=0;
      I=1;
      DO WHILE (I<=N);
           GET LIST (V);
           PUT SKIP LIST (V);
           SUM=SUM+V;
           I=I+1;
      END;
      AVG=SUM/N;
      PUT SKIP LIST ('AVERAGE IS ', AVG);
      RETURN;
   END;
```

"Procedure oriented" languages like those introduced in this chapter are suitable for widely varied applications. "Problem oriented" languages are tailored to specific uses.

Well, we won't tire you with more languages. Yes, there are many others. In fact, high-level languages are typically classified as procedure oriented or problem oriented. BASIC, Pascal, FORTRAN and PL/I are procedure oriented, that is, they can be used for many different types of computational need. Problem oriented languages are those which are designed for a specific problem class such as a simulation problem. Problem oriented languages are as common as bird species. You may even decide to write your own language compiler.

Before leaving our discussion, however, look at *Figure 4-9*. It gives the IBM 370 assembly language instructions for solving the average grade problem. The grades weren't read in order to keep it short. The actual machine instructions are listed in *Figure 4-9* as well as significant comments to the right. We won't go into what the instructions do, but if you have your own system handy, or can use the one at your school or work, you might want to learn how to code in the assembly level language. Assembly language is usually used for writing systems programs.

Figure 4-9.
IBM Assembly Language Program.

```
LOC      OBJECT CODE  ADDR1  ADDR2   STMT  SOURCE STATEMENT
130000                                1  AVERAGE  CSECT
130000   9 DEC D00C          000DC    2           STM    14,12,12(13)
                                       3  * THIS PROGRAM FINDS THE AVERAGE OF N INTEGER VALUES *
130004   05C0                         4           BALR   12,8
130006                                5           USING  *,12
130006   50D0 C03E           30044    6           ST     13,SAVE+4
13000A   41D0 C03A           30040    7           LA     13,SAVE
                                       8  * STANDARD LINKAGE FROM OPERATING SYSTEM *
13000E   5860 C082           30088    9           L      6,N        *REGISTER 6 USED TO INCREMENT *
130012   41B0 0000           00000   10           LA     11,0       *REGISTER 11 USED FOR SUMMING *
130016   4130 0086           3008C   11           LA     3,ADDR     *ADDRESS OF FIRST NUMBER
13001A   5AB3 0000           00000   12  LOOP     A      11,0 (3)   *SUM=SUM+NEXT NUMBER *
13001E   4133 0004           00004   13           LA     3,4 (3)    *GET ADDRESS OF NEXT NUMBER
130022   4660 C014           3001A   14           BCT    6,LOOP
130026   5CA0 C0A2           300A8   15           M      10,=F'1'   *EXTEND SIGN BIT TO HIGH ORDER
                                      16  *                          *REGISTER PAIR
13002A   5DA0 C082           30088   17           D      10,N       *INTEGER PART OF AVERAGE IS
                                      18  *                          *PLACED IN REGISTER 11 (IN HEX)
                                      19  *                          *AND REMAINDER IS IN REGISTER 10
13002E   E160 0000 0000 00000        20           XDUMP
130034   58D0 C03E           30044   21           L      13,SAVE+4
130038   98EC D00C           0000C   22           LM     14,12,12 (13)
13003C   07FE                        23           BR     14
130040                               24  SAVE     DS     18F
130088   00000006                    25  N        DC     F'6'
130080   0000001000000020            26  ADDR     DC     F'16,32,442,988,-26,388'
                                      27  END
1300A8   00000001                    28           =F'1'
```

WHAT HAVE WE LEARNED?

In this chapter we have learned about most of the commonly used languages for writing programs for a computer. We first investigated BASIC. This is an easy language to learn and is implemented on almost all small systems. In fact, if you have a personal computer in your home you probably already know BASIC.

Pascal was the next language we studied. Pascal is a relatively new language and has become quite popular. It has relatively few statements so it is implemented on many micro and minicomputer systems. Yet it is well designed and structured which permits its usage in structured programming.

FORTRAN is the most widely used language. Although it may not necessarily be the best, it's probably going to be around for a long time. It is well suited for scientific applications.

Then we took a brief look at COBOL. COBOL is primarily used for Business applications. Like FORTRAN it is also widely used, but also like FORTRAN, it was all we had to use for many years.

Finally, we discussed PL/I. It is a relatively new language and was designed to replace FORTRAN and COBOL. It was not widely accepted when it first came out but more and more organizations are beginning to use it. It is a very powerful language and can be used for writing well structured programs in any application area.

WHAT'S NEXT?

In the next chapter we will look at operating system programs. Both language translators and operating system programs are what we refer to as systems programs. They are written so that we can use the computer system to perform our task. The language translators provide a means for the conversion from human language to machine language to direct the computer to perform our application and the operating system programs manage the equipment so that we can get the task done.

Quiz for Chapter 4

1. Which of the following languages is not well suited for computation?
   a. Pascal
   b. FORTRAN
   c. machine

2. Which of the following languages is not well suited for business applications?
   a. COBOL
   b. PL/I
   c. Assembly

3. Which of the following languages is usually implemented with an interpreter?
   a. Assembly
   b. Pascal
   c. COBOL
   d. BASIC

4. Which of the following languages is often translated to pseudo code?
   a. Assembly
   b. FORTRAN
   c. PL/I
   d. BASIC
   e. Pascal

5. Which language is used for the following statement?
   A := C + D/E
   a. BASIC
   b. Pascal
   c. FORTRAN
   d. PL/I

6. Which of the following languages is more suited to a structured program?
   a. PL/I
   b. Assembly
   c. BASIC

7. Which of the following languages is the most widely used?
   a. PL/I
   b. BASIC
   c. FORTRAN
   d. Pascal

8. The following statement belongs to which language?
   FOR I = 1 TO N
   a. FORTRAN
   b. PL/I
   c. BASIC
   d. Pascal

9. An example of a problem oriented language is FORTRAN.
   True or False

10. Which of the following languages was developed first?
    a. Pascal
    b. COBOL
    c. BASIC

11. Which language would you expect the following statement to belong to?
    IF (A.GT.B) C = B
    a. Pascal
    b. BASIC
    c. FORTRAN

12. Pascal is implemented on many small computers.
    True or False

13. High level languages are generally easier to use than machine language.
    True or False

14. BASIC is well suited for structured programming.
    True or False

15. Even though Pascal is quite useful for many applications, PL/I is more powerful, ie., has many more options.
    True or False

(Answers in back of book.)

Operating Systems — An Overview

ABOUT THIS CHAPTER

Up to this point, we have discussed how the computer came about, what a computer is, how to program a computer, and what the various languages are that are available to program the computer. In this and the next chapter, we will discuss a computer program that has a very special function. This function is that of monitoring and controlling the computer system.

WHAT IS AN OPERATING SYSTEM?

Have you ever had somone constantly looking over your shoulder as you are working or doing something? That's what this special program does to your program as your program goes through the execution process. This special program, which actually is a collection of many different types of programs, is called an *operating system*. It is also sometimes called a *monitor*.

The operating system is a collection of "housekeeping" routines that govern system functions such as reading or writing data and loading or executing programs.

The operating system is what monitors and controls the execution of your program when you submit it via an input unit such as a card reader. An operating system program must instruct the card reader to read the cards which contain your program. If your program, or job as it is sometimes called, is written in FORTRAN, then the computer must be instructed by an operating system program to load and execute the FORTRAN compiler. (A different compiler is loaded for a different language.) After your high-level FORTRAN instructions have been converted to machine instructions, the computer must be directed by an operating system program to load these machine instructions and to begin execution of these instructions. When your program needs to print answers or results on the printer, an operating system program must direct this output to the proper printer. When your job has terminated, the computer must be directed by an operating system program to continue execution of other jobs. The collection of routines that read data cards, load the compiler, load and initiate execution of your program, control the output, and monitor your job's completion, is called the operating system.

Operating systems can be very simple for micro and mini systems to very sophisticated or complex for large general purpose systems. The size and complexity of the operating system for a computer system is a function of the type of functions the computer system is to perform.

OPERATING SYSTEMS FOR THE SMALL COMPUTER SYSTEMS

So that we can get a good handle on just what kind of things an operating system should provide, let's examine a small computer such as one of the popular personal computers. Let's first see how we execute a BASIC program and then we'll try a FORTRAN program. After that, we'll contrast this with running the same two programs on a large, general purpose system with a large and complicated operating system.

First, let's examine our small personal computer system configuration. It has two mini-floppy disks, a keyboard, CRT, and 64K of read-only and read-write memory as illustrated in *Figure 5-1*. Notice that we have divided the computer into four separate sections or modules — memory, CPU, I/O interfacing, and power. The semiconductor memory is further divided into read-write memory, labeled RAM, and read-only memory or ROM. Recall that the RAM semiconductor memory is volatile but the ROM is not. The CPU module contains the CPU and related circuitry. The I/O module provides electrical interfacing between the system busses and the I/O devices. It also has an I/O processor for the floppy disk. Finally, the power module contains the power supply and other electrical circuitry.

**Figure 5-1.
Personal Computer
System.**

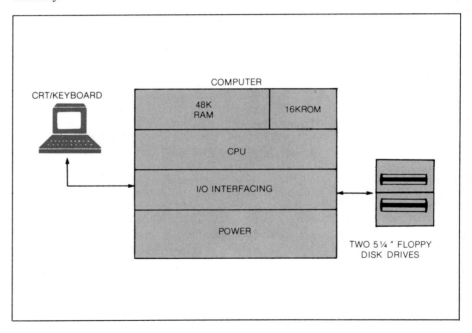

Executing a Program

To execute a BASIC program, we first turn the power on. As discussed in the preceding chapter, a prompt character on the CRT indicates the system is ready for BASIC. We may now enter

>PRINT 2*3

The computer immediately performs the multiplication and prints 6 on the CRT. How did this happen? First of all, where did the prompt character come from? Well, a set of instructions had to write it on the screen. And, how did the computer translate BASIC to machine language?

Let's go back to when we turned on the power. When power is applied to the computer, the CPU immediately begins executing a set of instructions at a pre-specified memory location. These instructions must direct the computer to begin its initialization process. Where did these instructions come from? You guessed it, they are in ROM. Remember, ROM is not volatile. These instructions in ROM are part of the systems Monitor or Operating System.

In this and the following chapter, we will consider the two terms, monitor and operating system, interchangeably. The term, operating system, though, is usually used when discussing a larger and more complicated system. The term, monitor, is usually used for describing a smaller system like our example personal computer system.

Functions of Monitor

Figure 5-2 illustrates the functions of the monitor. Notice that first some necessary 'house-keeping' functions such as zeroing accumulators are done in the initializing process. Next, an attempt is made to read the disk if one is connected. The disk operating system which has the instructions for the disk drive controller are kept on disk since these routines are too big to have in ROM and besides, they may change as updates to the program are made to accommodate more applications. The disk operating system routines are always at a specified location on the disk. This location is stored in ROM and the disk operating system routines are loaded in a special area of RAM, which is reserved for system use only, under control of instructions in ROM. So the sequence is as follows if a disk is attached: An instruction is sent to ROM to find the location of the disk operating system routine. After the routine is located it is read into the special area of RAM reserved for system use. Thereafter, other information can be written to or read from the disk.

The prompt character is next displayed on the screen and a wait for the keyboard input begins.

After a set of characters are entered at the keyboard and the carriage return or enter key depressed, the characters are scanned. If they indicate a BASIC command without a line number, such as PRINT 2*3, the command is immediately executed and control returned to the keyboard. If the BASIC command is a deferred one; that is, a line number is specified, the command is stored in a scratch pad area of memory as illustrated in the memory map of *Figure 5-3*. Notice that the BASIC interpreter is in ROM. It could have resided on disk and been read in. With it in ROM, however, the system may be used for BASIC programs without a disk.

The operating system, which begins to function as soon as you turn the computer on, may be either stored permanently in ROM or read from a disk into RAM at power-up.

The presence or absence of line numbers determines whether the system stores your commands as BASIC program statements or executes them immediately.

**Figure 5-2.
Personal Computer
System Operation Flow
Diagram.**

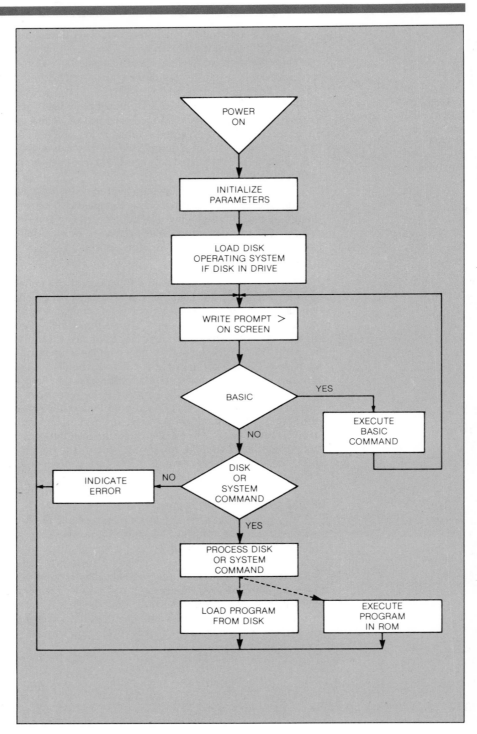

**Figure 5-3.
Memory Map for
Personal Computer
Example.**

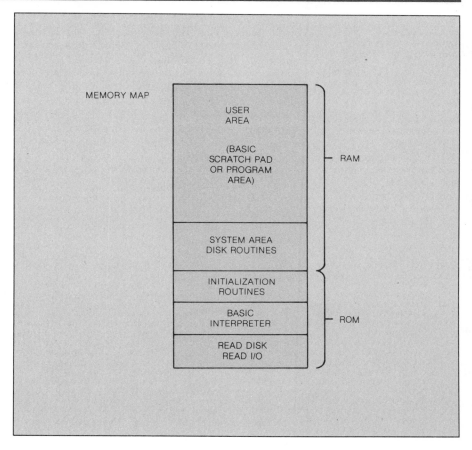

MEMORY MAP

USER AREA (BASIC SCRATCH PAD OR PROGRAM AREA)	RAM
SYSTEM AREA DISK ROUTINES	
INITIALIZATION ROUTINES	ROM
BASIC INTERPRETER	
READ DISK READ I/O	

The operating system distinguishes BASIC files from machine language files and processes them accordingly.

If the command specifies loading and running a program, first the program is loaded into the system's memory and then control is passed to the program for execution of the program. In addition to the file name given to the program, the type of file also is kept. Files such as a BASIC program file, binary or machine language program file, or a data file are examples. Then, if the loaded file is a BASIC program file, the BASIC interpreter is used. If a binary file is indicated, the instructions are already in machine language, therefore the CPU executes each instruction directly.

Notice that there hasn't been a lot of monitoring or controlling of your program. That's because there is no need for it, for dedicated systems. That is, your program is the only one in the system and you specify or direct its execution. The monitor, however, did provide you with the capability to control or direct its execution. That is, the monitor has the capability of reading the keyboard and interpreting special commands for program execution.

It passed control to BASIC if the instruction was a BASIC statement or to the disk operating system if it was a disk read or write instruction. It really had very simple functions to let you reference and work with files on the disk. But without the monitor you couldn't use the system very easily or as effectively. You certainly would have to write much more involved programs and enter them in machine language. Thus, a monitor is a 'must' even for this small system.

To run a FORTRAN program, the operating system must first load the FORTRAN compiler and let it translate the program to machine code, then store the code on disk and in RAM, and finally execute the program.

Now suppose that we have a FORTRAN program. In the creation of the program the instructions were written and saved on disk with an associated file name. To be able to run the program it must be in machine language. The conversion is done with the compiler, therefore, the system requires that the monitor load the FORTRAN compiler, which is in binary, and pass control to the compiler program. The FORTRAN compiler in turn reads your FORTRAN instructions and generates a binary file of the machine language instructions for performing the desired functions. This binary file of your program is then stored on disk by using the disk operating system commands.

Next, you load to RAM the file of all the machine language instructions of your program which has been stored on disk by the FORTRAN compiler. Then you are ready to run or execute your program.

The operating system functions and complexity vary depending on the class of computer system functions. Large general purpose machines typically have very large and sophisticated operating system programs, programs that monitor and control many users' jobs. The micro or personal computer and small minicomputers, on the other hand, typically have simple system programs whose functions are to aid in the development of your program and help in providing input and output functions. That is, we will see that the large computer systems not only execute many different types of user jobs, but have several in the system at the same time. At the other end of the spectrum, the small computer systems such as the personal computer used in small businesses or homes are typically dedicated to the user throughout the execution of a program.

In some respects, with the introduction of the small computer and accompanying system support programs, we have reverted back to the way we used the first generation of computer systems. That is, dedicating the computer to each programmer or user. However, now the hardware is much cheaper, smaller and faster, and the systems software is much better. Let's next look at the historical development of the operating system.

THE FIRST COMPUTERS — NO OPERATING SYSTEMS

The first generation of computer systems initially had little or no operating system. The computer was used by programmers one at a time. Each user had the computer to himself or herself while writing, debugging, and executing the program. Input/output was controlled completely by the user's program. Remember too that early programs were usually written in assembly language and some were in machine language.

Suppose you wanted to write 100 words from memory to the printer. First of all, recall that in order to specify alphabetic characters, coded data is needed — for example, the ASCII code. That is, there is a special coded number for a capital A and a second for a small a. Another for capital B, etc. The printer may not accept the same internal codes that are used by the computer so each character must be converted to the proper code. Next, you can't write to the same printer again until after it has finished the last write. Thus, you have to check and see if the printer has finished a previous print instruction. There may be more than one printer so you have to be sure you address the correct one. Or maybe you forgot to turn on the printer. All of these things must be checked or monitored when executing an I/O operation. During the first generation of computers, the user had to do all of these things, which made programming more complex for each application program.

These first computers also cost many thousands of dollars and required a lot of space, so there may have been only one computer to serve many programmers. As the numbers of applications increased, it soon became too expensive to have one person tie up the system for such a long period of time.

Operating systems were almost nonexistent on early computers. They evolved from a need for more efficiency and economy in the use of computer systems.

To alleviate some of these problems, routines were designed to aid the I/O process. They helped to connect to the I/O device, to insure that it was operational, and to carry out the desired operation. Also, so that more efficient usage of the computer could be obtained, batch processing was implemented. This was the beginning of the operating system.

BATCH SYSTEMS

In batch processing, the system reads in a job, passes control to this job, and when the job is completed, reads in the next job and passes control to it. Instead of each user operating the machine, one person called a computer operator, is in charge of collecting all the jobs and loading each one individually. This type of job submission is called closed shop operations. Each user submits his or her job to the computer operator and then returns later to get the output.

In batch processing, users submit their programs to an operator as "jobs" which are executed one after another in order of priority.

Typically, batch processing jobs are loaded from a card reader onto tape or disk. The monitor examines these jobs and selects one by the first-in first-out (FIFO) selection process. However, jobs may have priorities assigned, say a number between 0 and 9. Then the one with the highest priority is processed first. If the priorities of two or more jobs are the same, then the FIFO process is used to select between those of equal priority. That is, the control card information for the list of jobs which are in auxiliary storage is examined and the appropriate ones selected in the specified sequence.

The large variety of computers which occurred with the second generation of computers resulted in the need for more and more system functions. Input/output requirements became varied with the addition of more I/O device types. In early batch systems the operating system routines were called in from auxiliary storage when needed. However, as programs depended more and more on system routines it became more practical to leave many of these system routines resident in memory. Such operating systems were called *Resident Monitors*.

RESIDENT MONITOR

The Resident Monitor provides a collection of routines that watch over your job during its execution. It contains two basic parts, the Executive module and the Input/Output module.

Executive Module

Some early operating systems were called resident monitors. They had an executive module that managed the computer resources necessary to complete a given job.

The executive module contains routines that insure that all resources are available for your task. That is, you specify the language translator needed, the amount of memory needed, time requirements, input/output devices to be used, and job accounting information. Suppose for instance, you have a FORTRAN job and want your output to be punched on data cards. Recall that the following FORTRAN statement is used for output:

```
WRITE (7, 100) X
```

The 100 is the statement number of the statement which specifies the format; that is, where and how the data values of X are to be punched in the card. The logical unit 7 signifies that the output goes to the card punch machine. The programmer then has to tell the operating system that logical unit 7 is assigned to the card punch machine. The executive routine first checks to see if this card punch device is physically part of the system and then tells the input/output routine that whenever logical unit 7 is called for by the program, output is to be sent to the designated card punch.

The programmer could also specify a time limit for his or her program. That is, suppose the program had a 'bug' and under certain conditions executed a loop indefinitely. No one else could use the machine. The time limit specification is used by the executive to 'interrupt' your job if it isn't finished by the specified time. Then the executive reads in the next job. For accounting purposes, your job is given a name and the executive routine keeps track of how much computer time is used by your program.

Special system commands called "job control statements" communicate a program's resource requirements to the executive module.

How does the user tell the executive or the operating system all these things? A special set of commands or Job Control statements were developed just for this purpose. These statements are placed at the front of your program as shown in *Figure 5-4*. The executive routine reads in these job control cards first and insures that all resource needs can be provided. If not, an error is indicated as shown in *Figure 5-5* and your job is not run.

Figure 5-4.
Job Control Cards and
Program Deck.

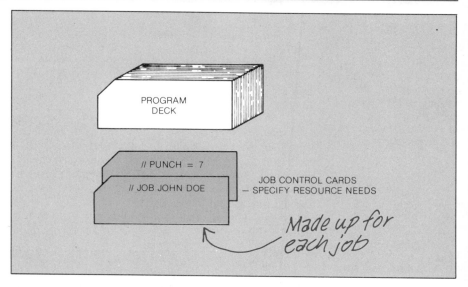

Figure 5-5.
Job Entry Flow Diagram.

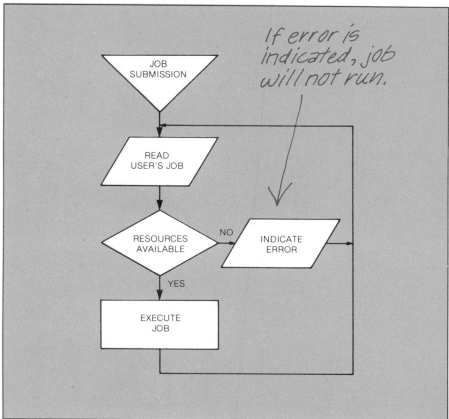

I/O Module

The input/output module contains routines that perform all input/output operations. They provide any code conversions necessary, insure the devices are ready, and monitor the I/O operation.

Recall that the I/O Processor or Data Channel is the hardware used for performing input/output. This hardware is allowed to perform its function at the same time as the CPU. For example, suppose a program specifies that 100 words are to be printed from some memory location. The CPU tells the I/O processor to start the print and then the CPU goes on to something else (*Figure 5-6*). The input/output routines monitor the I/O processor and record when they have completed the input/output operation. If a second output request is then made for the printer, it knows that the first has finished and initiates the second. If the first request had not finished, the second I/O request would have been placed on hold (in a queue) as shown in *Figure 5-6*. When the first operation is finished, the second I/O request is (or can be) initiated.

Since the data channel is reserved for input and output, the I/O processor and CPU can each attend to a different task simultaneously.

Figure 5-6.
I/O Output Request Flow Diagram.

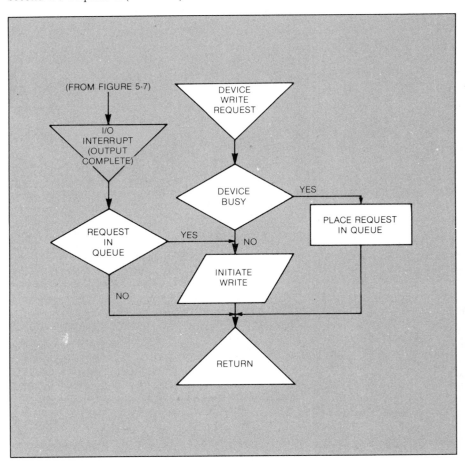

Interrupts

Computer systems recognize interrupts in order to act upon special conditions that have occurred, such as a programming error, a time limit exceeded, or an I/O device requesting service.

Interrupts are a means of interrupting the normal flow of instructions to the CPU to indicate that some special condition has occurred. Interrupts are implemented in hardware and used by software for enabling the operating system functions. By using interrupts, the normal program execution can be halted and control transferred to the executive module so that the interrupting condition can be examined. If the interrupt signifies the completion of an I/O operation by the I/O processor, then the executive transfers control to the input/output module as shown in *Figure 5-7*. This module then processes the interrupt as shown in *Figure 5-6*.

**Figure 5-7.
Processing Interrupts
Flow Diagram.**

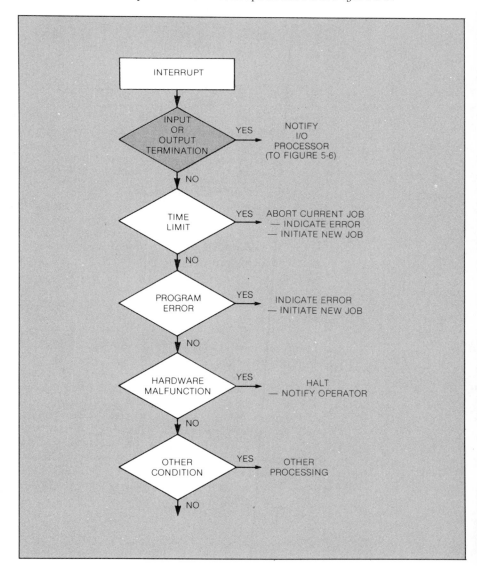

Other interrupt conditions are also possible. Maybe the programmer, by accident, tries to divide by zero or perhaps tries to reference a memory location that doesn't exist. Either condition is an error and the program should be halted and the programmer alerted. By using interrupts, the monitor does just that as shown in *Figure 5-7*. Also, if the preset time limit is exceeded, the program execution is interrupted and control transferred back to the executive module.

As you can see, the resident monitor is a fairly complex set of programs that performs many functions. So many options are possible for business applications that, when IBM introduced their System 360 family, the job control statements were renamed the Job Control Language.

The more general systems of today have essentially five major modules which manage the system's resources. These are called;

> Job Manager,
> Processor Manager,
> Memory Manager,
> I/O Manager, and
> Information Manager modules.

In the next chapter, we will discuss the role of each of these individual software manager modules and the type of hardware needed to implement them in a system.

As more and more people used the computer, another advancement occurred — the multiprogrammed operating systems.

With the growing complexity of computer systems, job control statements have evolved into a Job Control Language (JCL).

MULTIPROGRAMMED SYSTEMS

Resident monitors with batch processing capabilities were major developments which resulted in computer systems that were easier to use and more flexible. As noted, prior to this period the computer was used only by one programmer at a time. Batch capabilities enabled a number of users to submit their jobs and come back later for the results. These jobs were then processed mainly in the order received.

During the mid 1960's, another major step was taken in making the computer system more efficient — programmers began using multiprogrammed operating systems.

Multiprogramming is the process of having the system execute two or more jobs (programs) at the same time. Before explaining what this means, let's consider an example.

Multiprogrammed systems, which appeared in the mid-1960's, can process several jobs at once.

Suppose that you and a friend named Joe have programs to run on a batch processing system. Your program takes one minute to run. Joe's program, on the other hand, is used to solve a very complex mathematical algorithm and takes — get this — one hour. Now, if you see Joe taking his program to the operator, you will tend to hurry so that you can get there first. For if Joe gets there first, it will be an hour and one minute before your results are ready (*Figure 5-8*). By simply beating Joe to the computer, your job will be ready only one minute after submission of the job to the operator (assuming no other jobs are already ahead of yours).

**Figure 5-8.
Two Jobs Run in
Sequential Batch
System.**

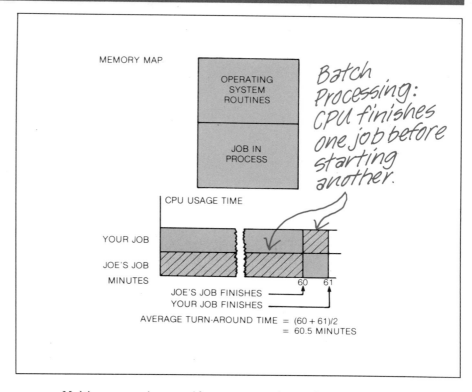

MEMORY MAP

OPERATING
SYSTEM
ROUTINES

JOB IN
PROCESS

*Batch
Processing:
CPU finishes
one job before
starting
another.*

CPU USAGE TIME

YOUR JOB

JOE'S JOB

MINUTES

60   61

JOE'S JOB FINISHES ———
YOUR JOB FINISHES ———

AVERAGE TURN-AROUND TIME = (60 + 61)/2
= 60.5 MINUTES

By dividing CPU time
among several programs,
multiprogramming often
results in quicker job completion than sequential
batch processing.

Multiprogramming provides a compromise to the sequential batch type of processing. Suppose the operating system reads both of your programs into memory as shown in *Figure 5-9*. The memory contains the resident monitor routines, the machine instructions for your program, and the machine instructions for Joe's program. In multiprogramming, the monitor lets both programs share the CPU. First, Joe's program gets the CPU for, say, a fourth of a minute, then it is interrupted and the monitor gives control of the CPU to your program for a fourth of a minute. This process continues with the CPU shared equally between the two jobs, until one completes its execution. Of course, yours will finish first, since it requires less time. Your job will finish in two minutes now instead of one. Joe's job will now take one hour and two minutes instead of one hour. Although yours would normally require only one minute to execute, you probably won't mind if it takes two. Joe on the other hand, would normally have to wait one hour anyway, so he doesn't mind waiting an extra two minutes.

Note that we have, in effect, two jobs in an execution state at the same time. An execution state consists of either using the CPU, or having once used it, waiting for its use again. The time required for a job from submission to getting the final results is usually referred to as job turn-around. Note, in *Figure 5-8*, that the average job turn-around time if Joe gets to the computer before you is (60 + 61)/2 or 60.5 minutes.

Figure 5-9.
Two Jobs Run in
Multiprogrammed
System.

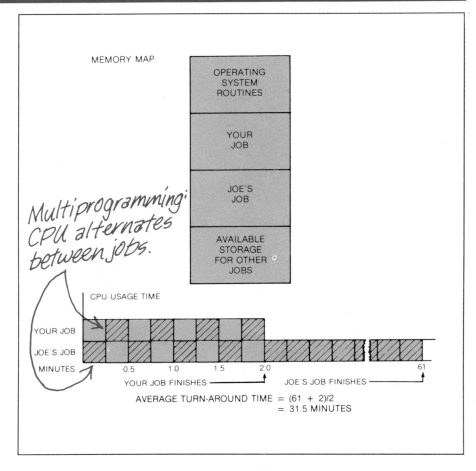

MEMORY MAP

OPERATING
SYSTEM
ROUTINES

YOUR
JOB

JOE'S
JOB

AVAILABLE
STORAGE
FOR OTHER
JOBS

Multiprogramming:
CPU alternates
between jobs.

CPU USAGE TIME

YOUR JOB

JOE'S JOB

MINUTES   0.5   1.0   1.5   2.0   61

YOUR JOB FINISHES ———→   JOE'S JOB FINISHES ———→

AVERAGE TURN-AROUND TIME = (61 + 2)/2
= 31.5 MINUTES

With multiprogramming, (*Figure 5-9*) assuming Joe once again gets the CPU first, it is (61 + 2)/2, or 31.5 minutes. This is clearly a significant improvement and of course, you actually get your job in two minutes. Thus, multiprogramming is great. Or is it? Well, maybe not every time. Let's try another example to see.

Figure 5-10 illustrates the execution time if three jobs are in the system and each one requires the same length of execution time. Notice in this case, without multiprogramming (*Figure 5-10a*), Job A finishes in one minute, Job B in two minutes, and Job C in three minutes. The average turn-around time is (1 + 2 + 3)/3 or 2 minutes. For the multiprogrammed system (*Figure 5-10b*), Job A completes at 2.5 minutes, Job B at 2.75 minutes and Job C at 3 minutes, so the average turn-around is 2.75 minutes. That is, when the jobs all require the same amount of CPU time, multiprogramming produces a greater turn around time for all jobs. Thus, the improvement provided by multiprogramming depends on the job mix or the mixture of CPU time requirements.

If all jobs in the system require the same amount of CPU time, however, multiprogramming may lengthen rather than shorten completion time.

**Figure 5-10.
Comparison of Three
Jobs of Equal Length
Run in Sequential Batch
and Multiprogrammed
Systems.**

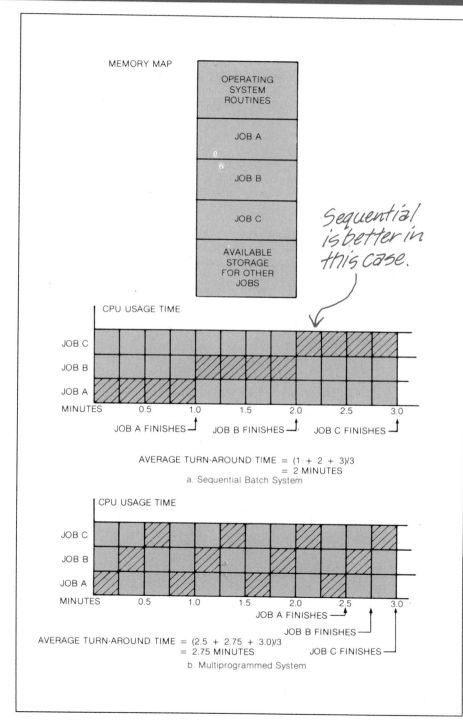

AVERAGE TURN-AROUND TIME = (1 + 2 + 3)/3
= 2 MINUTES

a. Sequential Batch System

AVERAGE TURN-AROUND TIME = (2.5 + 2.75 + 3.0)/3
= 2.75 MINUTES

b. Multiprogrammed System

A program cannot use the CPU while performing input or output. Multiprogramming's advantage lies in making the CPU available to other programs during these I/O intervals.

Now it seems that multiprogramming may not be so great after all. But let's look at another situation before passing final judgment. Suppose, in the second example where each job takes the same length of time, that Job A has to read data at the beginning of its execution. Furthermore, when the read request occurs, the program can't proceed until all of A's data is read in. Suppose that Job A really only needs the CPU for 0.25 of a minute for processing this data. That is, 0.75 of a minute is used for reading in the data. Jobs B and C, on the other hand, don't require such input. Referring to *Figure 5-11*, we see that the turn-around time is decreased for Jobs B and C because the CPU is equally shared between Jobs B and C while Job A is reading in data. There is certainly no need to give the CPU to A, when A can't use it anyway until after the data has been read. With this scheme, jobs waiting for I/O are always in a wait or hold state. In this case, Job A finishes after 1.25 minutes, Job B at 2 minutes and Job C at 2.25 minutes for an average turn-around of 1.83 minutes. Furthermore, we have 100 percent CPU utilization. (If the three jobs had been processed sequentially, then the CPU would not have been used for 0.75 of a minute of the total 3 minutes of processing and we would have had only 75 percent utilization of the CPU). In this last example of using multiprogramming, a net improvement of both turn-around time and resource utilization was achieved.

Thus, we see that a major advantage of multiprogramming is in CPU utilization when I/O operations are lengthy. When a job is not using the CPU due to I/O requirements, then the CPU can be assigned to another task. Also, as we saw in the first example, a net improvement in job turn-around time results when a stream of jobs with unequal time requirements are multiprogrammed.

The development of operating systems with multiprogramming capabilities required changes to the hardware to permit efficient system utilization. Such things as monitor states and user states were introduced. When in the monitor state, for instance, information could be read from memory at any address. In the user state, only particular memory locations within a certain boundary were allowed to prevent one program from interfering with another. Also during the monitor state, additional groups of instructions could be executed that were not allowed in the user state. These instructions were called privileged instructions. One told how to specify memory boundaries. Procedures for relocating jobs to different memory areas were also needed to efficiently process the various mixtures of jobs. Most of these features are still used in today's complicated operating systems and we will look at them in more detail shortly.

Let's continue into our historical view of operating systems development. Notice that the trend has been to make better utilization of the computer system or not to let the processor be idle when it could be assigned to another task. Such changes increased CPU utilization and the average number of jobs processed over a given time period. The next major change was to provide a time-sharing capability.

**Figure 5-11.
One of Three Jobs has
I/O in Multiprogrammed
System.**

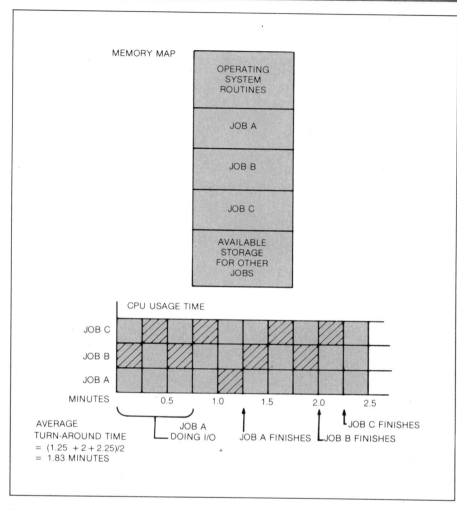

MEMORY MAP

OPERATING
SYSTEM
ROUTINES

JOB A

JOB B

JOB C

AVAILABLE
STORAGE
FOR OTHER
JOBS

CPU USAGE TIME

JOB C

JOB B

JOB A

MINUTES   0.5   1.0   1.5   2.0   2.5

AVERAGE
TURN-AROUND TIME
= (1.25 + 2 + 2.25)/2
= 1.83 MINUTES

JOB A
DOING I/O

JOB A FINISHES

JOB B FINISHES

JOB C FINISHES

TIME-SHARING OPERATING SYSTEMS

Time-sharing systems can interact with multiple users while appearing to be dedicated to each individual user.

In some respects, multiprogramming is a kind of time sharing of the CPU and memory. Time sharing, however, is so named because the time-sharing operating system permitted many individual users to interact with the system in such a manner that the system appeared dedicated to each user. Remember that the computer is very fast and can execute millions of instructions in one second. Since typically, you or I can't respond much faster than one or two seconds, the computer can service you, then me, then perhaps fifty more people before we punch in another character on a keyboard. Users typically interact with the system by using a keyboard and display. This is, in fact, what led to the development of interactive languages such as BASIC. Users wanted to get quick results for small computational needs.

Time sharing in the 1960's became the "in thing" for computer systems. Systems which provided both time sharing and batch processing were developed, making them much more versatile for general computer needs. Hardware capabilities were introduced which allowed a user to dial up a computer on the telephone from a remote location and use it for running, say, a BASIC program, or perhaps for generating a file of instructions or data. A FORTRAN program could be one file and its data a second. Special system instructions were available which would let a user submit the program for execution in the system in a batch mode.

Figure 5-12 illustrates how the computer can be used for both batch and time sharing. That is, the CPU cycle time utilization can be divided into two parts — a cycle time for batch jobs and a cycle time for time-shared jobs. Each processing requirement, whether coming from a batch job or a time-shared job, gets its respective share of the system resources for a specified time during each processing cycle in the same manner as before. The amount of time alloted to batch or time sharing during each cycle is selected by the operator and directly affects job through-put and turn-around for the various job classes. The same is true for memory allocation. The more memory available for a particular job, whether it be batch or time shared, means that either more jobs or larger jobs can be stored. (Actually, the memory requirement for individual jobs is a problem in itself and typically, there is always a job needing more memory than is available).

Some techniques allocate CPU time and system resources alternately to time-shared jobs and batch jobs.

Figure 5-12.
CPU Usage for Batch and Time-Shared Jobs.

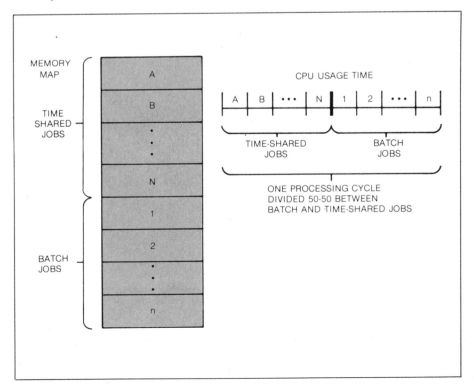

In the development of operating systems, time sharing tended to make them even more complicated. The original goal of using time sharing was to improve the usage and efficiency of the computer, but as we have seen, the opposite effect could occur under certain conditions. Therefore, the computer operating personnel had to constantly "tune" the system, that is, they had to select a mixture of jobs and had to set priorities so that the computer system was used effectively.

ADDITIONAL OPERATING SYSTEM FEATURES

As previously mentioned, memory is one bottleneck that is common to most computer systems. It seems like jobs almost always need more memory than is available. That is, the program often has more instructions and needs more data storage than the main memory can accommodate. One way to solve this problem is through the use of overlays.

When main memory space is a problem, one solution in large systems is to divide programs into sections which are processed by bringing each section into a given area of main memory in sequence.

As illustrated in *Figure 5-13*, programs are separated into parts or sections, where any individual section is small enough to reside in main memory. When section A completes execution, section B is loaded into the same area of main memory where section A had been and control passed to section B. All sections reside on auxiliary storage and the next specified section is simply overlaid on top of the previous section when needed. It is the responsibility of the operating system to load the next section, when so directed by the user through special commands, and pass control to the loaded section for execution. Therefore, the user has the responsibility of dividing his or her program into these sections and directing the overlay process, when needed.

**Figure 5-13.
Memory Overlay Method.**

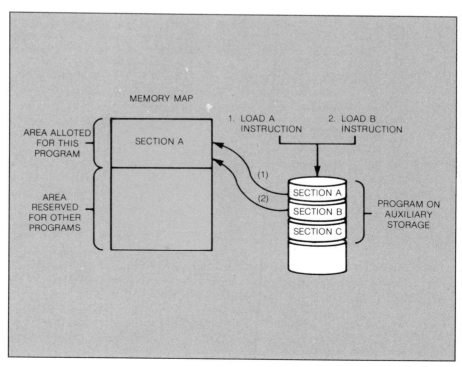

Memory Overlay

Today's systems can auto-
matically divide programs
into "pages" of equal length
and load the pages, singly
or in groups, as needed in
order to run the program
in sections.

Someone got the idea to let the computer do this work, that is,
have the computer automatically section or overlay modules. For this
method, the needed memory space (the address space) of a program is
defined as all addressable instructions and data. The address space can be
greater than available main memory. The address space is divided into
equal size pages as shown in *Figure 5-14*, and pages are loaded into the
allotted memory as needed by a combination of hardware and the operating
system software. Control can be passed to another job while this loading
takes place. Once the referenced page is loaded, control is returned to the
program. When a location is referenced that is on a page that is not in
memory, it is said that a page fault occured. The memory available to a
program can usually accommodate more than just one page. When a page
fault does occur, the page in memory that is replaced by the referenced
page is the one least used over a specified time period. This strategy of
replacing those pages used the least is called the *least recently used*
strategy or LRU. It is still commonly implemented in today's systems.

**Figure 5-14.
Virtual Memory and
Paging.**

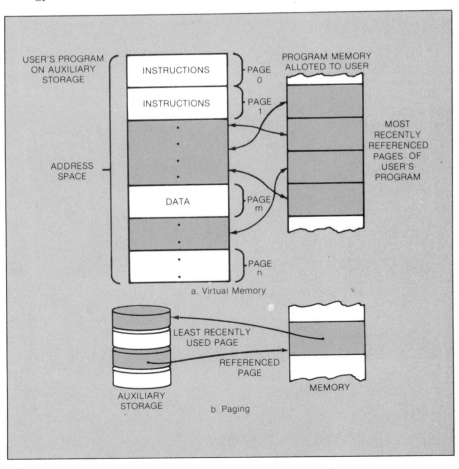

a. Virtual Memory

b. Paging

The page being replaced is rewritten to auxiliary storage if any changes occurred. Remember that when we talk about instructions or data being moved from memory or auxiliary storage to another location, we actually mean that a *copy* of the memory or storage contents is moved while the memory or auxiliary storage still holds the original information. Therefore, in this case, if no changes were made on the page, the auxiliary storage contents are still valid so it is not necessary to rewrite it.

Virtual Memory

Because the program now appears to reside in much more memory than actually is available, as illustrated in *Figure 5-14*, and the swapping of pages is automatic and completely unknown or transparent to the user, the term *virtual memory* is used to describe this process. That is, it appears to the user that he or she has much more memory than actually is available. The portions of the program not in main memory are simply kept on disk.

Systems which use virtual memory require even more careful 'tuning' by system personnel. For example, if a job is allowed only one page of real memory, and if instructions tend to frequently reference locations on two different pages, then frequent swapping or paging occurs. This is illustrated in *Figure 5-15*. As noted in this figure, first page 0 is referenced, then 1, then 0 once again and so forth. This frequent paging takes time and soon the system may be spending more time paging than executing the user's program. This phenomenon is called *thrashing*. Thrashing can easily occur under the right conditions, so programmers and system personnel have to be careful to try to avoid those conditions.

Automatic memory overlay makes the system appear to have more memory than it has in fact. This effect is called "virtual memory."

**Figure 5-15.
Thrashing.**

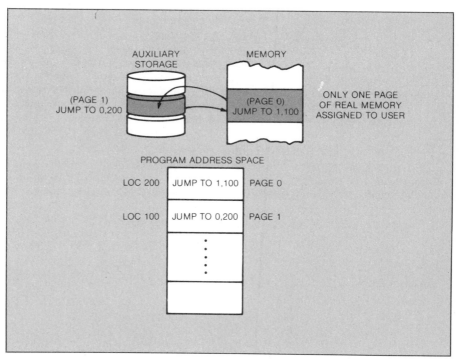

UNDERSTANDING COMPUTER SCIENCE

Some of the more recent changes to operating systems were made to accommodate more varied and flexible data or file management features. A group of data instructions, etc. can be treated as a separate entity, given a name, and placed in a file or auxiliary storage according to this name. Data within each file is broken up by records and information within records by fields. Numerous data bases can then be structured accordingly. System instructions for searching, editing, sorting, or referencing this data by other programs are provided.

Use of Multiple Computers

Recent operating system innovations enable networks of computers to interact and redistribute work loads among each other.

The most recent advancements have permitted computers to talk to other computers. This permits sharing of work loads in much the same fashion as that of an electrical power distribution system. As a result, a computer is called for use but it doesn't do the processing. It assigns a second computer to actually do the processing. Of course, this occurs without the knowledge of the user.

Rapid growth of operating systems has accompanied the rapid growth of hardware. As operating systems provided more features in attempts to maximize system efficiency and usability, the fine tuning required to make all the features work properly became more complicated and difficult to achieve. In many instances, systems have become so complicated that no one individual knows how the whole system works. It takes several highly skilled systems personnel to effectively tune, control, and use these systems.

AN OPERATING SYSTEM FOR A LARGE GENERAL PURPOSE SYSTEM

Earlier we described the process for executing a BASIC program and a FORTRAN program on a small personal computer. We said that running these same programs on small minicomputer systems instead of the personal computer were not too different. That is, the operating systems for most small computers are not complex. Large computer operating systems, on the other hand, are complex and capable of running many different types of jobs and executing many jobs at the same time.

First, let's consider what is involved when running a BASIC job on such a large system, and then we'll run a FORTRAN job.

BASIC Program

The first step in communicating with a large system from a terminal is to "log in".

Suppose we have a CRT terminal that is connected by a direct line to the computer, which say, is located in another room or in some other remote location. First, we must 'log in' to the system. This is typically done by an instruction similar to,

```
LOGIN CS.B815 JONES
```

The LOGIN tells the computer that you want to use its resources. A time sharing manager routine and one of the job manager routines process your request. Your account number is CS.B815 and your password is JONES.

The account number is used to keep track of the time you use the system for each job. You will be charged at the end of the month for the accumulated time. The password is included so someone else can't use your account or gain illegal access to the computer.

When you log in, processing is done by the job manager routines; first reading the LOGIN parameters and second, insuring that your account is not delinquent. The processing may be done by either the main CPU or by a general purpose programmable data channel or I/O processor. The job manager must read and record each character and check the account number and password for validity. If this processing is done by the main CPU, only a portion at a time may be done because the CPU is also being used for batch processing and for reading and executing other user programs at the same time.

After the computer confirms that your log-on data is correct, the interpreter must be loaded to run BASIC.

If the account number and password are legal, the computer responds to the user by some type of verification procedure such as,

```
JOB 542 LOGGED IN. ASSIGNED TTY 14
```

This simply indicates the number assigned internally to your job is 542 and your terminal device is assigned logic unit number 14. Future references within the system will be by these numbers. The operating system then reserves a portion of memory and CPU time to run the job.

Next, the need for the BASIC interpreter must be indicated. This is done by the command,

```
BASIC
```

The system then responds by telling you that BASIC has been loaded and is ready for use. That is, the operating system, after seeing the command BASIC, loads the BASIC interpreter for execution. From this point on, the system is simply used to run your BASIC program. The memory map of the system is illustrated in *Figure 5-16*. Notice that there are several other users shown. Some of these are also using BASIC. Others are using batch.

The BASIC interpreter has some of its own system commands for writing BASIC programs or executing these programs. It must do these things through the operating system. Control is first passed to each BASIC program where BASIC instructions are converted to machine language and executed. Control also is passed to each batch program that is sharing memory; first passing control to one program, then the second, then the third, etc.. That is, each unit of processing time, say one second, is divided into many parts. Then the CPU is used for batch programs for 50 percent of the unit time and for time-sharing programs for the other 50 percent.

Referring to the example we've been using throughout the book, averaging N numbers, suppose we have already written our program and it was stored by the name AVERAGE. Then, we simply use the command

```
OLD AVERAGE
```

**Figure 5-16.
Memory Map of Large
General Purpose
System.**

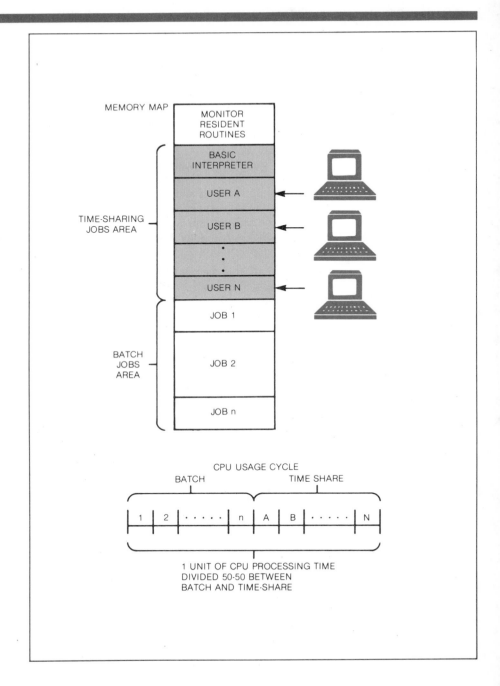

This command is interpreted by BASIC when it's our turn for the CPU and the command directs the operating system to locate and load a set of BASIC instructions or file called AVERAGE. (OLD tells the system that it's a previously stored program.) Control is then transferred by the operating system to other programs while this file is being loaded into the memory area assigned to our program. Next we type,

```
RUN
```

If you want to run a previously saved BASIC program, you load it with the OLD command and enter the RUN command to execute the program.

This command, when control is passed back to our program, instructs BASIC to begin executing the BASIC instructions in our program named AVERAGE.

BASIC is an interpreter and is not part of the operating system. However, the operating system is responsible for transferring control to each of the BASIC jobs as it becomes their turn.

In our personal computer example, BASIC is located in ROM. This is so the BASIC interpreter is immediately available when power is turned on; otherwise, the BASIC interpreter would have to be loaded each time at start up. In the large system, BASIC is located on disk and is loaded when needed. It can be shared by other BASIC programs.

The operating system is also responsible for reading and writing to the terminal device. All I/O is handled by the input/output Manager. That is, BASIC requests output but it's the operating system which actually writes the output.

BASIC, as mentioned, has many of its own system functions. The operating system lets BASIC take care of setting up the environment for the BASIC program. BASIC interacts with the operating system on input/output and when loading from memory or saving program files to memory.

FORTRAN Program

FORTRAN is designed for batch processing. The operating system regulates all processing steps.

For the FORTRAN program, things are different. This is because FORTRAN, unlike BASIC, doesn't have as many system functions and all operations must go through the operating system. FORTRAN is structured for batch processing. It is a compiler and not an interpreter. *Figure 5-17* illustrates the job processing function of the operating system. As discussed earlier, your job consists of your control cards, complete program, and data. To execute this job, it is broken up into processes or tasks. The operating system initiates each task.

First, your job is read in along with other jobs and loaded or 'spooled' to disk. As it is read, its entry time, priority, and resource requirements are noted. A set of routines, called the Job Manager, examines the priority and entry time. If the job is of the highest priority and first in line of the other jobs with the same priority currently in the system, the job manager examines your resource needs. These needs include memory and I/O as specified by your control cards.

**Figure 5-17.
Large General Purpose
Computer System
Operation Flow Diagram.**

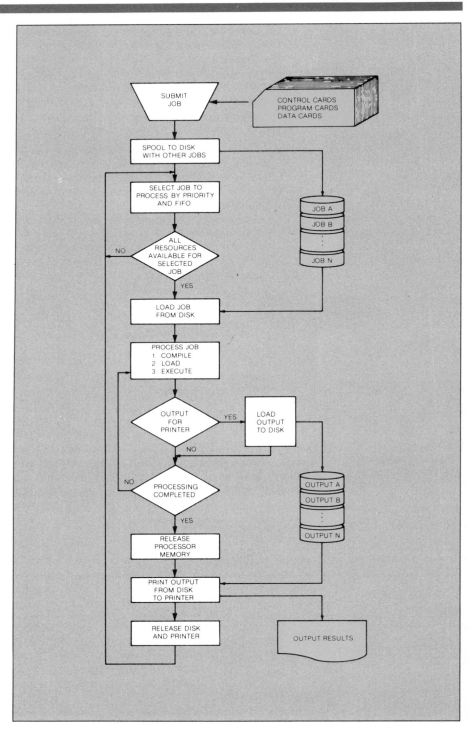

As a result, a request is made to the memory manager operating system routines for memory needs by a subroutine call made by one of the job manager routines. Consequently, the memory needed by the job, which has been indicated on the input cards, is noted. The memory manager checks its tables to see how much memory is available and where. If sufficient, then an area of memory is marked for use by your job and control is returned to the job manager. If not enough memory is available, your job is placed in a 'hold state' until enough is available. Your input/output needs are handled in a similar fashion through the input/output manager.

When resource needs are met, the first step or task of your job is initiated. This may be loading the FORTRAN compiler if it's not already loaded. Control is then transferred to this routine to compile your program. Note that the processing time is shared with other jobs in the system.

When your job has been compiled, the job manager requests that a loader program load your job into the system. Finally, control is passed to your job and its execution is started.

When your program requests output to the printer, this output is read ('spooled') to disk as are outputs from other jobs. When your program has finished, your output is transferred from disk to the printer. This processing feature, which makes better use of system resources, will be discussed further in the next chapter. Meanwhile, the resources used by your job are released for use by other jobs.

Thus, we see that a lot of operating system routines get into the act just to process our simple FORTRAN program. These routines initiate our job, monitor its execution, and stay with it until its completion.

Each job in the system, and there can be many, will likewise have a manager controlling and monitoring its processing. Some of the operating system modules are shared between the time sharing and batch applications. Both make requests to the job manager, however, the job manager handles each type differently. Here are some examples. The time-sharing job is usually processed immediately, whereas the batch job is 'spooled' or stored on disk. The time-sharing job requests BASIC. This loads the interpreter. After it is loaded, BASIC processes the BASIC statements. The batch job takes a different route. First, the input program is compiled by the FORTRAN compiler, then loaded into the system and executed. Output from the batch job goes to disk, then to the printer. Output from the BASIC job goes directly to the terminal device.

There are many functions performed by the operating system as your job is processed. In the next chapter, we will examine these functions in more detail.

After the operating system allocates system resources for the job, the program is compiled, loaded into the system, run, and printed.

The various modules of the operating system collectively monitor the execution of every job submitted to the computer.

WHAT HAVE WE LEARNED?

In this chapter, we have examined the concepts of operating systems. When you run a program on the computer, there has to be another program already in the computer to read your program.

If your program, which is often called a job, consists of FORTRAN statements, they must be converted to machine instructions. Thus, the FORTRAN compiler must be read into memory to perform this conversion. After the translation is complete, the resulting machine instructions must be loaded into the computer's memory and then executed.

This program within the computer which reads in your job, has it compiled or converted to machine instructions, and executed is the operating system program. It is very complex and consists of many subroutines or parts. It may also have many other functions such as running several jobs concurrently.

Most of the first computers didn't have an operating system program. The few that did had very simple operating systems. Each user had the computer to himself or herself while running a program. This was a very inefficient usage of the computer and as the number of users increased, batch systems were implemented. For these systems, a program within the computer loaded and executed each program in sequence. An operator was in charge of submitting each job and getting the results back to each user.

Systems progressed to the point where several programs could be in memory at the same time with each job having use of the CPU during alloted time intervals. Such multiprogrammed systems resulted in even more efficient usage of the computer's CPU and other resources such as memory and I/O devices.

Time-sharing operating systems were developed which allowed programmers from remote locations to dial in over a telephone line and use the computer with the aid of a teletype or CRT terminal.

Since micro or small minicomputer systems are typically used by only one user at a time, the operating systems on the small computers are much simpler than those on the larger computers.

WHAT'S NEXT?

Computers could not be as useful as they are today without some type of operating systems. The subprograms of the operating system for large computer systems provide efficient management of the CPU, memory, and the various I/O devices. In the next chapter, we will examine how such subprograms are structured to accomplish these functions.

Quiz for Chapter 5

1. The first computers permitted several programs to be executed concurrently.
True or False

2. Resident Monitors were developed because the many functions required of the operating system needed to be in memory for speed purposes.
True or False

3. Which of the following operating system functions would you not expect on a small personal computer?
a. Time sharing
b. Input/Output support
c. BASIC interpreter
d. Disk operating system routines

4. Multiprogrammed systems were implemented before virtual memory.
True or False

5. A user could run a program larger than main memory by which of the following techniques?
a. Multiprogramming
b. Time sharing
c. Overlays
d. Multiprocessing

6. Systems which implement virtual memory must be 'tuned' for efficient operation.
True or False

7. Most operating systems for micro-computers permit multiprogramming.
True or False

8. Paging is a concept used when implementing virtual memory.
True or False

9. The term 'LRU' is most often mentioned when describing the interaction between a user and the operating system of a personal computer.
True or False

10. Which concept was not implemented when the resident monitor was first introduced?
a. Input/output support routines
b. Batch processing
c. FIFO in job processing
d. Distributed processing

11. Match the terms, best describing the functions of each operating system class.

1. Multipro-grammed Systems

2. Distributed Processing Systems

3. Batch Processing

4. Time Sharing

5. Resident Monitor

a. More than one computer used in a network for job processing.

b. Several users at remote locations using the same computer.

c. Current processing of jobs.

d. Leaving the implementation of most commonly used system routines in memory.

e. A group of jobs submitted in sequence for processing.

12. Many personal computers implement BASIC in ROM, however, it can be maintained on disk. One disadvantage of having BASIC on disk is;
    a. Execution time is increased
    b. A disk drive is required
    c. Multiprogramming is precluded
    d. None of the above

13. Closed shop operation is preferred for large general purpose computer systems.
    True or False

14. Job Control Language usually requires a compiler.
    True or False

15. Interrupts are one means of ensuring that jobs execute only for a given time period.
    True or False

16. Multiprogramming essentially means that a computer system has two or more CPUs.
    True or False

17. Assume two jobs, A and B, are to be executed in a multiprogramming system where job A requires 2 minutes of CPU time and job B 2 hours. The average turnaround time that can be expected, assuming no other jobs in the system is:
    a. 63 minutes
    b. 2 hours
    c. 31 minutes
    d. 2 hours 1 minute
    e. none of the above

18. For a sequential batch system, the average turnaround time for jobs A and B of problem 17 is:
    a. 63 minutes
    b. 2 hours
    c. 31 minutes
    d. 2 hours 1 minute
    e. none of the above

19. In virtual memory systems, the swapping of pages is usually transparent to the user.
    True or False

20. Thrashing is where a user spends too much time performing input or output operations in a program.
    True or False

(Answers in back of book.)

Resource Management

ABOUT THIS CHAPTER

In the last chapter, we discussed the basic functions provided by an operating system. Essentially, the operating system provides a monitor and control function. It monitors the total execution of your job; controlling or directing its initiation, execution and completion. The operating system is not just one program, but many programs or routines which manage the computer system's resources. The larger the computer system, the more general purpose capabilities it provides, and as a result, the more complex these system resource manager routines or programs become.

Actually, there are other system programs which are not considered part of the operating system. Such programs are software resources and include the utility routines, the loader and the language translators. Utilities are system routines which the user may call to perform frequently needed functions by many application programs; such as sorting a file, copying data or a program from one tape to another, or copying from tape to disk, etc. The loader is the program which loads your program into memory for execution, and language translators have already been discussed in previous chapters. These translators include the FORTRAN compiler, the COBOL compiler, the PL/I compiler, and the various assemblers. We will have more about compilers in Chapter 8.

"System programs" that support many users include utilities, loaders, and translators as well as the operating system.

The term 'system programs' is used when referring to the operating system routines, utilities, loaders and translators. They are called this because they support the computer system. They are not written to support only a program for one specific application such as one to compute the average of a number of grades. They are written to support all programs written by the many users for a particular computer system.

In this chapter, we will examine in detail how the operating system performs the resource management functions. By resource management, we mean managing the various system resources used by an application program as the system executes the program. The memory, CPU, I/O devices, and various system programs are the system resources.

AN OPERATING SYSTEM — A COLLECTION OF RESOURCE MANAGERS

The resources of a system include both hardware and software.

A computer system consists of a number of computing resources which include both hardware and software. Hardware resources are the CPU, memory and I/O devices. Software resources are the loader program, utilities, language translators, and data file manipulation programs.

The operating system consists of resource managers to manage these resources. Resource managers can be divided into these five classes:

Job Manager,

Memory Manager,

Processor Manager,

I/O Manager, and

Information Manager.

The job manager is responsible for reading in your program, determining the resource needs, ensuring that these resources are available, scheduling the job for execution, monitoring the job throughout execution, and releasing the resources used when the job terminates.

The memory manager is responsible for assigning memory and releasing memory as a job executes.

The processor manager is responsible for assigning computation time or processor time.

The I/O manager is responsible for assigning and performing all I/O operations to specific devices.

The information manager handles requests for filing in auxiliary storage a specific group of data items under an assigned file name. When the data items are needed, the information manager finds the file and gives the location to the I/O manager.

Five categories of "resource managers" — job (program), memory, processor, I/O, and information (data) managers — make up the operating system.

**Figure 6-1.
Mythical System CS
Computer System.**

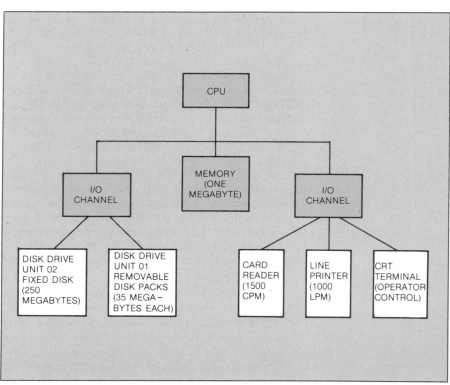

An Example System

Let's see how these resource managers control a job by following the submission and execution of a job in a large computer system. We will define our own job control language (JCL) and use a mythical machine called the System CS. The configuration of our computer system is illustrated in *Figure 6-1*. As shown, the system has two disk drives, one for a fixed disk with 250 megabytes (250 million storage locations with 8 bits in each location) of storage and the other one with removable disk packs where each disk pack can hold up to 35 megabytes of storage. Memory consists of 1 megabyte of semiconductor storage. A card reader capable of reading 1,500 cards per minute and a printer capable of printing 1,000 lines per minute provides the necessary I/O devices. A CRT terminal is used by the operator for controlling the system.

JOB EXECUTION

Suppose the job we want to run is, once again, to compute the average of a set of N numbers. Only this time, suppose that the N numbers are located on the disk pack under the file name DATA. Let's see how the resource managers perform as our job is executed.

We must, however, first define some terms. Jobs generally consist of steps of processing. The execution of our job to compute the average of a set of numbers for instance, consists of these three steps:

Compile,
Load, and
Execute.

Each step may require one or more processes or tasks. *A process is a set of related instructions to perform a specific function.* Processes may be user processes or system processes. The resource managers themselves consist of many processes. For example, the job manager assigns a separate process to each job to guide and monitor the job throughout its execution. The actual execution of a process occurs when a processor (CPU) is assigned to a process. If there is only one CPU in a system, then there is only one processor.

Processing within the system is implemented by a number of lists associated with each resource manager. Requests for servicing by a resource manager are made by placing an entry in the service list of this manager (*Figure 6-2*). The manager then examines this list and performs the appropriate processing to service this request. If the processes of the resource manager itself are to be executed, they are placed in the request list of the processor manager.

Each step of running a job — compiling, loading, and executing — may involve several related processes.

Figure 6-2.
Process Implementation.

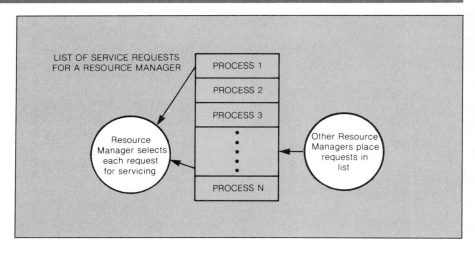

Program Deck and Control Cards

Job control cards at the beginning of a FORTRAN program supply accounting information and specify the system resources required by the program.

     Let's now specify the needed system resources for our example job. Let's say our job is written in FORTRAN; therefore, the FORTRAN compiler must be specified. Other information about the job includes; the job name, account number, job priority, memory requirements, time requirements and data file needed. As noted in the last chapter, this information is specified by control cards preceding the program deck. There are several formats used for specifying this information on control cards by the various operating systems. Our format is as follows:

```
// JOB AVERAGE, ACCNT = CS – 12
// MEM = 48K, TIME = 1 MINUTE, PR = 2
// FT5 = CARD, FT6 = PRINTER, FT20 = DATA.DISK01
// FORTRAN
   PROGRAM CARD DECK FOLLOWS CONTROL CARDS
   .          .          .
   .          .          .
   .          .          .
```

     The "//" indicates a control card. The job control cards specify the job accounting information and the resource needs. The job accounting information includes the name of the job, AVERAGE and the user account number, CS-12. The program requires 48K (49152 bytes) of memory and has a 1 minute time limit. Actually, the memory requirements for our AVERAGE program would probably be much less than 48K, however, the memory used by the FORTRAN compiler must be included for the compile operation (or step). The job is assigned a priority 2 where priority 1 is the highest. The card reader is assigned the logical unit 5 and the printer is assigned the logical unit 6. The file DATA has the values to be averaged and is found on the disk drive with removable disk pack, which is disk unit 01. This unit is assigned logical unit 20. (The fixed disk is on disk unit 02. The numbers 01 and 02 are obtained from the initial physical system hardware configuration). The last control card which immediately precedes the program deck specifies the FORTRAN compiler.

**Figure 6-3.
User Jobs Spooled to
Disk.**

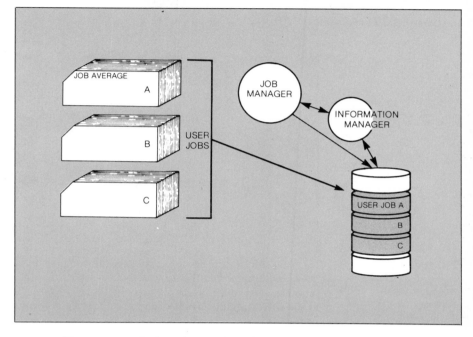

The program deck and control cards for our job AVERAGE are placed on the card reader along with two other jobs. We'll call our job A and the other two B and C for simplicity in the following discussion. As these three jobs are read in they are stored or "spooled" on the fixed disk unit 02 (*Figure 6-3*).

Job Manager

As the job is read into the system, each of the resource managers plays a role in preparing the system to execute the program.

The job manager requests space on the disk from the information manager. The information manager ensures that there is room on the disk by looking into a disk directory. This is a table, usually kept on the disk, listing all current files on the disk, their starting location, and the amount of storage used. A new file name is assigned for each of the spooled jobs.

As each job is read and placed on disk, a job control block is generated (*Figure 6-4*). This is simply an internal table used by the job manager for executing each job. Each job read is now placed in a *hold* state; that is, it's in the system but execution has not yet begun. The job manager then looks through the job control blocks and finds the job with the highest priority. If two jobs have the same priority, the one read first is selected first. Requests are made to the memory manager, I/O manager, and information manager to see if the needed resources are available for job execution. If sufficient resources are not available, the job is left in the hold state until such resources are available. Requests for unavailable resources are usually set up on a waiting list so the resource can be obtained as soon as it becomes available. When the resources become available, they are assigned to the appropriate requesting job.

6 RESOURCE MANAGEMENT

Figure 6-4.
Job Control Block.

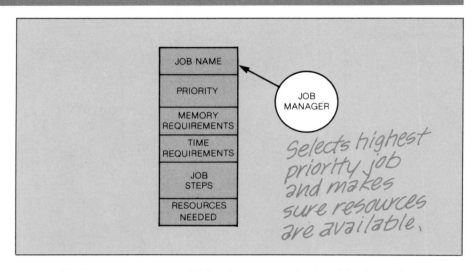

When the needed resources are available, the system queues the job for execution.

If all resources are available, the program is placed in the *wait* state and attached to the service request list of the processor manager to wait for a processor. In this state, the job is ready for CPU usage. All jobs in the wait state are maintained in this service request list as illustrated in *Figure 6-5*.

Figure 6-5.
Processor Manager
Service Request List.

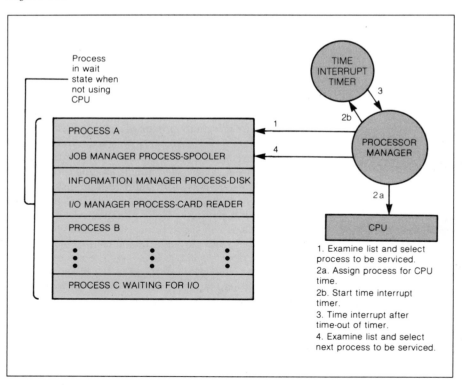

Processor Manager

The processor manager examines this list and assigns each of these tasks a specified amount of CPU processing time. Note that other resource management routines are included in this list. This is because these managers are programs and need CPU time for execution. Thus, they are always in the list when management functions are to be performed. The main difference is that these system routines can place themselves in the processor's list, but user programs must be placed in this list by a resource manager as the need arises.

The processor manager sets a time interrupt to occur when the task assigned has used its portion of the CPU time. When this interrupt occurs, the next task on the list is given some CPU time. When a process is performing I/O and the CPU is not needed until the I/O is complete, that process is kept in a wait state until the I/O operation has completed. When the last item in the list has been serviced, the processor manager assigns CPU time to the first item and the loop is continuously repeated until no requests for service remain.

The method just described of allowing each process in the list an equal share of the CPU during a time cycle is referred to as a "round-robin" assignment procedure. More complex processor assignment algorithms can be implemented, such as giving priority to certain processes, or locking out certain processes in the list during a cycle while others of higher priority are given use of the CPU.

Thus, the processor manager is responsible for assigning the CPU or processor to a process. Of course, this processor manager program itself also requires CPU time and receives its time between usage of the CPU by each of the other processes. That is, control is passed to it when the time interrupt occurs.

Releasing Resources

When the application program completes its execution, the resources that have been used are released. Typically, output is not sent directly to the printer during program execution but 'spooled' to the disk, once again, via the information manager. When the job has completed its execution, the output is then printed from this spooled file along with output from other jobs. The overall process from job submission to job completion is illustrated in *Figure 6-6*.

Let's next examine in more detail each of these resource managers that make up the operating system.

**Figure 6-6.
Job Execution.**

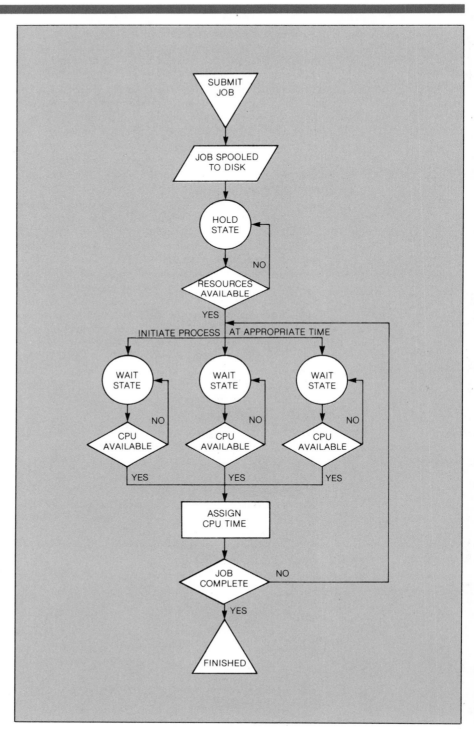

JOB MANAGER

As noted previously, the job manager is responsible for first spooling jobs to the disk. As each job is read, a job control block is generated which provides an internal table for keeping track of each job as it is executed. Among other things the job manager reads the job control statements and records all resource requirements. All of the control blocks are then placed in a list. Jobs spooled onto the disk are said to be in a hold state. They remain in this state until necessary resources are available and the job enters into a state where it is ready to be executed.

The job manager consists of a number of processes. One of these is responsible for determining which jobs are permitted into the system. This process is attached to the processor manager request list. When the job permission process receives the use of the CPU, it examines the control blocks of all jobs in the hold state on a first-in basis and/or priority assignment and determines if all necessary resources are available for the specified job. If so, the first step of the job is set for processing.

After a job is set for processing, the job manager coordinates the need for other resource managers and places requests on the list for the respective manager.

This is done by attaching a second type of job management process, unique to the job in consideration, to the processor service list of the processor manager. If, for instance, a FORTRAN compilation is required, the special process attached to the list is a request to run the FORTRAN compiler. The process requesting execution of the FORTRAN compiler specifies where the program to be compiled (source statements) are located. Once the process receives its share of the CPU, control passes to the FORTRAN compiler which initiates a read request for the FORTRAN source statements. The read request is processed by the information manager to obtain the FORTRAN statements on disk 02 where the jobs were spooled.

When the FORTRAN compiler has generated the machine language program (relocatable object module) and completes execution, the object module is stored to disk via the information manager. The job manager process assigned to monitor this task next requests that the object module generated by the FORTRAN compiler be loaded into system memory by the system loader program by attaching the appropriate request to the service list of the processor manager. After the loading is complete, the user program is ready to be executed. Then the job manager process attaches a request to the service list of the processor manager to execute the user program.

Recall that the AVERAGE program requires the data file, DATA. The I/O request for this file is made when the logical unit 20 is referenced. The information manager locates this file and it is read into an I/O buffer area in memory that has been assigned by the memory manager. When the program completes its execution, the job manager process makes the appropriate request to the memory manager to release the memory area assigned.

Output spooled to disk during execution is then noted and a process attached for transferring this output from disk to the printer. This completes the execution of the job manager process for this job.

Summary

In summary, the job manager is responsible for getting each job processed. It does this by generating a special job control block for the specific job. The job control block is an internal table containing all necessary information about the job so it may be executed. The job manager then initiates a separate job manager system process which monitors this particular job throughout its execution. All necessary resources needed by the job are obtained by this system process.

If jobs are initiated via terminals a separate time-share process of the job manager is attached to the request list of the processor manager. When the time-share process receives control, it monitors any request by the terminals that are time sharing the computer system. During its execution, it checks the account number and then processes the control statements. If a file is called for during execution, the time-share process sees that it is loaded by the information manager and executed by assigning a unique job related process to it.

Remember that this whole procedure is possible because of multiprogramming which we discussed in Chapter 5. That is, many different types of system and user processes are using the CPU and memory at the same time.

Let's next examine the function performed by the memory manager and see how several jobs can be contained in memory at the same time.

MEMORY MANAGER

The memory manager attends to the memory requirements of each job in the system. The complexity of the task depends on the number of jobs being processed.

The memory manager has responsibility for obtaining memory for processes. If memory only accommodates one job at any one time, then memory management is relatively simple as illustrated in *Figure 6-7*. In this figure, the total memory is 128K bytes with 24K bytes allocated for system programs. The user job requires 20K bytes . The loader simply places the user program in contiguous (in numerical order, one after the other) memory locations, beginning where the resident system routines end at location 6000 hexadecimal (24576 decimal).

Figure 6-8a illustrates how three user jobs can be loaded to share memory. As long as free memory is available for processes, they are simply placed in adjacent locations. Memory management for this scheme also is relatively easy. However, a problem with using memory as one contiguous block is illustrated in the following case. Suppose Process A and C finished but Process B has not finished. Process D is ready for execution, however, it is larger than either A or C but not the combination. This is illustrated in *Figure 6-8b*.

**Figure 6-7.
Memory Map for Single
Process.**

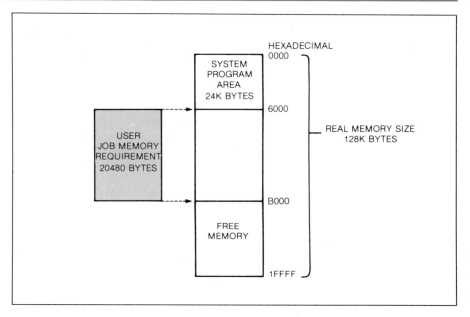

**Figure 6-8.
Memory Map for
Multiprogramming.**

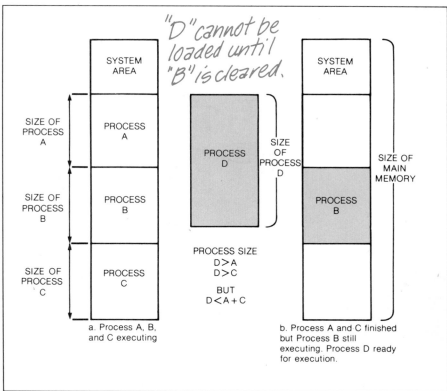

"D" cannot be loaded until "B" is cleared.

a. Process A, B, and C executing

b. Process A and C finished but Process B still executing. Process D ready for execution.

Note that Process D cannot be loaded until Process B finishes or is moved. However, moving B would be difficult after it has already started execution, since some of the original tables indicating memory reference instruction, etc. may have changed. Besides, relocating B would take considerable time and a similar situation may occur again when another job is ready.

Relocation Registers

Relocation registers are a means of indexing the memory locations and memory references of individual programs so that several jobs can share the available memory.

One solution to the problem is to use relocation registers. In this method, all programs are assembled or compiled relative to location zero. Then, when each process receives use of the CPU, the actual beginning memory location where each process is loaded is placed in the relocation register.

The relocation register is a register within the CPU and when any memory reference occurs, including fetching of instructions, the actual memory address is the specified address plus the contents of the relocation register as illustrated in *Figure 6-9a*. With three such registers, Process B can be moved and its relocation register changed to indicate the new position as shown in *Figure 6-9b*. Then Process D can be loaded. The use of such relocation registers makes job movement easier. However, each job loaded in the system requires a relocation register.

**Figure 6-9.
Memory Map Using
Relocation Registers.**

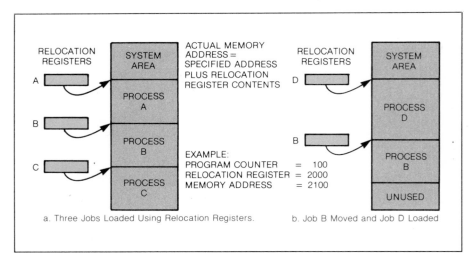

a. Three Jobs Loaded Using Relocation Registers.   b. Job B Moved and Job D Loaded

Fixed Pages

Segmenting programs into "pages" which are copied into memory as needed is another way to make the system's memory available to several jobs at once.

There is yet a better way and it's the way most large computer systems handle dynamic memory requirements. For this method, memory is divided into fixed pages of, say, 2048 (2^{11}) bytes each. Furthermore, suppose that the available system address space is 16,384K (2^{24}) bytes, which is much greater than available main memory. Remember that address space is defined as the maximum number of unique locations that can be identified by the number of bits contained in the system binary memory address.

The memory manager sets up a page table to track the locations of individual program pages.

The address space of each program is divided into 2048 byte pages, and as each process is prepared for processing, the memory manager generates a page table, as shown in *Figure 6-10a*. This page table indicates where pages of the process are located. Initially, the process or object module is a file located on disk as generated by the compiler. Note in *Figure 6-10a* the first page is on track 2, sector 0. When the process is scheduled for execution, one or more pages are loaded into memory. In *Figure 6-10b*, the first two pages are in memory and the other 8 are still out on disk.

**Figure 6-10.
Memory Paging Method.**

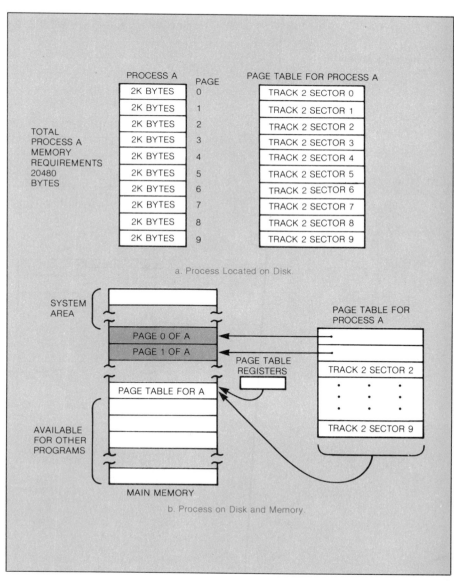

When Process A receives use of the CPU, it begins processing in page 0 and page 1 of the program. Actual memory locations are computed by the hardware as in the relocation case, except that instead of going to a register to get the relocation displacement address, the hardware goes to the page table which is in memory (*Figure 6-10b*). The CPU contains a page location register whose contents contain the page table of the current process being executed. Thus, as each memory fetch or reference occurs, the actual memory location is automatically computed by the hardware by first going to the page table, fetching the address of the page in real memory, and adding it to the memory location specified by the instruction or program counter. This procedure is illustrated in *Figure 6-11*.

**Figure 6-11.
Computation of Memory
Address Using Page
Table.**

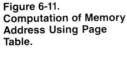

Page address + instruction's location within page = real memory location.

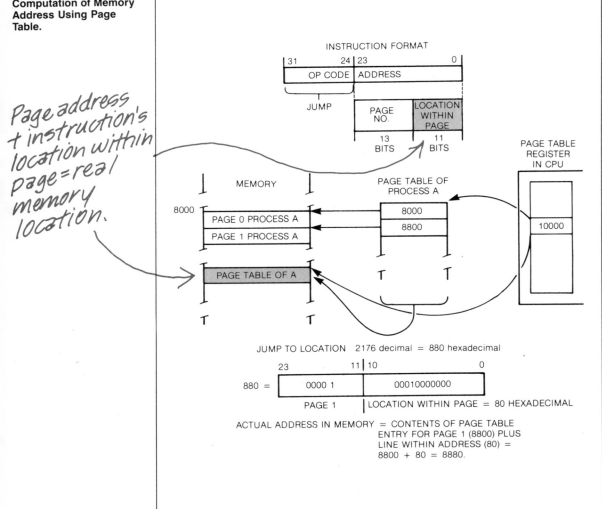

For example, in *Figure 6-11*, the address space is 24 bits. The first (least significant) eleven bits specify one of the possible 2048 locations within a page and the remaining 13 bits specify one of the 8192 possible pages. An address of 2176 decimal or 880 hexadecimal is equal to 100010000000 binary. This address indicates the location of 80 hexadecimal (least significant 11 bits) within page 1 (next 13 bits). If page 1 begins at real memory address 8800 hexadecimal as specified by the page table, then the hexadecimal address 880 is translated as real memory location 8880.

Page Fault

If a program segment references a page not currently in memory, control passes momentarily to another process while the needed page is loaded.

If a memory reference is made to a page not in memory, a "page fault" occurs and control is transferred to the next process while that page is placed in memory. Most systems implementing memory in this fashion have registers associated with each page of real memory. This register keeps track of the number of references made to each page. When a page fault occurs, these registers are examined, and the page whose register has the smallest value (referenced the least) over a given time period is 'paged out' or transferred back to disk while the new page is 'paged in' or loaded. This *least recently used* (LRU) paging strategy is implemented by many systems. Other methods have been introduced, but the LRU method is the most popular.

**Figure 6-12.
Determination of
Memory Address for a
Page Not in Memory.**

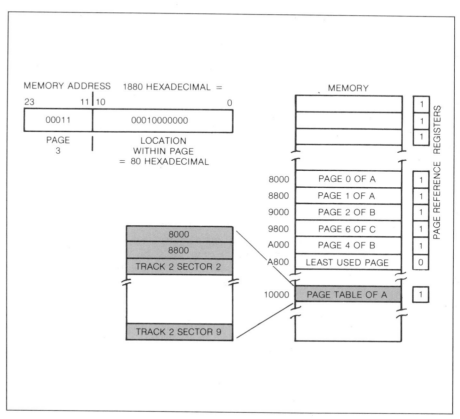

The memory manager contains tables to indicate which pages are free for assignment. *Figure 6-12* illustrates the complete process of determining a memory address for a page not in memory. In *Figure 6-12*, a memory reference to hexadecimal 1880 occurs. This reference is translated by the hardware, as location 80 in page 3. The hardware then fetches location 10000 (the address in the current page table register from *Figure 6-11*) +3 and finds that this is a disk location, not a memory location. That is, the page is not in memory and a fault has occurred. An interrupt indicates this and control is passed to the memory manager. The memory manager then examines the one bit registers associated with each page and finds that page 21 was not referenced since the last examination of these registers. The memory management program then resets all of the page reference registers to zero and pages out the contents of page 21 to the disk location where it was originally contained. The contents of disk location track 2, sector 2 is then "paged in" or loaded into memory location A800 thru AFFF. This memory location is then fetched and execution continues.

Some computers indicate not only when a reference is made to a page, but if the reference was a read or store. If for instance, no memory stores occurred on the page in question, then no changes to that page in memory ever occurred and thus, the contents do not have to be paged out to disk since the contents on disk are still valid. The contents of that page in memory are simply overwritten or replaced by the new page.

Virtual Memory

"Virtual memory" is an attribute of systems that are able to run large programs in relatively small amounts of memory.

When a program's address space can be greater than actual real memory as just discussed, the system is said to implement virtual memory. In the previous example, a 24-bit address space permits a possible 16,384K byte program while real memory is only 128K bytes.

Virtual memory works very well because in most cases, a memory fetch (read) will be to a location close to the current memory location. For example, unless the instruction requires a memory reference (an instruction which references another address for the purpose of obtaining an operand from the referenced location, or a jump to that location), then the next memory fetch will be to the next consecutive location. Therefore, all pages of a program do not always need to be in memory. The LRU method keeps the most used pages in memory. The hardware automatically computes the absolute or real memory location from the relative location plus the offset amount from the page table. So we see that for systems using virtual memory, the memory manager is responsibe for keeping track of available memory and assigning the most used pages to real memory.

Next, let's look at the Processor Manager.

PROCESSOR MANAGER

Multiprogramming

Recall from Chapter 5 that *multiprogramming* permits two or more processes (programs) to be in an execution state at the same time. In a multiprogrammed system, the processor manager is responsible for assigning the CPU to each program for a certain amount of time during each CPU cycle.

Equal-time Processing

In computer systems that support multiprogramming, the processor manager allots a certain amount of CPU time to each job in progress.

Let's consider an example where we have 3 processes named A, B, and C all in memory and sharing the one processor. The systems personnel who run the computer have specified that the CPU is to be equally shared by all jobs in the system. If there are n processes in the system then each process should get approximately 1/n second of processing time for every second. With three processes and a CPU usage cycle set for one second, each process is assigned approximately 333 milliseconds (⅓ second) of computer time.

The processor manager examines the processor service request list (*Figure 6-13*). From this list the amount of time to be assigned to each executable task or process for a given cycle is computed. The CPU is assigned to the first process and the processor manager directs the hardware to interrupt the computer after 333 milliseconds. When this interrupt occurs, the second process is assigned the CPU for 333 milliseconds. Finally, the third process uses the CPU for the last 333 milliseconds.

**Figure 6-13.
Processor Sharing.**

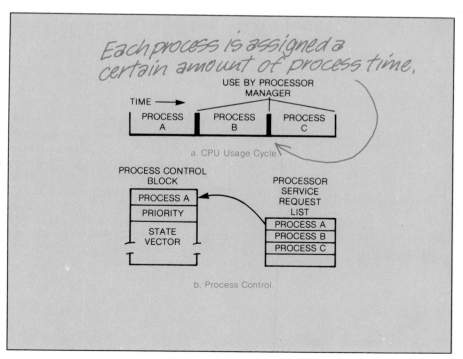

Each process appended to the list is assigned a processor control block (*Figure 6-13*). This block is somewhat similar to the job control block discussed earlier. It contains information about the specific process. It is needed by the processor manager so that the process can be assigned to the CPU. It also is the place where the contents of all registers are stored when a process is interrupted. When the CPU is returned to the interrupted process, these registers must be restored. That is, the CPU must be returned to the state that it was in before it was interrupted.

The contents of all registers used by the process and any other process related information is called the process state vector. This state vector is stored in the process control block as illustrated in *Figure 6-13*. Also included in this block is the name of the process or program, where it is located, the address of all tables used by the program, and its priority if used by the processor manager for assignment purposes.

More Complex Schedules

For some processes a different distribution of CPU time other than equal division may be desirable. That is, those processes associated with batch jobs may need more time alloted than those associated with time sharing jobs. Such assignment parameters are set by the computer system operator and the processor manager then assigns CPU time according to these parameters.

Multiprocessing

"Multiprocessing" systems have two or more CPU's, each working independently on different tasks.

A system may have more than one CPU working at the same time. If so, the system is said to permit *multiprocessing*. Each of the CPU's may have two or more programs in execution at the same time. So you can see that the assignment of CPU time by the processor manager is more complex. That is, you can't have one CPU working on part of a process and a second CPU working on another part without a lot of coordination. For this reason it's not usually done. Multiprocessor systems with independent CPU's typically have each CPU working on completely different tasks.

Synchronization

Because tasks or processes may be related, yet can be executed independently, some method of process or task synchronization is often required. In our earlier example the three job steps involved were compile, load and execute. That example illustrates a simple order and you can easily see that it is important that the load step doesn't occur before the compile step, or the execute step before the load step.

The process execution order of *Figure 6-14* is somewhat more complicated. Here process 7 cannot be executed before 5 and 6 have finished since processes 5 and 6 generate results necessary for proper execution of 7. Process 6 cannot occur before processes 2, 3 and 4 have completed for the same reason. Finally, processes 2, 3, 4 and 5 cannot occur before process 1 has finished.

If all of these tasks are appended to the processor manager's service request list at the same time, how does the processor manager control the steps to accomplish this desired order?

**Figure 6-14.
Process Execution
Order.**

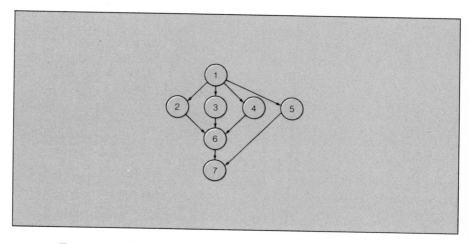

The processor manager software uses global variables called "flags" to ensure that related tasks are completed in the proper sequence.

To remedy this problem, the processor manager provides added software to each process to let the process prevent execution of itself until all required preceding processes have completed. Flags, which are often referred to as global variables, are used by each process. If a process should not execute until N preceding processes have completed execution, this global variable that we shall call P is orginally set to the value $-N$. When this process receives control by the CPU, the process first checks the value of the variable P. If it is zero, then the process will execute. If P is not zero, then the process will not execute and the processor manager gives the CPU to the next process in the list. That is, before each process begins execution, it checks this global variable as follows:

IF $P < 0$ THEN RETURN to processor manager
ELSE process is executed.

The variable P is called a global variable because the other tasks or processes which must be first executed may change this variable. They do so after they have completed execution by incrementing P. Thus if the three processes 2, 3 and 4 must complete before process 6 can begin, the global variable associated with process 6, P_6, is initially set to -3. As each process 2, 3 and 4 completes, they increment P_6 so that P_6 equals zero when all three processes are complete (*Figure 6-15*).

So we see that the processor manager has an important function in the operating system. It is directly responsible for assignment of the CPU to each task. If processes are related to one another as in *Figure 6-15*, then process synchronization is required. If there is more than one CPU, then the processor manager has a very complicated function.

Let's next look at the functions of the I/O processor. This manager, like the others, is very necessary for the efficient operation of the operating system.

**Figure 6-15.
Process
Synchronization.**

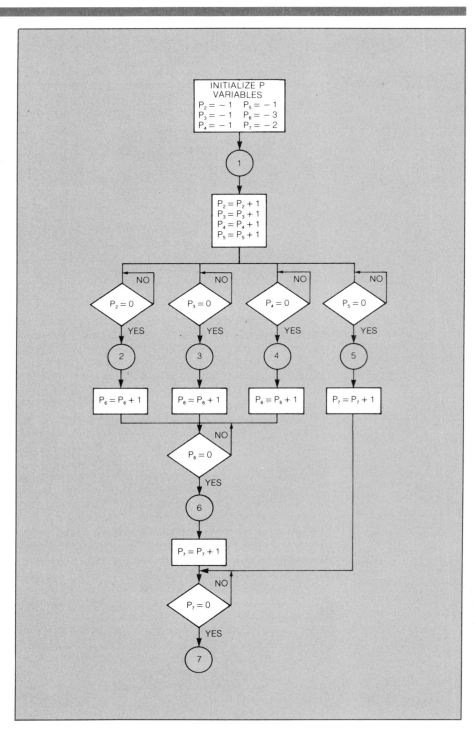

I/O MANAGER

The I/O manager is responsible for all input/output operations. The information manager locates the physical device and address of a data file that has been referenced by a program and passes this information to the I/O manager which then performs the actual input/output functions. It does so by setting up the appropriate channel word for a particular I/O operation and directs the data channel or I/O processor to start this operation. The channel word is usually a block of information contained in main memory which specifies the external device that will send or receive, whether the transfer is an input or an output operation, the number of words to transfer, the locations in memory where data is to be sent or obtained, and what to do when the I/O operation is finished.

If a request is made to a device that is busy, the I/O processor usually queues this request. Then, when the process to which the device is assigned completes its execution, all requests queued for the device are serviced in the order received on a first in, first out basis.

The I/O manager maintains tables for associating logical units assigned by a program to actual physical units. A table of all system I/O resources is maintained to show the physical address, status, logical unit assigned, data channel, and process assigned at all times. The I/O manager examines and updates this table while performing I/O assignments and operations.

When an I/O operation is finished, it usually is indicated by an interrupt, as discussed in Chapter 5. However, some I/O managers on minicomputers and microcomputers do not use interrupts. For these computers, when an I/O operation request occurs, the I/O manager connects to the equipment and initiates an I/O operation. The I/O manager then continually checks the status and does not return control to the calling program until the I/O operation is complete.

An I/O operation is initiated by the following calling sequence:

```
CALL I/O manager (starting location)
Read or Write           ┐
Number of words         │
Logical unit number     │   Calling
Buffer address          ├─  Parameters
Where to return control │
when I/O is complete    ┘
```

The first statement is a CALL instruction to the appropriate memory address of the I/O manager routine. The memory locations following the CALL instruction specify the type of I/O operation, that is, a read or write. The remaining locations of the routine specify other I/O parameters such as; the number of words or bytes to be transferred, the logical unit number of the device, the operation that is involved, the memory address or buffer address of the data that is to be read from or stored to, and where control is to be transferred after the I/O operation is complete.

Certain problems can develop when performing I/O operations if the operations are not synchronized properly. In the next section, we will examine some of these problems and how they can be avoided.

Buffers and I/O Synchronization

Small blocks of memory called "buffers" are reserved for temporary data storage during input and output operations. Buffer size depends on the characteristics of the external device.

When performing I/O operations the I/O manager reads data into a buffer within the I/O manager. The I/O manager usually has a fixed number of buffers and of a specified size for each job. Different devices have different buffer sizes. Buffer sizes are either equal to or mutiples of the physical record size of the I/O device. Remember when we talked about data cards in a previous chapter, we saw that the typical data card has a maximum of 80 characters on a card. Thus, the buffer size when reading a set of data cards should be a multiple of 80 bytes. It wouldn't be practical to have a buffer size of 810 bytes or characters as this would accept all 80 characters of each of 10 cards but only the first 10 characters of the eleventh card.

Buffer sizes are also structured according to logical record sizes. Recall from Chapter 2 that logical records may include several physical records. The physical record size of magnetic tape or other devices with variable record lengths usually directly affect the amount of storage possible for a given tape length. In general, the greater the physical record size the more data that can be stored. This is because each gap between physical records takes up space that could be used for storage. Conversely, the smaller the record size the more gaps required, and thus, the more space lost. Disk units with fixed physical record sizes are not hampered by smaller records as are tape units.

Increasing buffer size increases memory requirements, but may decrease total throughput time enough to offset the extra cost if high-speed processing is needed. For example, suppose a program is to read and process 5000 bytes and the buffer size is only 1000 bytes. It takes more time to initiate five separate reads than to have one read of 5000 bytes.

Figure 6-16 illustrates an I/O operation where data is read into a buffer. The program that initiated the input operation usually cannot continue until the input is complete, so the program is left in the wait state until completion.

**Figure 6-16.
I/O Operation with Single
Buffer.**

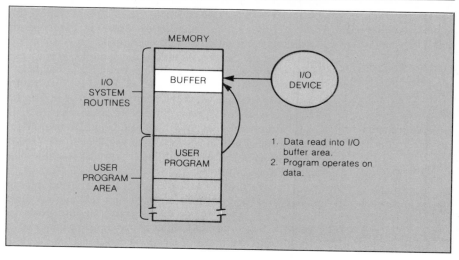

Double Buffering

　　Double buffering or ping-pong buffering is used when inputting from one device and outputting to a second. This procedure is illustrated in *Figure 6-17*. First data is read from an input device into buffer A by an I/O processor until buffer A is filled. Then a second I/O processor is assigned the task of writing this data from buffer A out to the output device. The first I/O processor then begins reading data from the input device into buffer B. Thus buffer A is being emptied while buffer B is being filled. When both operations are completed the two buffers are exchanged. Buffer B is then emptied while buffer A is being filled.

When information is transferred through the computer from one external device to another, double buffering speeds the flow of data.

**Figure 6-17.
I/O Operation with
Double Buffer.**

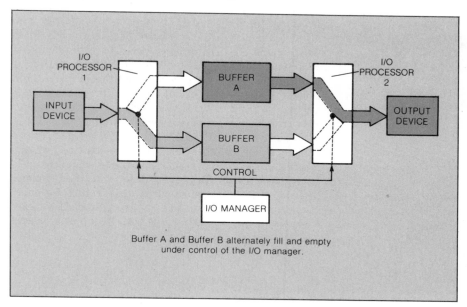

Buffer A and Buffer B alternately fill and empty
under control of the I/O manager.

Shared I/O Race Condition

When I/O resources are shared by two or more processes in a multiprocessor environment, conditions may develop where two or more such processors are assigned to the same I/O resource at the same time unless proper caution has been exercised. For example, suppose that the printer can be shared by processes A and B. Suppose further that a flag, F, is used to indicate when the printer is busy or in use. Process A examines F and sees that it is zero. But before A can change F, B also sees that F is zero. Process A changes F to 1 and begins to use the printer. Process B also writes a 1 to F and begins to use the printer. The result is what is referred to as a 'race' condition (*Figure 6-18*) and a mess of jumbled characters are printed.

To prevent a race condition, most computers provide a special hardware instruction for performing a test and set function. This instruction, when executed by a processor, first tests a flag; and if zero, sets the flag to one. All other processors are inhibited or prevented from referencing the memory location containing the flag until the test and set instruction is complete.

If process A starts the test and set instruction and an interrupt occurs because CPU time has run out, the interrupt will not be processed until the instruction is completed. If a second CPU tries to reference the flag, it cannot do so until after the first test and set operation is finished. Thus, the race condition is prevented. Computers without such hardware capability, or systems using a network of processors, have to solve this problem using other procedures.

Shared Resource Dead-Lock Condition

The second condition that computer systems with process sharing must guard against is preventing system dead-locks. A dead-lock occurs when two or more processes need the same two or more resources and can never get these resources.

Suppose process A needs devices 1 and 2. Process A requests device 1 and the I/O Processor assigns this device to A. Meanwhile process B is requesting device 2 and the I/O Processor assigns this device to B. Next process A requests device 2 but this device is already assigned to process B. So A holds device 1 and waits for device 2. Meanwhile B, which still has device 2, now asks for device 1. But device 1 is being held by A. Process B then holds device 2 while waiting for device 1. Well you can see what has occurred. Process A holds device 1 and waits for 2 to be released. Process B, on the other hand, holds device 2 and waits for 1 to be released. Neither process can continue until the other process releases the device it holds (*Figure 6-19*). To prevent dead-locks, the I/O manager never lets a processor hold a shared resource while waiting for another shared resource. If resources are shared and busy, the process is not executed. Any available resources which are free can be used by the next process.

**Figure 6-18.
Race Condition.**

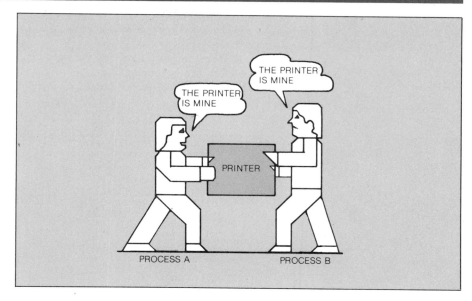

**Figure 6-19.
Dead-Lock Condition.**

Synchronizing Buffers

Finally, let's see how we can have a process which is filling a buffer communicate with a process which is to use or empty the same buffer. For illustration, we could say that process 1 reads data and process 2 uses the data read; or perhaps process 1 sends data to be printed and process 2 prints the data. In either case, process 1 is the 'producer' and process 2 is the 'consumer'.

To synchronize data transfers from one device to another through a single buffer, the I/O manager alternately sets and resets flags that enable the buffer to be filled from one device or emptied to the other device.

**Figure 6-20.
Dual Process Buffering
Concept.**

To enable this capability, we use the synchronization variables discussed in the processor manager section. We use the term WAIT (P) to inhibit a task or process from execution where P is once again a global variable; that is, P can be changed by another process. We use the term SEND (P) to indicate the increment of the global variable. Then to prevent process 2 from executing and using a buffer until process 1 has filled the buffer, the process will be appended with the send and wait terms as illustrated in *Figure 6-20*.

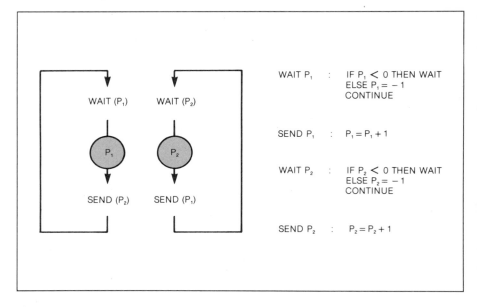

P_1 is initially set to zero and P_2 is initially set to -1 as shown in *Figure 6-21*. With P_2 equal to -1, process 2 cannot execute. Process 1, however, can execute since P_1 is zero. P_1 is then set to -1 and the data is obtained and placed in the buffer. Next P_2 is incremented to zero and process 1 waits because P_1 is set to -1.

Since P_2 is now zero, process 2 can execute. P_2 is set to -1 by the WAIT (P_2), process 2 is executed, and the data is consumed or read from the buffer. Once the buffer is free or process 2 has completed, P_1 is incremented to zero by SEND (P_1). Now process 2 waits and process 1 may continue once again.

This same procedure can be expanded to handle multiple producers and consumers. I/O management thus like processor management requires synchronization to handle the many processes which can be in various states of execution. Multiprogramming provides more efficient usage of the system resources but requires more complex managers.

Let's next look at the information manager which works closely with the I/O Manager.

INFORMATION MANAGER

The information manager controls the storage and retrieval of data files. A unique file name identifies each file.

The information manager is primarily responsible for locating a specified file. This typically involves examining a directory of some type. Essentially, the information manager uses the directory much like you or I use an indexed dictionary to look up a word. That is, if the word you are looking for begins with a C, you use the "C" tab on the dictionary to open the book to the place where words beginning with C are located.

Figure 6-21.
Dual Process Buffering Flowchart.

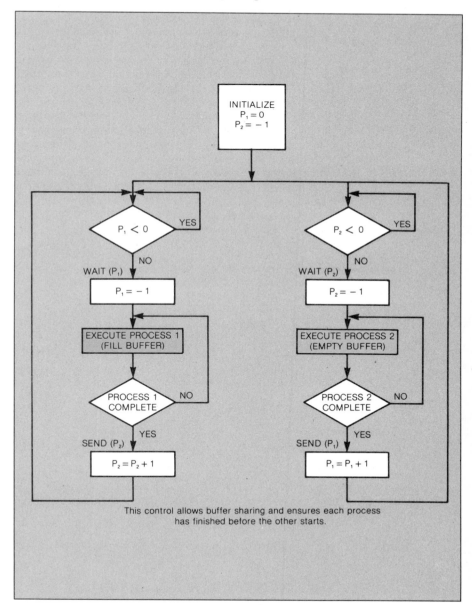

This control allows buffer sharing and ensures each process has finished before the other starts.

An information manager's directory works somewhat the same way. File names are listed in the directory in alphabetical order. The information manager locates a file by first finding the "tab" and then by looking up the file name in the directory. The directory organization and directory search will be discussed in more detail in the next chapter.

The information manager is also responsible for storing data under a specified file name. When a request is made by the program to store a file, the information manager first checks its directory to see if a file with that name already exists. If so, an error is indicated. If not, then a list of all available sectors is examined and one or more are assigned to the file. The I/O manager is then instructed to store the data for the file into the assigned disk location. The directory is then updated to add this new file.

How does the computer actually perform the searches for a particular file name? How is the directory actually updated to add, change or delete files? There are several methods to do this. These methods come under the topic of data structures and are discussed in the next chapter.

Thus, we see that the information manager is responsible for locating and assigning files. Large computer systems may use many complex methods for accomplishing this function because such systems must reference many and varied file types. Algorithms and data structures are implemented to minimize the use of system resources while working with these files.

WHAT HAVE WE LEARNED?

In this chapter we have looked in detail at the various system resource managers used by a computer system for controlling jobs. The collection of such managers make up the operating system. We learned in Chapter 5 that multiprogramming can be quite useful, but in this chapter we learned that multiprogramming causes a number of problems that must be handled by the resource managers. We learned, for instance, that without proper process synchronization, the system could become dead-locked and certain tasks or processes would never be executed. Or we could have two processes outputting to the same device at the same time which produces incorrect results.

The memory manager becomes involved when memory paging is introduced. The job manager must determine when a job is allowed into the system and, when it is actually entered, the job manager must monitor the job throughout its execution. The information manager locates or sets up programs and data files on various devices.

In summary, the resource managers are responsible for managing the system hardware and software resources. The hardware resources are the CPU, the memory and the I/O devices. The software resources are the loader, language translators, utilities and other such system programs.

WHAT'S NEXT?

In the next chapter, we will see how to further implement the resource managers. We will also see how the software resources function by examining the way data and programs are structured.

Quiz for Chapter 6

1. Match the following operating system functions with the correct manager.

b **1.** Paging

c **2.** Double Buffering

a **3.** Spooling

b **4.** LRU

d **5.** Locating a file

c **6.** Race condition

e **7.** Multipro-gramming

    a. Job manager

    b. Memory manager

    c. I/O manager

    d. Information manager

    e. Processor manager

2. The use of a global variable of $P = -3$ will require how many processes to have executed?

    a. 2

    b. 3

    c. 4

    d. 1

3. A page address of 3 and a line within page address of 640 will generate which decimal address for the following page table?

0	5000
1	2000
2	4000
3	1000
4	3000

    a. 5640

    b. 4640

    c. 1640

    d. 5003

    e. 1003

4. Match the following blocks with the manager primarily responsible for it.

a **1.** Job control block

c **2.** Process control block

d **3.** Channel control block

    a. Job manager

    b. Memory manager

    c. Processor manager

    d. I/O manager

    e. Information manager

5. When two processes think they have the same resource it is called.

    a. Dead lock

    b. Race condition

    c. Page fault

6. A page fault is handled by which manager?

    a. Job manager

    b. Memory manager

    c. Processor manager

    d. I/O manager

7. Which manager reads the control cards?

    a. Job manager

    b. I/O manager

    c. Memory manager

8. The Least Recently Used strategy is used for.

    a. Determining available I/O resources

    b. Determining available memory pages

    c. Determining file locations

9. The round robin algorithm is used often for assigning processes to processors.

    True/False

10. Which manager is responsible for preventing a deadlock condition?

    a. BASIC

    b. I/O Manager

    c. Job Manager

    d. Memory Manager

    e. Processor Manager

(Answers in back of book.)

Data Structures

ABOUT THIS CHAPTER

By now you should have an understanding of the two major categories of software; that is, application programs and operating system programs. We saw in Chapter 3 some of the methods used to develop and write programs, and in Chapter 4, the various languages used to write or code these programs. In Chapters 5 and 6 the various operating system programs were discussed.

In this chapter we are going to further examine programs that are used for manipulating data. The particular way that a program is structured to solve a specific task is called an *algorithm*. We'll look in detail at some algorithms, specifically those used to facilitate rapid search of data files. These techniques are developed into system programs where the minimum resources must be used, and they also are often used in various application programs where the structuring of data is critical. These methods provide special ways to structure data in memory so that the data may be more easily referenced and updated.

What is a Data Structure?

The procedures for structuring data and the algorithms for referencing this data are grouped under an important topic in computer science. This topic is usually referred to as data structures. Like some of the other topics we have discussed, data structures is far too complex and involved to completely describe in only one chapter. Therefore, we will only introduce some of the more commonly used techniques, ones that occur quite often when writing programs. There are several books available that specialize in data structures that you will probably want to study as you develop the need for more sophisticated programs.

"Data base programs" manage data files that are available to a variety of application programs.

Some of the systems routines which use data structuring techniques extensively are those dealing with data files, that is, files that store information for use by various applications programs. Programs used for storing, altering and/or accessing this data are often referred to as *data base programs*.

Let's look at some of the functions which may be provided by a data base program for a small personal computer system.

DATA BASE PROGRAM FOR THE PERSONAL COMPUTER

Suppose you are in charge of an organization such as the Boys Club, Boy Scouts, or Girl Scouts and you want to keep track of the monthly membership. Suppose further that membership reports are to be provided each month for the various local clubs at different building locations. For instance, if you live in New York City, the city could be divided into fifteen regions, each of which is responsible for the membership for that particular region. During each month, membership applications are completed by either of two types of applicants, a previous member (renewal) or a new member. The data base consists of all members for a given year grouped by month and region.

Each month a summary report is prepared for the directors of the organization to review the makeup of the membership. A representative report for Region 15 is illustrated in *Table 7-1*. The number of new members versus renewals is indicated both for the month and cumulative for the year. The number of members in each age bracket and school grade bracket are provided. The membership totals of boys living with both parents or who are living only with their mother or father are next given. Finally, the size of the family from which the member comes is shown in the last three rows of *Table 7-1*. All statistics are provided for the current year and for the same period of the previous year.

There could be other information of interest but the example report of *Table 7-1* was selected primarily to show the kinds of things the program can summarize. In order to prepare such a report, membership information is entered each month for each member into the data base.

Table 7-1.
Monthly Membership Report for Boys Club — Region 15.

	THIS YEAR		LAST YEAR	
	MONTH	TOTAL FOR YEAR	MONTH	TOTAL FOR YEAR
New Members	165	948	225	810
Old Members (Renewal)	80	420	65	510
Total Members	245	1368	290	1320
AGE				
6-8 Years	95	625	110	612
9-11 Years	50	175	28	210
12-14 Years	54	270	35	225
15 and over	76	298	117	273
Grade in School				
1-3	97	630	95	605
4-6	55	162	58	212
7-9	31	280	29	230
10-12	62	296	108	273
Living With				
Mother and Father	155	742	145	851
Mother Only	70	431	82	271
Father Only	20	195	63	198
Number in Family				
3 or Less	123	803	173	740
4-6	110	480	102	510
7 or more	12	85	15	70

A data base program uses data structuring techniques to maintain the contents of the data base.

How does a data base program provide the capabilities to obtain such information? The data base program is responsible for providing the ways and means for keeping track of each member. Recall from Chapter 2 that when data is stored on an auxiliary storage device such as a floppy disk, the data is stored by the use of physical records or sectors as illustrated in *Figure 7-1*. Each disk contains a number of tracks and each track a number of sectors. For a floppy disk, the sector size is usually fixed and a common sector size is 256 bytes.

Figure 7-1.
Physical Records on a
Floppy Disk.

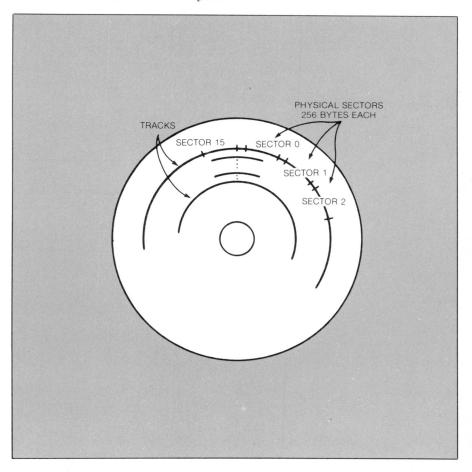

The Data Base

Collections of logical records containing "fields" of information compose the files in a data base.

The data base consists of logical files. Each logical file contains a collection of logical records which have common characteristics. These characteristics are usually called fields. For example, the names and addresses of all Boys Club members could be a logical file with the information for each member making up a logical record. The name and address are two fields of each logical record.

Notice in *Figure 7-2* that a logical record can encompass one or more physical records. Conversely, a logical record can be smaller than a physical record. Thus, a logical record (one associated with each member) can consist of less than a physical record or one or more physical records or sectors. By the same reasoning, a logical file can consist of one or more tracks. A directory table associated with each file keeps up with which physical records are associated with each file. An example of the directory table is:

```
File    BOYSCLUB.80.R15
    SECTOR 5 TRACK 6
    SECTOR 6 TRACK 6
    SECTOR 6 TRACK 5
    SECTOR 7 TRACK 5
```

Figure 7-2.
Relationship of Logical File, Logical Record, and Physical Record.

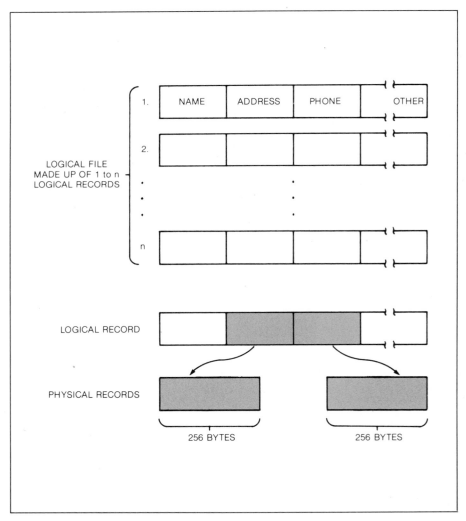

Hardware characteristics determine "physical" record length. Data characteristics determine "logical" record length.

In this example, each physical sector consists of 256 bytes with two adjacent sectors linked together. That is, the information on sector 6 track 6 follows that of sector 5 track 6, and that on sector 7 track 5 follows sector 6 track 5. This is illustrated in *Figure 7-3*. Notice in this figure that a logical record consists of two fields. The first field is the name field which requires 20 bytes. The second field is the address field which contains 50 bytes. Thus each logical record consists of 70 bytes. Therefore, each 256 byte physical record can contain up to 3 complete logical records and 46 bytes of a fourth. The last 24 bytes of the fourth logical record are carried over to the next sector.

**Figure 7-3.
Logical Records Placed in Physical Records of a Floppy Disk.**

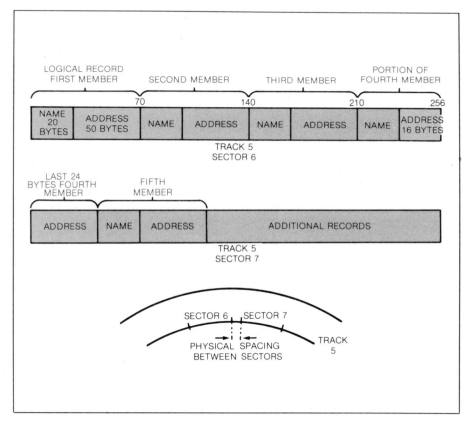

Each file carries with it information that identifies the file and describes its data structure.

A second table is associated with logical records and indicates how many bytes in each field, the number of fields, and the number of logical records. An example of this table is:

```
File    BOYSCLUB.80.R15
Fields:
    Name,20,C
    Address,50,C
Records:   245
```

Notice once again the name of the file, BOYSCLUB.80.R15 is included. The file currently has 245 logical records and each record consists of two fields. The name field consists of 20 bytes and contains character or coded (ASCII) data (as opposed to strictly numeric data) as indicated by the letter C. Similarly, the address field contains 50 bytes of character data. Thus, by using these kinds of tables, the assignment of data files, records, and fields can be related to physical records for easy access to stored data.

Actually, for the example report listed in *Table 7-1*, each record would need to contain more than just two fields. More likely, the following fields would be specified for the Boy's Club application:

```
NAME                    ,20,C
ADDRESS
    Street Number       ,10,C
    Street              ,15,C
    P.O. Box            , 6,C
    City                ,20,C
    State               , 2,C
    Zip                 , 5,I
PHONE                   ,10,I
AGE                     , 2,I
SCHOOL                  ,20,C
NUMBER YEARS MEMBER     , 2,I
NUMBER IN FAMILY        , 2,I
LIVING WITH
    Mother              , 1,C
    Father              , 1,C
    Both                , 1,C
    Other               , 1,C
SCHOOL ATTENDING        ,20,C
GRADE                   , 2,I
```

This file structure requires a total of 18 fields per record and a total of 140 bytes. Fields contain either ASCII coded character data as specified by C or simply a binary number which is specified by I. Fields could also be designated to contain floating point numbers.

Data bases are structured so that programs can access either whole files or parts of files, according to the requirements of a given application.

When the file is first established, it is defined by specifying the various descriptive information mentioned above. Data is then entered in the file or data base according to this format. Then the data base system programs provide an interface so that application programs can easily access a given field, record, and file within the data base. Access may be required to change (rewrite) a particular field to update the data base, or to read the file to prepare a report. The report program reads various fields of each record and summarizes the appropriate data to prepare the desired summary report.

Data Base Commands

Data base access consists of opening a given file, reading or writing data, and then closing the file.

Typically a minimum of four commands are used in all data base systems; the OPEN, the READ, the WRITE, and the CLOSE commands.

The OPEN command is used to tell the data base program of the intent to use the file named in the command. Prior to using any file the tables discussed earlier are read in for reference so that the file name, the number of records, the fields in each record, the length of each field in the record and the type of information in each field (ASCII or binary) is known. The data base program provides commands to read in this reference material.

The functions of the READ and WRITE commands are fairly obvious. They cause the transfer of data from (read) or to (write) the specified file. The CLOSE command releases memory used by the file description information so that the space can be used by subsequent files.

When files are opened, buffers are also specified in addition to the space alloted for the file description. Thus either small or large systems have a definite maximum on the number of files which can be opened at the same time because of memory requirements.

Additional Features

Data base programs often support such functions as querying files for specific items, generating and formatting file reports, and modifying file structure.

Data base programs usually provide several additional features. A set of commands are generally available that permit the data base to search for specific data (querying the data base). Typically, the more sophisticated the data base program, the greater the query capability.

For instance, if we want to know the number of members which are age 8 and live only with their mother in families of 6 or more, the following commands can be used:

```
OPEN BOYSCLUB.80.R15
TALLY IF AGE = 8 AND LIVED WITH = "M" AND
NUMBER.IN.FAMILY > 5
```

The OPEN command opens the specified file for members of the current year from region 15. The TALLY command tells the data base query system to count the number of members of age eight, living only with their mother (M) and in families greater than 5 (6 or more).

Data base programs also usually provide a procedure in which the query commands can be grouped together, assigned a procedure name, and then executed. For instance, in the above case, we can define a procedure named SUM with the following commands.

```
DEFINE PRO SUM
10 OPEN BOYSCLUB.80.R15
20 TALLY IF AGE = 8 AND LIVED WITH
= "M" AND NUMBER.IN.FAMILY > 5
30 END SUM
```

The procedure can then be executed by a simple command such as:

```
DO    SUM
```

This command can direct the data base program to execute the query commands much as if they were entered directly. (This is similar to a BASIC program with line numbers. Recall that a BASIC program can be executed by first loading the program and then entering the simple RUN command.)

In addition to the query procedure, procedures are often provided for generating reports of all kinds. The one described earlier was one example. Other commands may be provided so that a report could be printed under a separate heading that contained the number of boys of age 8 and living only with their mother in families of 6 or more.

Commands can also be provided that convert one data file type to another one. The conversion procedure can change a file with the detailed field descriptions that we discussed to a file like the first one we discussed which consisted only of name and address information.

How does a data base perform such functions? That is, how can it keep track of fields, records and file names particularly when new records are added or old ones deleted or modified?

We will look next at data structuring procedures which can provide this capability.

Linear List

Linear lists are a funda-
mental data structure.

Data structures is the study of techniques used for organizing data or information so that it may be easily updated and read. By updated we mean modified, replaced, deleted or appended. Data structures also cover the actual mathematical algorithms or techniques for such updating.

One of the basic data organizations is the linear list. This is a sequential list of data items. For instance the following list of numbers forms a linear list of two digit numbers.

01
04
52
25
22
45

If this list is sorted according to increasing numerical values, the list is still linear but rearranged as follows:

01
04
22
25
45
52

In general a linear list consists of a set of n values where n is equal to or greater than zero (n > = 0). We can subscript each value as X (I), where I is the Ith element in the list. Then if n > 0, X(1) is the first element in the list and X (n) is the last element in the list. In the sorted list above, X(1) = 01 and X(n) = X(6) = 52. The variable n is equal to six; that is, there are six elements in the list. Furthermore if $0 < k < n$, then the kth element is preceded by the k − 1 element and followed by the k + 1 element. If k = 3 then the fourth element, 25, follows the third, 22. The list need not be sorted for the list to be linear. The linear list simply says that the k + 1 element in the list always follows the kth element, etc.

Data is stored in memory in the computer as a linear list. The k + 1 memory location follows the kth memory location which is preceded by the k − 1 memory location. If the unsorted data list discussed previously were stored in memory beginning at location 100, it would be stored as follows:

LOC	CONTENTS
100	01
101	04
102	52
103	25
104	22
105	45

Stacks and Queues

Linear lists may be configured either as stacks (meaning data is added or deleted only at the top) or as queues (meaning data is added at one end and deleted at the other).

The two commonly used procedures to insert or delete items from a linear list are the stack and the queue.

In the stack, insertions or deletions are always at the front or top of the list (*Figure 7-4a*). That is, if a new number, 41, is added to the list we have been discussing, the new list would look like this:

41
01
04
52
25
22
45

Similarly, if an element is deleted, it is always the one at the top. This type of list is referred to as a stack. Stacks are like a line of people getting on an elevator. The first on is usually the last off as that person goes to the back of the elevator. The term POP is used when deleting an item from a stack and PUSH when inserting an item into the stack. Thus, to place 41 in the list we say, "push 41". Taking items from the list with POP's gives first 41, then 01, 04, 52 and so forth.

**Figure 7-4.
Construction of Stacks
and Queues.**

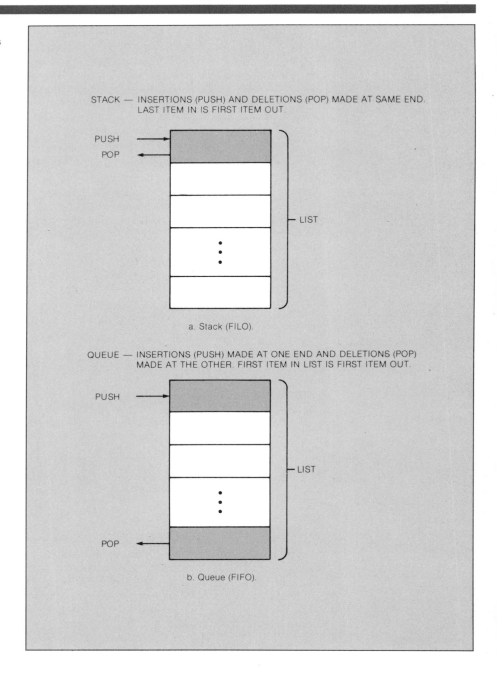

STACK — INSERTIONS (PUSH) AND DELETIONS (POP) MADE AT SAME END.
LAST ITEM IN IS FIRST ITEM OUT.

PUSH

POP

LIST

a. Stack (FILO).

QUEUE — INSERTIONS (PUSH) MADE AT ONE END AND DELETIONS (POP)
MADE AT THE OTHER. FIRST ITEM IN LIST IS FIRST ITEM OUT.

PUSH

LIST

POP

b. Queue (FIFO).

The queue is a list of items in which insertions are made at one end and deletions at the other. In this case, to place 41 in the original list of items, it is once again placed at the top. However, when we take an item from the list structured as a queue, the last item 45, is removed rather than 41 as in the stack (*Figure 7-4b*). In the queue, the first item in is the first one taken out. The term FILO (first in last out) is often used to describe a stack and FIFO (first in first out) is used to describe a queue. Both stacks and queues are very useful for maintaining lists.

Lists do not always have to be placed in consecutive memory locations. Instead they can be linked by a set of pointers. Let's next look at the linked list structure.

LINKED LIST

A linked list is another way of structuring data such that the $k+1$ data item in a list is not necessarily the $k+1$ memory location. That is, the data items are not in the same order as their respective memory locations. A linked list requires one or more additional memory locations to contain pointers. The pointers are used to link the various data items. Some explanation of a pointer may be in order. A pointer is either a register or memory location whose contents serve as a reference from which other memory locations are determined or the contents itself which directs the program to a new next memory location.

Suppose, for example, we have the original linear list discussed earlier but want the items ordered by increasing numerical values. The linked list to accomplish this looks like *Table 7-2*.

Notice in this table that twice as many memory locations are required as before. The additional locations 101, 103, 105, 107, 109 and 111, are used for pointers. These pointers point to the next data item according to the desired ordering. The data items are in memory locations 100, 102, 104, 106, 108 and 110.

The contents of location 100 is 01, the smallest number in the list. The next smallest number is 04 which is in memory location 102. The data value 22 which follows 04 in numerical sequence, is in location 108. Therefore, the pointer in location 103 (the pointer with data value 04) points to location 108. The pointer with data value 22 is in location 109 to point to location 106 which holds the next data value, 25, in numerical sequence. Its pointer in location 107 points to location 110, and so forth.

Linked lists appear to be linear but are not necessarily stored sequentially in memory. "Pointers" link successive items in a list.

**Table 7-2.
Linked List.**

MEMORY LOCATION	CONTENTS (DATA)	MEMORY LOCATION	CONTENTS (POINTER)
100	01	101	102
102	04	103	108
104	52	105	− 1
106	25	107	110
108	22	109	106
110	45	111	104

Links

The last element in the list is the number 52 at location 104. Notice at pointer location 105 is the value −1 which is used to indicate the end of the list. In linked list procedures, a special symbol or a value which won't usually occur is used to indicate the end of the list. This symbol is useful when the length of the list is unknown. As each pointer is read, it is checked for the special end indicator. When the end indicator is detected, the search or read is terminated. Sometimes a pointer having the same value of the memory location (that is, the link points to itself) is used to indicate the end of the list.

Data Structure

The elements of a linked list can have multiple pointers and data fields.

In a linked list structure, the number of words per element may be greater than 1. Also if the memory is byte oriented (separated into 8-bit locations), the pointer can require two bytes instead of one. The general structure of each data item of a linked list is illustrated in *Figure 7-5*. Notice in this figure that three fields are illustrated. The key field is used to order or sort the various data items or records. The second field contains the pointer(s). (We will see later that there can be more than one pointer; that is, some linked data structure organizations, one of which is called a tree, have multiple pointers). Finally, the third field contains the data items.

**Figure 7-5.
Linked List Record
Format.**

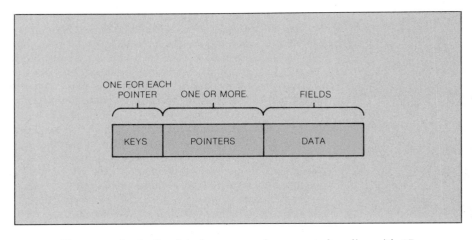

For example, in the data base example presented earlier with 17 fields, each group of 17 fields can be a record. The records are then linked according to the alphabetical order of the last names (which is in the key field) of the Boys Club members with the pointer indicating the alphabetical order. The data field of the format in *Figure 7-5* consists of all the other fields listed earlier such as age, address, grade, etc.

In a linked list data structure, a starting pointer is necessary to indicate where the data file begins. This is where the first record in the data organization exists. The pointer points to the first record or cell (sometimes called a node). The first record then points to where the second record exists and so on.

Record Additions and Deletions

You can add or delete items in a linked list by changing the pointer values of the elements concerned.

Two operations must be accounted for in referencing data files. First, we must be able to add or append new records to the list and the new record must be placed in the appropriate order according to the key. Second, we must be able to delete records from the list. *Figure 7-6* illustrates the procedures necessary to add or delete records to or from a linked list. The procedures are simple but care must be taken to ensure the proper sequence of operations.

**Figure 7-6.
Record Addition and
Deletion in a Linked List
Structure.**

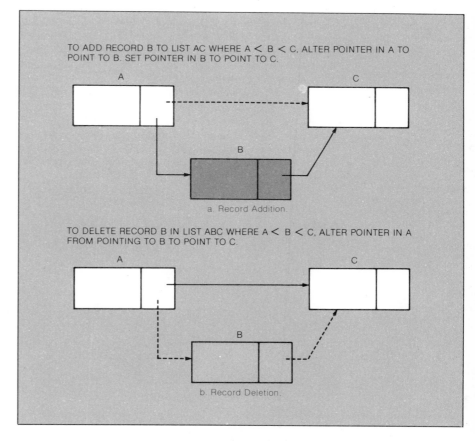

TO ADD RECORD B TO LIST AC WHERE A < B < C, ALTER POINTER IN A TO POINT TO B. SET POINTER IN B TO POINT TO C.

a. Record Addition.

TO DELETE RECORD B IN LIST ABC WHERE A < B < C, ALTER POINTER IN A FROM POINTING TO B TO POINT TO C.

b. Record Deletion.

Figure 7-6a illustrates how a record is added to the list. The initial list consists of two records with keys A and C and the record with key B is to be added. The list is arranged according to the alphabetical order of the keys, therefore, record B must be placed between records A and C. To append record B to the list AC, the pointer of record A is changed to point to record B, then the pointer of record B is set to point to record C.

Figure 7-6b illustrates the procedure for deleting record B from the list of records with keys A, B, and C. To delete record B, the pointer of record A is simply changed to point to C.

Thus we can see that it is relatively easy to append or delete records from a linked list. However, there is something else to consider when adding or deleting records to or from a list. Where does the storage space for a new record come from? Where does the storage location for a deleted record go?

Space List

The spaces that are taken up or created by insertions or deletions are maintained as a linked list of empty cells.

Most systems implement a space list to account for this storage space. A space list is a linked list of empty cells and the space list is pointed to by the space list pointer. The list is maintained as a stack or FILO structure. Whenever a new cell is needed during an add operation, the cell is popped from the top of the space list. The space list is then updated to indicate this deletion of a cell from the space list. That is, when a space deletion occurs, the space list pointer is simply changed to point to the next available set of cells.

When a cell is returned to the space list, it is pushed to the top of the space list stack. Thus cells at the top of the space list are more likely to be used than those cells at the bottom of the list.

Several linked lists and a space list can occupy the same general area, taking or releasing cells. *Figures 7-7* and *7-8* illustrate the general way of changing list updates using a space list.

**Figure 7-7.
Record Addition Using a
Space List in a Linked
List Structure.**

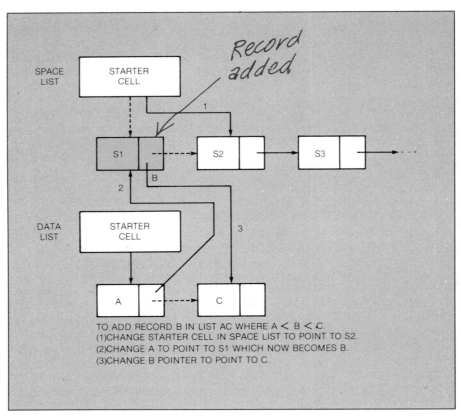

TO ADD RECORD B IN LIST AC WHERE A < B < C.
(1)CHANGE STARTER CELL IN SPACE LIST TO POINT TO S2.
(2)CHANGE A TO POINT TO S1 WHICH NOW BECOMES B.
(3)CHANGE B POINTER TO POINT TO C.

The space list starter cell is changed each time an addition or deletion occurs.

In *Figure 7-7* the record with the key B is once again to be added to the list A, C. First the space list starter cell is changed to point to S2. Next the pointer in cell A of the linked data list is changed to point to S1 which is given the key B. Finally the pointer of S1 or B is changed to point to C.

In *Figure 7-8* the cell with key B is to be deleted from the list A, B, C. Here the pointer of cell A is first changed to point to C. Next the starter cell of the space list is changed to point to the deleted cell B. Finally, the pointer of the deleted B cell is changed to point to S1.

Figure 7-8.
Record Deletion Using a
Space List in a Linked
List Structure.

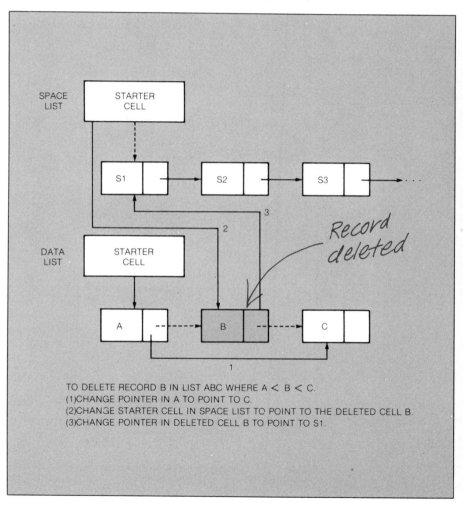

TO DELETE RECORD B IN LIST ABC WHERE A < B < C.
(1)CHANGE POINTER IN A TO POINT TO C.
(2)CHANGE STARTER CELL IN SPACE LIST TO POINT TO THE DELETED CELL B.
(3)CHANGE POINTER IN DELETED CELL B TO POINT TO S1.

Linked List Use for Disk Files

Linked-list techniques can be used to manage files on disk as well as files in memory.

As mentioned, the linked list can be used for dynamically assigning disk space for adding or deleting records in a file. Suppose, for example, we have a list of Boys Club members as illustrated in *Figure 7-9*. The list is to be kept in alphabetical order by member name with the last name first. Then, as shown in *Figure 7-9*, the record for Jones can be added easily by first going to a subroutine which assigns an available sector of consecutive bytes from the available sector list. The Jones record is added and pointers are changed to put Jones in alphabetical sequence. When a member is deleted, the sector that had been used for that member's record is returned to the available sector or space list.

**Figure 7-9.
Linked List Implemented
on a Floppy Disk.**

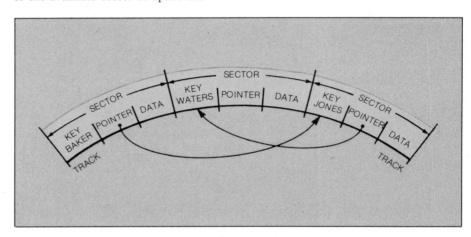

When a record is added, care is usually taken to assign sectors which are on or close to the same track as other sectors in the list. This is because the disk read head must move when referencing sectors from different tracks. Since a certain amount of time is required for the head to move from one track to another, the access time is considerably greater when the desired record is on a different track rather than the same track. In most systems, more time is required for access as the distance between the desired tracks increases.

Multiple space lists associated with closely grouped tracks can be used to accomplish the goal of keeping the physical distance between consecutive records to a minimum. Then, when a new sector is needed, the available sector assignment routine tries to assign a sector on or near the same track as the preceding and following records where the new record is to be attached.

Example BASIC Program

Let's consider the BASIC instructions used for working with a linked list. For our example, let's assume that we have a list consisting of two entries with the keys A and C. It is desired to append a new entry with the key B to the list. *Figure 7-10* provides the BASIC instructions for first initiating the linked list and then for inserting the new key, B.

Figure 7-10.
BASIC Instructions for
Initializing and Adding to
a Linked List.

```
100   REM   LIST = STARTER CELL POINTER TO DATA LIST
110   REM   SPACE = STARTER CELL POINTER TO SPACE LIST
120   REM   KEY$ (100) = KEYS IN LIST
130   REM   DATA (100) = DATA IN LIST
140   REM   POINT (100) = POINTER OF LIST
150         SPACE = 1
160   REM   SET UP POINTERS
170         FOR I = 1 TO 99
180         POINT (I) = I+1
190         NEXT I
200         POINT (100) = -1
```

a. Initialize List.

```
1000   REM   KEY$ (1) = A; KEY$ (2) = C; SPACE = 3; LIST = 1
1010   REM   APPEND NEWKEY$ = B
1020   REM   1. CHANGE SPACE TO POINT TO
1030   REM   SECOND ENTRY   S2, IN SPACE LIST       COMMENTS
1040         TEMP = SPACE                           TEMP = 3
1050         SPACE = POINT (SPACE)                  SPACE = 4
1060   REM   2. CHANGE A TO POINT TO B (S1)
1070         I = POINT (LIST)                       I = 2
1080         POINT (LIST) = TEMP                    POINT(1) = 3
1090   REM   3. CHANGE B TO POINT TO C
1100         POINT (TEMP) = I                       POINT(3) = 2
1110         KEY$ (TEMP) = NEWKEY$                  KEY$ (3) = B
```

b. Add Data Item.

When using a linked list which obtains storage from a space list, the space list must initially be structured. That is, the pointers within this list must be linked. We will assume that the data list will be less than 100 entries. Furthermore, we will let the variable array KEY dimensioned for 100 entries contain the keys in the data list. The array DATA also dimensioned for 100 will contain the data items to be stored and finally, the array POINT dimensioned for 100 will be used to contain the pointers. The variable LIST is the starter cell pointer for the data list and points to the first entry in the data list. Similarly, the variable SPACE points to the first entry in the space list.

**Figure 7-11.
Linked List Structure
Before Adding Item.**

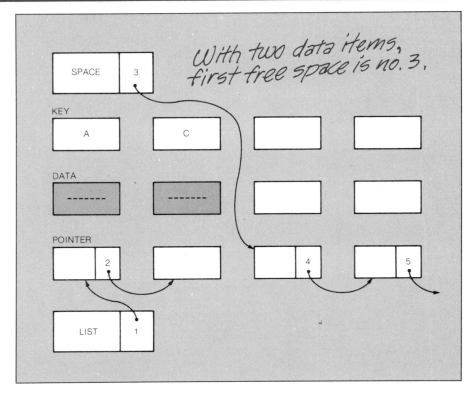

In the first set of code, lines 100 through 200 of *Figure 7-10a*, the space list is structured. That is, the pointers are set to the index values in the arrays. Initially, the space list pointers are set to point to each other. That is, the starter cell pointer, SPACE, is set to 1, the first entry. The pointer of the first cell is set to 2, the pointer of the second is set to 3 and so forth. The pointer of the last entry is set to −1 to indicate the end of the list.

We will assume that the first index value is for the key A and the second is for the key C as illustrated in *Figure 7-11*. LIST points to 1 and POINT (1) points or is set to 2.

The code in *Figure 7-10b*, lines 1000 through 1110, provides the instructions for adjusting the pointers to add a new key, B, to the key list. In line 1040, the third entry in the list is assigned for use by setting the variable TEMP equal to SPACE (which is given as 3 in line 1000). In line 1050, SPACE is set to the value of the pointer of 3, which is 4, to point to the fourth entry. Now SPACE points to the first free space available as shown in *Figure 7-12*. In line 1070, the current value of the pointer of 1 (LIST = 1 in line 1000), which is 2, is saved in I. In line 1080, the pointer of 1 or A is changed to 3 to point to the new entry B. In line 1100, the pointer of 3 or B is set to 2 to point to C. In line 1110, the key value of key 3 is set to B.

**Figure 7-12.
Linked List Structure
After Adding Item.**

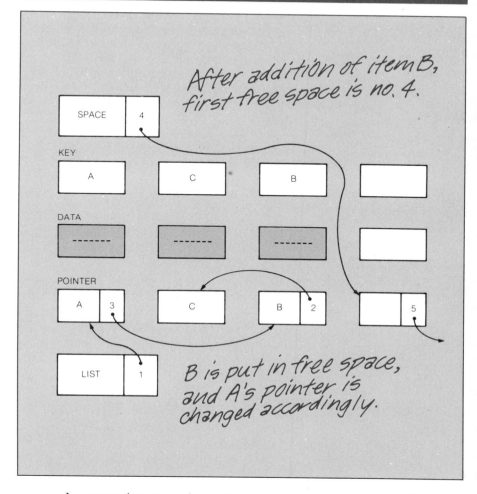

*After addition of item B,
first free space is no. 4.*

SPACE — 4

KEY: A | C | B

DATA

POINTER: A | 3 | C | B | 2 | 5

LIST | 1

*B is put in free space,
and A's pointer is
changed accordingly.*

In an actual program, instructions are also necessary to locate the position in the list where the new key should be inserted. That is, suppose there are 20 entries (instead of only 2 as in our example) ordered according to increasing key values. The appended key has to be inserted in the appropriate place to maintain the ordering. Thus each key in the list has to be compared to the new key to determine where in the key order the appended cell should be placed.

The process of ordering an unordered list is called sorting and is also a part of the topic of data structures. However, sorting algorithms will not be discussed in this chapter, but will be included in application examples in Chapter 9. In the next section the techniques involved in implementing a queue will be discussed.

Implementing a Queue Using a Linked List

With separate pointers to mark its beginning and end, a linked list can operate as a queue.

We have seen that it is easy to implement a stack using a linked list and that only one pointer is needed for a stack. Let's now look at how a queue is implemented in a linked list. Recall that a queue is a FIFO organization. Notice in *Figure 7-13* that there are two starter pointers, one for the beginning of the list where the first item entered is located, and the second for the end of the list where the last item entered is located. To add an item, E, to the list A, B, C, D, the front pointer (PF) is used to find the front of the list, D. The front pointer is then changed to point to E. The pointer of D is also set to point to E. To delete an item, A, from the list, the end pointer (PE) is used to find A. The pointer of A is used to find the cell with the key B. The end pointer is then changed to point to B.

Figure 7-13.
Queue Implementation.

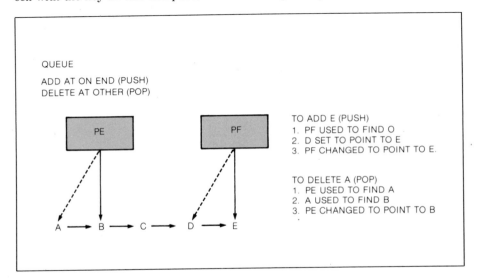

Searching for a Record in a Linked List

A linked list is useful for dynamic storage allocation, however, it requires extra memory, and maintenance of the list requires additional CPU time. If data items are simply placed in consecutive memory locations, memory overhead is reduced but updates are much more involved if records are to be placed anywhere except at the end of the list. That is, if a record is placed anywhere except at the end, existing records will have to be moved up or down to accommodate the insertion of the new record. This can be very cumbersome and time consuming especially when the list is kept on disk. Thus linked lists are often used for maintaining files on disks.

Searching for a Record in a Linked List

So far we have only discussed methods for updating lists or data files. But, suppose we want to find a particular name in the existing membership list. If the list is N records long, it will take an average of N/2 looks to locate a name in the list and N looks if the name is not in the list. If the list is long and the list is stored on several tracks, considerable search time may be required. Let's see if we can reduce this search time.

The binary search method, used with sorted lists in sequential memory locations, divides the number of items to search by 2 after each unsuccessful scan.

First let's search for a record in a linear list within memory that is not linked. Once again, to locate the record will take an average of N/2 looks assuming the record is in the list. Suppose, however, we have sorted the list so that the records are ordered according to increasing numerical values of the key as illustrated in *Figure 7-14*. Then to find a particular key we can look at the key of a record half way into the list rather than at the first. Upon examining the key of the record at the half-way point, we find that it is greater than the desired key, so we need to look in the lower half of the list. If the key at the half-way point is less than the desired key, we can confine our search to the upper half of the list. That is, we can cut the number of records to search in half by our first look. We then make the next look halfway into the upper or lower half of the list. The second look reduces the number of records to search to one-fourth the original size. The third look, assuming we haven't yet found our desired record, is half way into the remaining records which further reduces the number of records to search to 1/8 the original size.

**Figure 7-14.
Binary Search for Key
04.**

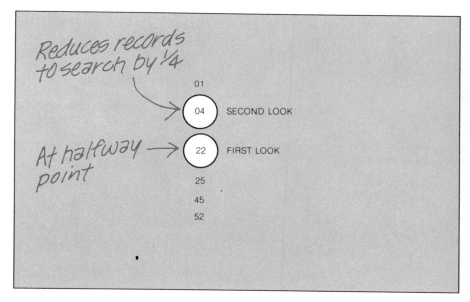

This type of search is called a binary search and the average number of looks required to find an item in the list is $(\log_2 N) - 1$. The number of looks will never exceed $(\log_2 N) + 1$. If a list has 1024 records, the most looks required to find a particular key is 11 ($1024 = 2^{10}$, $10 + 1 = 11$) and the average number of looks is 9 if the binary search is used. This is considerably less than the 1024 maximum looks or 512 average looks required for a sequential search.

Example Program

A BASIC subprogram which uses a binary search for locating a key, KEY, from a list of N items in an array, K, is given below. The program assumes that the key is located in the list.

```
10      L=1
20      U=N
30      I=(L+U)/2
40      I=INT (I)
50      IF KEY < K(I) THEN U=I-1
60      IF KEY > K(I) THEN L=I+1
70      IF KEY=K(I) THEN RETURN
80      GO TO 30
```

In this program the variable L is used to keep track of the lower search limit and the variable U for the upper search limit. Initially L = 1 and U = N. The variable I is the search index. At line number 30, I is set for the first look at the halfway point in the list. I must have an integer value since the index or subscript of an array cannot be a fraction. Therefore, in line number 40, the BASIC function INT truncates the floating point number within parentheses (deletes all digits to the right of the decimal point) to the largest integer less than or equal to the floating point value. In line numbers 50 and 60 the new upper or lower search bounds are changed depending on the relationship of KEY to the value in the array K(I). If KEY is equal to K(I) then the subprogram returns control to the calling routine. Otherwise, control transfers back to line number 30 where I is recomputed for the next halfway point.

Figure 7-15.
Binary Search for Key 3.

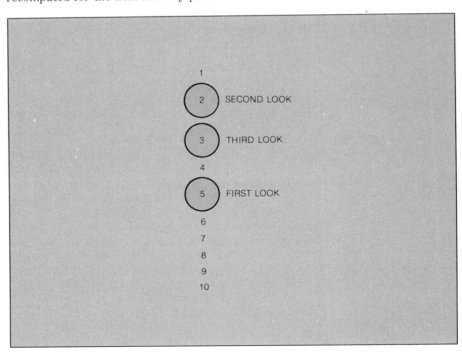

For example, suppose we are looking for a key of 3 (KEY = 3) in a list containing the keys 1 thru 10 (*Figure 7-15*), that is, K(1) = 1, K(2) = 2, etc. The first look is at INT ((1 + 10)/2) so that K(I) = 5. Since 3 is less than 5, U is changed to 4 in line number 50 and the next look is at INT ((1 + 4)/2) so that K(I) = 2. Since 3 is greater than 2, control passes to line number 60. Therefore, L is now set to 3 and U is still 4. The third look then yields the desired key 3 as INT ((3 + 4)/2) = 3.

Remember that this search method requires that the list be in consecutive memory locations and sorted. Can we use this procedure to search through a linked list in memory or on disk? Well we can't use our linked list previously discussed with just the one pointer. That is, when we look halfway into the list, the record examined won't necessarily be the appropriate record as the records are not ordered. So let's examine another method which is illustrated in *Figure 7-16*.

**Figure 7-16.
Ideal Binary Tree Linked
List Structure.**

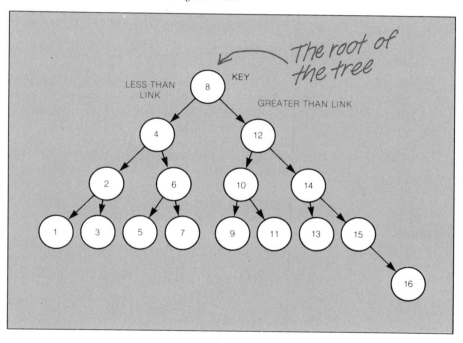

Binary Tree

A binary tree is a sorted linked list structured to facilitate binary searches.

A list structured as shown in *Figure 7-16* is called a binary tree. There is a beginning node which represents the root of the tree. In the ideal balanced binary tree, the key of the root node is that associated with the middle record of an ordered list. For example, if we had a list of 16 keys with values 1 thru 16, the root node has the value 8. The right link points to a subtree of all nodes greater than 8 and the left link points to a subtree of nodes less than 8. This is true for each subtree, that is, the right link is always to a subtree or new tree with keys greater than the root and the left link is always to a subtree or new tree with keys less than the root.

The root of the tree is the middle element of the linked list. Branches form in pairs from the root. The branches to the left of the root contain items preceding the middle element in sequence; those to the right contain items that follow the middle element.

To implement a binary tree, two pointers are necessary instead of one as in the list discussed earlier. However, we have traded the requirement for more space for reduced search time. If the list is maintained on disk, the reduction in search time can be significant since track to track moves would probably be involved in a large list.

One problem with constructing the ideal, balanced binary tree is that it must be arranged after all records have been entered or arranged by a time consuming process while they are being entered. Then, when additions or deletions are made, the tree has to be rearranged to maintain the balance, For example, suppose we initially have a list of 6 keys. The first root node should be the third or INT $((6+1)/2)$ item in the list. If, however, we add an item to the list, the root node should be the fourth item in the list. A number of more complicated pointer changes are necessary rather than the simple one discussed earlier.

In reality, though, we don't have to be concerned whether or not the binary tree is balanced to make use of it since the nodes of a binary tree do not have to correspond to the binary search values obtained from $(L+U)/2$.

Assigning the Nodes

Additions to the tree are placed according to their position in the data sequence.

A binary tree by definition is simply a tree which has a maximum of two branches each of which forms a new binary tree. The first node is the root node. Therefore, we can add data or delete data items from a binary tree structure and not worry if it is well balanced or not. As each record is entered, we place it on a right branch when it is greater that the root of a subtree and on the left branch if less than the root of a subtree. In the example illustrated in *Figure 7-17*, the keys are received in the order 5, 2, 8, 9, 3, 17, 12. As each key is received, it is placed in the tree according to the right-left procedure just described.

**Figure 7-17.
Dynamic Binary Tree
Implementation.**

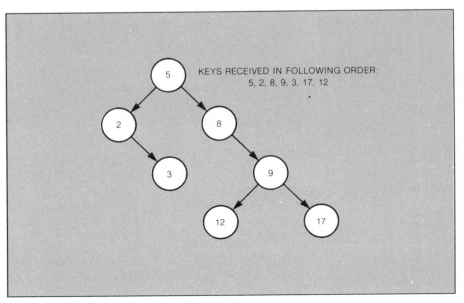

KEYS RECEIVED IN FOLLOWING ORDER:
5, 2, 8, 9, 3, 17, 12

As shown in *Figure 7-17*, key 5 is received first and is assigned the root node. Next, 2 is to be added. Since 2 is less that 5, it is placed on the left branch. That is, the left link of 5 is set to point to the record with key 2. Next key 8 is received and, being greater than 5, it is placed on the right branch. Next the key 9 is received. Nine is greater than 5 so we take the right branch. Nine is next compared to the subtree with the root node 8. Nine is also greater than this node, so it is placed on the right branch of 8. This procedure continues until all keys received are properly placed on the tree of *Figure 7-17*.

Searching the Nodes

Searches begin at the root. Within each subtree, higher values are on the right and lower values are on the left.

To search for a given node on this tree, the same procedure is followed. That is, suppose we want to find the node 12. We first go to 5, then 8, 9 and finally 12. Searching for a key will still be less than N/2. In fact, it turns out that if the keys are randomly received, the average number of looks for a record in the list approaches about 1.38 log₂N. This is still a significant savings over N/2.

The worst case is illustrated in *Figure 7-18* in which the keys are entered in increasing order. In this situation, the search time increases to N/2 and it would be better to have a single pointer list since the extra memory isn't required. However, if records are not expected in a particular sequence such as in *Figure 7-18* the binary tree structure is a useful way of maintaining files because search time is minimized and record updating is still easily accomplished.

Figure 7-18.
Worst Case Condition for a Binary Tree.

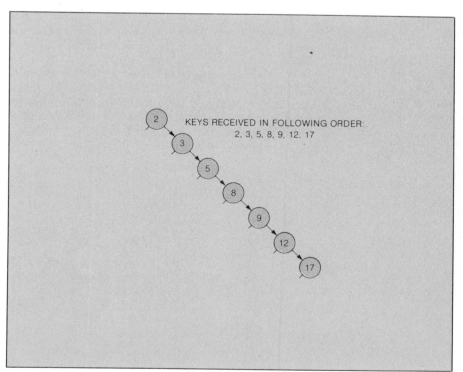

KEYS RECEIVED IN FOLLOWING ORDER:
2, 3, 5, 8, 9, 12, 17

Other Linked List Organizations

There are other forms of linked list which use two or more pointers. In general, more pointers permit faster searches but additions or deletions to the list become more difficult.

You can establish more than one data sequence within a linked list by using multiple pointers.

Multiple pointers can be used to provide dual ordering on a data list; that is, the data can be linked by two keys. Multiple key ordering is illustrated by this example:

```
LOCATION      23    26    33    43    55
KEY 1          A     C     B     D     E
KEY 2          1    10     4     5     2
POINTER 1     33    43    26    55    12
POINTER 2     55    12    43    71    28
```

Here five records are illustrated out of a number of such records in a double linked list. The first record is located at index 23, the second at 26, then 33, 43 and 55. Each record has two keys. The first key, KEY 1, provides the alphabetical ordering A, B, etc., and the second key, KEY 2, identifies the numerical ordering 1, 2, 3, etc.

Each record also has two pointers. The first is used for the first set of keys and the second pointer for the second set of keys. Record 23 with the keys A and 1 point to records 33 and 55 respectively. Record 33 has the key B for the first set of keys and record 55 has the key 2 for the second set. The records pointed to by pointer 2, (12, 71 and 28), are not shown because they are not in key 2 order. The doubly linked list provides searching for items according to two key types but insertions and deletions are much more involved. For instance, if record 33 with keys B and 4 is to be deleted, pointer 1 of record 23 must be changed, and pointer 2 of a record (not shown) which links that record to KEY 2 = 4 must be first found then changed.

Another type of linked list is the ring structure which is illustrated in *Figure 7-19*. In this case, either the last item points back to the first or various items will point one or more links back. With sub-rings as illustrated in *Figure 7-19*, previously related keys can be quickly found without having to go all the way back to the beginning of the list to search for an earlier noted key.

Figure 7-19.
Ring Structured Linked List.

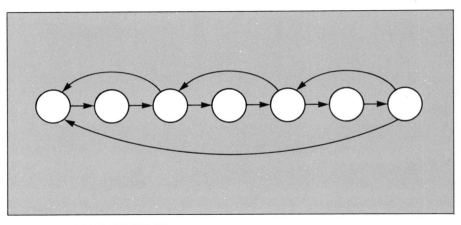

SEARCHING WITH A DIRECTORY

In data base maintenance as well as many other applications, a list must often be searched while looking for a particular record. We have just discussed the binary search procedure for a linked list as a way of performing such a search, and found that the linked list has an advantage when data items are to be inserted or deleted. A second search procedure that can be used is the directory.

Directory searches divide data lists into sublists.

For the directory method, the data list is divided into sublists and keys within each sublist are sorted. The directory indicates where each sublist is located. Thus, the search procedure for a desired key begins by searching the directory, then the sublists specified in the directory are searched. *Figure 7-20* shows an example directory and two sublists.

Figure 7-20.
Example of Data List
Directory and Sublists.

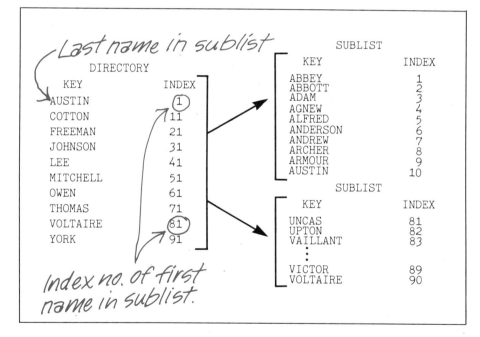

The directory is usually structured so that the key given in the directory is the last key in each sublist and the index is the location of the first key in the sublist. This organization is used so that when searching for a given key, say UPTON (*Figure 7-20*), the last keys of each sublist are compared to the desired key. If the desired key is greater than the key for a given sublist, then you know that it isn't in that sublist. When a key is found which is greater than the desired key, say VOLTAIRE, then you know that the search for the desired key should be confined to that sublist and the search should begin at the location index for that key, which for VOLTAIRE is 81. Therefore, UPTON should be found by a sequential search that begins at location 81. If UPTON is not in the list the search ends at VOLTAIRE.

Since the directory and sublists searches are usually performed sequentially, the size of the sublists and directory becomes important. For example, if the size of the directory is n_1, and that of the particular sublist referenced is n_2, then the average number of looks to find a data item would be $n_1/2 + n_2/2$. Calculations have shown that the optimal sizes for n_1 and n_2 for a list of N items turns out to be equal to the square root of N for both n_1 and n_2. Therefore, if we have a list of 10,000 items, the optimal sublist size is 100 and the average number of looks is 100. Contrast this with a binary search which takes approximately 13 looks average. (Recall that for a binary search, average looks = $(\log_2 N) - 1$; therefore $(\log_2 10,000) - 1 = $ approximately 13.)

Directories are used in many disk organization schemes because they are easy to implement, and because it is convenient to keep sublists on specific tracks where the data is then stored sequentially.

There is yet another searching procedure that is faster (requires fewer looks) than either the directory method or the binary search. This method, which is called hashing, will be discussed next.

HASH CODING TECHNIQUES

The hashing method of building a list positions items in the list according to the results of a mathematical operation on each item.

Hashing is a procedure which is used for structuring a list. For this method, the address in the list for each key is obtained directly from a mathematical operation on the key itself. There are several ways of computing the address from the key, but the one most commonly used is to divide the key by the size of the table in which the list is to be placed. This assumes that the value of the key is greater than the table size. The division then results in a quotient Q and a remainder R. The location in the table for the particular key is R; that is, the remainder is used to specify the address within the table for a given key.

Suppose for instance the key is the number 001053972 which could be a person's identification number. Dividing the key by a table size of, say 1019, yields a quotient of 1034 and a remainder 326. The key would thus be placed at location 326 in the table.

Now you may ask, what happens if two keys yield the same remainder? Not only is this possible, but it can easily occur. However, chances of two keys hashing to the same address is somewhat reduced if a table size equal to a prime number is used. Furthermore, the prime number should be one which is also equal to 4K + 3 where K is any positive integer. For example the number 1019 is a prime number. It is also of the form 4K + 3 where, in this case, K is 254. That is $4 \times 254 + 3$ is equal to 1019.

Collisions

If a computation assigns an item to an address already occupied, a new address is generated.

Even with table sizes selected by these values, keys can still hash to the same address. When this happens a collision is said to have occurred and a new address must be computed. One method to compute the new address is to add R to the quotient. If the resulting sum exceeds the table size, a table wrap around is used; that is, the table size is subtracted from the sum to bring the new address within the range of the table. If, for example, the remainder is 1018 and the quotient is 7, the new address is location 6 (from 1018 + 7 – 1019).

If the new address also already has an entry (another collision), then the remainder is added to twice the quotient, once again providing wrap around if needed. In general, the address is computed by the following in descending order until a non-collision address is found:

$$R$$
$$(R + 1Q) \bmod N$$
$$(R + 2Q) \bmod N$$
or $$(R + 3Q) \bmod N$$
$$\cdot$$
$$\cdot$$
$$\cdot$$
$$(R + kQ) \bmod N$$
$$\text{where } k = 1, 2, \ldots, n$$
$$\text{and } N = \text{table size}$$

The mod (modulo) term is the mathematical way of describing the wrap around procedure. This hashing procedure is illustrated in *Figure 7-21*. There are several other methods for handling collisions but the method just described is one of the better ones. It is usually referred to as the Linear Quotient Method.

**Figure 7-21.
Example of Hashing.**

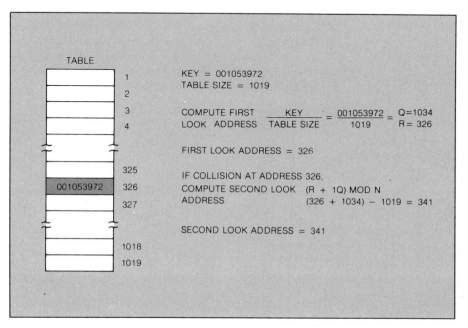

Inserting

Addresses for inserted items are computed in the same way as the addresses of the previous items in the list.

The following procedures would be used for inserting an item in a list using the linear quotient method for handling collisions.

1. Divide the key, K, by the table size N yielding the quotient Q and remainder R.
2. Look at location R in the table, and if there is no entry at this location, insert the data item with the key 'KEY'. If there is already a data item at this location, then compute the new address $(R + Q)$ mod N.
3. If the calculated address still has an entry, compute another address $(R + kQ)$ Mod N and try again. First $k = 1$, then 2, then 3 and so forth.

Searching

The hashing procedure is an extremely fast way to search a data list.

Searching for an item in the table involves the same procedure except that at each computed location the key at that address is compared with the desired key. If it is not the right key, then a new address is computed. The process repeats until either the desired key is found or an empty location occurs, in which case the desired key is not in the table. A way to minimize collisions when using this procedure is to never completely fill the table. That is, if the table size is 1019 then use only, say, 500 entries. Then collisions are not as likely as if, say, 700 entries are made.

It has been found that, generally, if the table size is half full, then on the average it will take about 2 looks to find the desired key. If the table is 60 percent full, then an average of about 2.5 looks is required. A seventy percent full table requires about 3.3 looks. With a table 90 percent full, almost ten looks are required. Thus, if the table is kept only 50 to 60 percent full, generally no more than 3 looks are needed to find a data item in the list. Thus, we see that hashing by far requires the fewest number of looks for searching a list than the other methods discussed up to now. However, this fast search method requires additional memory.

Assemblers and compilers often use hashing methods when identifying symbols. We will look at how an assembler or compiler is constructed in the next chapter.

WHAT HAVE WE LEARNED?

In this chapter we have examined several techniques used in structuring data so that it can be more rapidly accessed and used. Such structuring techniques are referred to as data structures in computer science. Data structuring techniques are often found in system programs such as data base programs, compilers, assemblers and operating systems. They are also often used in application or user programs.

We looked at the linked list structure for keeping track of data items and saw that this structure can be used for dynamically allocating storage. By using double pointers, a binary tree can be constructed which reduces search time for allocating various data items in a linked list. Directories were examined and we learned that they are often used to maintain data files on disk. Hashing was introduced and we saw that it provides one of the fastest searching procedures.

WHAT'S NEXT?

In the next chapter the various concepts in construction of assemblers and compilers will be examined.

Quiz for Chapter 7

1. Most system programs employ one or more data structuring techniques.
   True/False

2. Data structuring techniques can provide more rapid data searching but often at the expense of memory.
   True/False

3. Which of the following search procedures on the average provides the fastest search for a given data item?
   a. sequential search
   b. binary search
   c. hashing
   d. directory

4. Match the following terms and/or relations.
   a. FIFO   1. (R + Q)MOD N
   b. Hashing   2. square root of N
   c. FILO   3. stack
   d. Binary tree   4. queue
   e. Directory   5. dual pointers

5. When constructing a directory, what size should be selected for each sublist if the list has a total of 100 items?
   a. 100
   b. 10
   c. 1
   d. 20
   e. 25

6. What would be the average number of looks required to find a particular record in the list of question 5 with the optimal sublist size selected?
   a. 50
   b. 10
   c. 1
   d. 20
   e. 12

7. If the list in question 5 above was restructured for a binary search, what would be the maximum number of looks ever required?
   a. 6
   b. 7
   c. 8
   d. 9
   e. 10

8. Suppose table A will accommodate 503 records and table B 1019 records. Suppose further that table A has 251 entries and table B 509 entries. All entries were made using the linear quotient hashing technique. How many looks would be expected for locating a record in table A?
   a. 2
   b. 3
   c. 4
   d. 10
   e. 125

   In table B?
   a. 2
   b. 3
   c. 4
   d. 11
   e. 254

9. A space list is usually constructed as a:
   a. stack
   b. queue

10. A queue implemented in software requires how many pointers?
    a. 1
    b. 2
    c. 4
    d. 8

(Answers in back of book.)

Language Translators

ABOUT THIS CHAPTER

In this chapter, the concepts of language translators will be discussed. You recall from previous chapters that, in general, a language translator translates one computer language to another, and that the assembler and compiler are two types of translators. The assembler converts mnemonic-coded machine instructions (assembly language) to binary-coded machine instructions (machine language). The compiler translates instructions in a high-level language (such as FORTRAN) to machine instructions. Remember also that the language translator itself is a program and must be written in some language. Initially, translators were written in assembly language, however, now they are often written in a high-level language.

Cross Translators

A language translator program that generates machine code for computers other than the unit running the program is called a cross translator.

The translator may also generate object code for a machine other than the machine on which the translator is executing. This is common for microcomputers. For such cases, often the target machine, that is, the machine for which the object code is being prepared, does not have the necessary resources (disk, printer, etc.) to support an assembler or compiler. In this situation, the assembler or compiler may execute on a different system, say another microcomputer, minicomputer, or even a large general purpose machine. The object code generated by the translator however, can not run on the machine the translator ran on because the object code is coded for the target microcomputer. Such translators are referred to as cross translators. A cross compiler, for instance, is a program which converts high-level source statements into machine code for a machine other than the machine on which the cross compiler is executing. For example, a compiler may be executed on a DEC PDP 11 computer to generate object code for a TI-9900 microprocessor based microcomputer.

The discussion begins with loaders. Even though a loader is not a translator, we will do this first so that we can obtain a good understanding of the form of the instructions that are generated by a compiler or assembler. Then we'll see how these instructions can actually be placed in the machine so that program execution can occur.

LOADER

The loader is a program
that reads translated programs into memory for
execution.

     The loader is the program which loads your program into memory
for its execution. Now, this may seem a simple task, especially if the
language translator has generated an object file (the machine instructions)
which need only to be placed in memory at a specified starting address.
However, for multiprogrammed systems, the translators do not know what
part of memory will be free to use by the time the machine instructions are
ready and selected for execution. Also we may want to use previously
assembled or compiled subroutines. Thus, the translators usually generate
what is called relocatable code or a relocatable module. A *relocatable
module* is a machine code program file that has one or more tables or ways
for keeping track of memory dependent instructions. *Memory dependent
instructions* are instructions which will not perform properly unless they
are placed at an exact location relative to other instructions, or data or
operands which these instructions reference.

Memory Dependent Instructions

Some machine code in-
structions, to execute
properly, must occupy specific memory locations.

     An example of a memory dependent instruction is the instruction
that unconditionally transfers control, such as

         JMP 300

This instruction, which has a unique instruction code or op code for JMP,
causes a transfer of control to the instruction at memory location 300.
Obviously, the program containing this instruction will not execute properly
if location 300 does not contain the proper instruction.

     An example of a machine instruction that does not reference
memory is,

         MOV A,C

This instruction causes a transfer of the contents of register C to register
A where both registers A and C are in the CPU. No reference to memory
is made. This instruction could be in any memory location and still perform
properly. Instructions are executed in sequence, therefore, their location
relative to one another is important. The starting address and the
particular memory block where they are loaded is also important for
memory reference instructions.

Relocatable Modules

Relocatable modules are
machine code program
files that provide for keeping track of memory
dependent instructions.

     A program often consists of a number of relocatable modules.
Since any module may reference locations within another module of the
same program, a table is used to keep track of such references. As these
modules are placed in memory by the loader, the actual memory addresses
of the memory dependent instructions are placed in correct locations
by using the reference table. These loaders, often referred to as linking
loaders since they can link various relocatable modules, will load a program
when the operating system has specified a block of available memory.
Let's now look at an example of each of two types of loaders; the absolute
loader and the linking loader.

Absolute Loader

An absolute loader reads absolute (non-relocatable) machine code into specific memory locations.

The absolute loader simply loads a set of machine instructions referred to as an absolute module. Such loaders are very simple as nothing needs to be done except to read the machine instructions into the specified memory locations.

As shown in *Figure 8-1* the assembly or high-level language instructions (source code) are converted to machine instructions (object code) by the language translator. In this case an assembly language source is indicated which includes the instructions MVI A,4 and JMP 300. The MVI A,4 causes a transfer of the value 4 to register A. The translator or assembler for this example determines that a MVI, A instruction has the opcode 26 and an operand of 4, the machine instruction in hexadecimal is 260004.

**Figure 8-1.
Translation Process.**

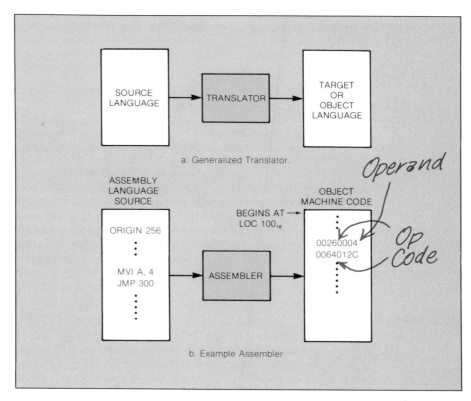

a. Generalized Translator.

b. Example Assembler

As discussed previously, JMP 300 is a memory reference instruction. The translator sees the JMP and determines that the opcode for an unconditional jump is 64. Since 300 decimal is equal to 12C hexadecimal ($1 \times 16^2 + 2 \times 16 + C = 256 + 32 + 12 = 300$), the machine instruction in hexadecimal is 64012C. Note that the op codes 26 and 64 could be, and usually are, entirely different for different machines; that is, machine level instructions are almost always machine dependent.

One instruction in the source module, ORIGIN 256 in the example, is used to tell the assembler that the machine instructions generated are to be loaded beginning at memory location 256 decimal or 100 hexadecimal. Therefore, the absolute loader takes the machine instructions and loads them directly into memory locations beginning at hexadecimal memory location 100 as shown in *Figure 8-2*.

Figure 8-2.
Module Loading by
Absolute Loader.

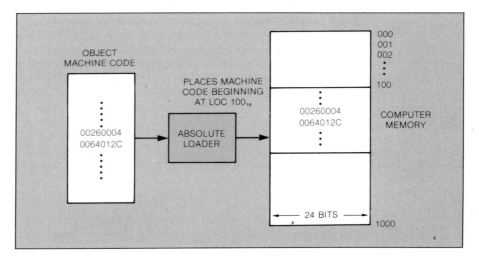

As previously mentioned, this absolute loader program is very small and simple. It reads the first word from the load module which tells the loader where in memory to place the instructions that follow. The loader then reads each instruction and stores it at the appropriate sequential memory location beginning with location 100. If no ORIGIN instruction is given in the source code, the loader is responsible for determining or allocating available memory for the block of object code, the object module.

Linking Loader

A linking loader reads modules of relocatable machine code into any part of memory that has enough space for the entire program.

The linking loader is more complicated than the absolute loader as it provides more functions than simply placing object code into memory. Basically, this loader takes relocatable object modules generated by the language translator, links these modules, and then stores them into the appropriate memory locations.

Recall that we said earlier that a relocatable module is a machine code program that has one or more tables for keeping track of memory dependent locations. Also recall that these tables are the primary difference between a relocatable module and an absolute module. The absolute module has machine language instructions which cannot be moved once compiled or assembled because the memory reference instructions expect to find operands or other instructions at the specified memory locations. Thus, if the program was designed to begin at location 100, it can't be placed at location 200 and still have it execute properly.

In most programs, particularly those designed for large machines, the user doesn't care where in memory the program is placed just as long as it executes properly. For multiprogrammed computers, that is, those with two or more jobs in an execution state at the same time, programs are loaded or placed in memory in accordance with available space at the time the program is to be executed. Therefore, the compiler or assembler doesn't know where the loader will actually place the instructions. In fact, to specify that instructions must begin at a specific memory location limits the ability of the system to handle multiple jobs.

Thus the compiler or assembler generates relocatable object modules which can be placed anywhere in *contiguous* memory space. To accomplish this, the translator first assumes that the program will be loaded beginning with location zero. Next, two tables, the relocation directory table and the external symbol table, are generated as the instructions are converted to actual machine code.

Relocation Directory

A relocation directory, generated for the loader during the translation of relocatable code, keeps track of memory references that may need adjustment when the code is read into computer memory.

The first table, the relocation directory, keeps track of all memory reference instructions. It does this by simply recording those memory locations which must be changed if the program doesn't begin at location zero. An alternative way that doesn't use a table is to use a bit associated with each instruction. If the bit is 1, then the instruction is a memory reference instruction. If the bit is 0, it is not.

The relocation directory table is then sent along with the machine instructions to the loader. After the loader has decided where the program is to be loaded, say beginning at location 1000, it examines this directory and adds the actual starting location to the address given in the memory reference instructions in the list. For instance the relative machine code illustrated in *Figure 8-3* was assembled to begin at location zero. If the loader decides to place this code beginning at location 1000, then the instruction "load the accumulator register with the contents of memory location 100" or LDA 100, and the unconditional jump instruction to location 200, JMP 200, need to be changed to LDA 1100 and JMP 1200 respectively. The relocation directory points to these locations so that the loader knows which instructions to modify. (Of course the actual machine codes are used rather than the mnemonic codes, LDA, JMP, etc. that are shown in *Figure 8-3*.)

Figure 8-3.
Module Relocating and
Loading by Linking
Loader.

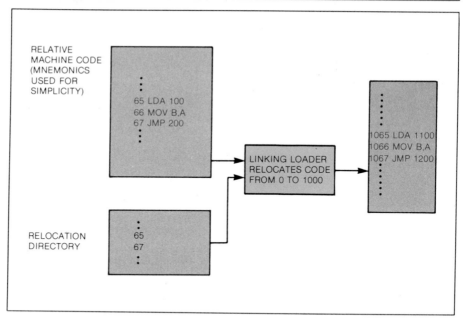

External Symbol Table

An external symbol table, generated during the translation of relocatable code, enables the loader to link the various modules that make up a program.

The other table used by the linking loader is often called the external symbol table. This table is used by the loader to link various modules to be used as one program. For instance, suppose we have three modules of subroutines which perform computations needed by a main program. Assume that the first subroutine is given the name SUB1, the second SUB2 and the third SUB3. The main program calls these routines with the instructions:

    CALL SUB1
    CALL SUB2
    CALL SUB3

This is illustrated in *Figure 8-4*. Each module is assembled separately with each beginning at location 0.

The loader must first decide where in memory the modules will be placed. Next, as each memory reference instruction is modified, the instructions CALL SUB1, CALL SUB2 and CALL SUB3 must be assigned the appropriate addresses for the subroutines. When the main routine was assembled, no address was specified for the CALL instructions because the assembler was told by a special instruction that these locations would be external to the main program. This special instruction, called a directive, is used to indicate external symbols, that is, symbols within the program which are references to other modules. The loader looks in the external symbol table of the main program and looks in the external symbol table of each of the modules to be linked. When a match is found, the appropriate address is determined.

**Figure 8-4.
Linking Process.**

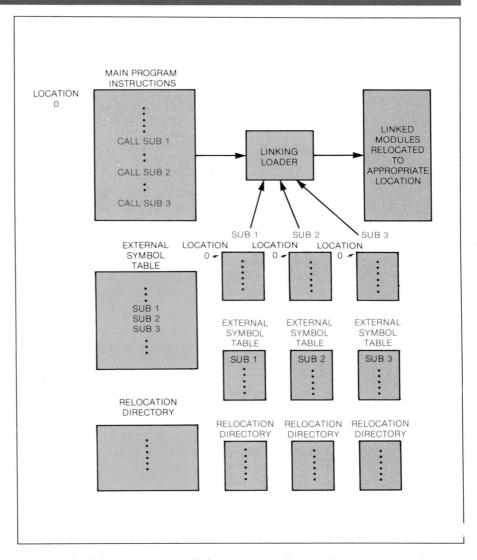

The linking loader thus links various modules and generates an absolute object file (non-relocatable machine instructions) for the total program. It can then load these instructions directly into memory.

Relocatable modules are useful in that a compilation or assembly only needs to be performed once. The resulting load modules are then stored and referenced when needed. Also modules generated from different languages can be linked. For instance, FORTRAN generated modules can be linked to assembly language generated modules.

Let's next look at the assemblers and compilers which produce these load modules.

Relocatable modules do not need to be retranslated each time you run a program. You simply store the machine code and re-load it when necessary.

ASSEMBLERS

An assembler is a program that translates assembly-language instructions into machine code.

We have already seen that language translators which generate machine code directly usually provide three files. The text file is often the name given to the actual machine code. The other two files are the relocation directory and the external symbol table. Most computer systems provide a linking capability. However, for some microprocessors which provide only a simple absolute loader, the language translators need only generate an absolute text file and linking and relocation is not permitted.

The assembler is responsible for reading the symbolic instruction codes, operands, and memory locations and converting them to the actual machine level instructions. That is, an instruction such as,

MVI B, 6

must be changed to a machine instruction, say 260006. Here 26 is the machine op code and 06 is the operand to be placed in the B register within the CPU. For the instruction

MVI B, DATA

the assembler has to find where the symbol DATA is assigned to a numeric value and then assign the appropriate operand.

The assembler first scans the program and generates a symbol table. Then it assigns machine-code values to the symbols.

To perform this process, generally the assembler will take two passes at reading the source or symbolic instructions. During the first pass the assembler reads each instruction, checks the syntax of the instruction, and generates a symbol table. The symbol table identifies all symbols used in the program and the address or operand value assigned to these symbols. (The symbol table can be constructed by using the binary tree structure or the hashing technique described in the preceding chapter.) Once the program has been read as signified by the END instruction, the assembler assigns the appropriate values to these symbols. It also keeps track of the total amount of memory needed in a memory location counter.

Example Program in Assembly Language

Let's take a simple example to illustrate this process. Consider a program consisting of the following assembly language instructions.

```
BEGIN:   LDA ZERO
         STA SUM
         MVI B, 10
LOOP:    IN 6
         ADD SUM
         STA SUM
         DEC B
         JNZ LOOP
         HLT
ZERO:    DW 0
SUM:     DS 1
         END
```

These labels are placed in a symbol table.

These instructions give the assembler values for "zero" and "sum".

This program sums a set of 10 numbers as illustrated in *Figure 8-5.* The ten numbers are read from I/O port 6 and the program stops after reading and summing these ten numbers.

The program begins by setting the memory location SUM to zero and the register B to 10. The LDA ZERO instruction sets register A to the value in the memory location with the symbol 'ZERO'. Looking at the third instruction from the bottom, we see that the symbol ZERO is set to the value 0 by the instruction:

ZERO: DW 0

**Figure 8-5.
Flow Diagram for
Summing Program.**

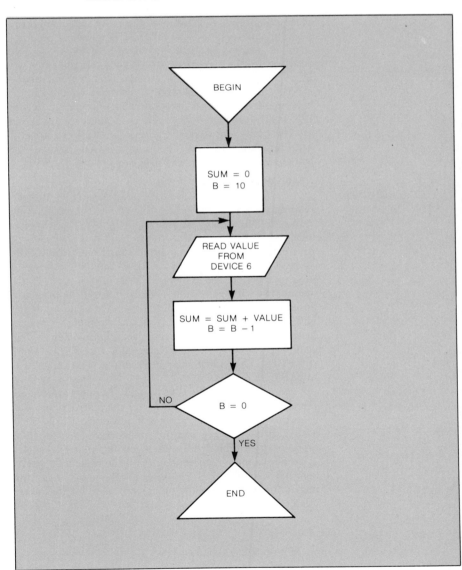

Assembly-language programs may contain special translating instructions ("directives" or "pseudo instructions") for the assembler.

This instruction is referred to as a directive or pseudo instruction. It is not an actual machine instruction but an instruction to the assembler to tell it to set the value 0 to the storage location ZERO. The instruction, SUM: DS 1, tells the assembler to define a storage location or memory word to be referenced by the symbolic name SUM. The contents of this location is then set to zero by the instruction STA SUM which means "store the value now in register A in memory location SUM". Register B is set to the value of 10, the number of values to be read and summed, by MVI B, 10 which means "move immediately the value 10 to register B."

Values are read from port 6 by the instruction IN 6. This instruction reads a value from the input device 6 and places it in the accumulator register. The ADD SUM instruction adds the contents of memory location SUM to the contents of the accumulator and places the results into the A register. The STA SUM then stores the new sum back into memory location SUM. The DEC B decrements (decreases the value) the B register by 1. The JNZ instruction which means "jump if not zero", is a conditional jump instruction which jumps to the symbolic location LOOP if the B register is not zero. Another value is read and the sum and store process repeated. If the B register is zero, then all ten values have been read and summed. The jump to LOOP is not executed and the next instruction, HLT, stops the program.

Assembly of Example Program

Labels like BEGIN and ZERO make up the symbol table that the assembler generates on its first pass through the program.

Let's see how the assembler assembles this program. It begins by reading each instruction and placing each symbol in a list. Appropriate values are then assigned to these symbols. The symbol BEGIN, which is a label, is the first to go into the list and it is assigned the value 0 for the first memory location. The assembler doesn't know yet where ZERO is located, so it simply places ZERO in the list for later assignment. In the next instruction, the symbol SUM is encountered. It is also placed in the symbol list without a value. The label LOOP is placed in the list and assigned the value 3 (the fourth memory location) as it will be associated with the fourth instruction. (For this example we are assuming that each instruction requires one memory location.) When the label ZERO is finally read, the assembler knows what value to assign to this symbol. It assigns 9 to ZERO for the ninth memory location. The value 10 is similarly assigned to SUM.

With the symbol table set up, the assembler translates the instruction mnemonics to machine code, adding the values of labels when appropriate.

The assembler is now ready to generate the object code. It begins the second pass to once again read the instructions. As each instruction is read this time, the assembler can determine the correct machine code to assign. It does this by locating the correct code for the symbolic op code in a prespecified table where the symbolic op codes are already related to the appropriate numerical values. Then the assembler assigns the symbolic operand variables that are referenced. Thus, the machine code for each instruction consists of the numerical value for the op code plus the numerical value of the operand, if any.

The assembler process is illustrated in *Figure 8-6*. Note in this figure that the first pass of the assembler uses the memory location counter to specify appropriate address values to labels and eventually determine the total program length requirements. The symbol table keeps track of symbols and their values. The op code table provides the relationship between the symbolic op code and the numeric machine op code value. In the first pass any unidentified op codes or other symbols are denoted as error conditions. The second pass is where the actual object module is generated along with the program listing. The program listing usually provides both the assembly language instructions and the corresponding machine instructions.

**Figure 8-6.
Assembler Process.**

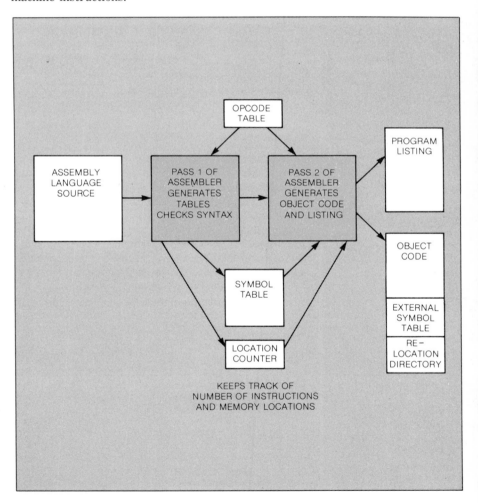

FORMAL LANGUAGE SPECIFICATION

The assembly level language essentially provides a symbolic method of programming with the actual machine instructions. Such programs are machine dependent as few computers utilize the same machine instructions unless they are from the same family. As discussed, programming in assembly language is usually very complex, particularly when writing mathematical algorithms. Higher level languages, such as those we discussed in Chapter 4, provide a much easier method of writing application programs. Then, as we have previously discussed, the compiler does the tedious work of translating the high-level language to machine language.

The BNF Specification

The BNF specification is a format for describing the grammar of high-level programming languages.

In order to describe these high-level languages, we need to put what they say in a form that the computer can easily interpret. In order to do that, a method needs to be defined to specify the grammar of these languages. One method often used for specifying the grammar of programming languages is referred to as BNF, an abbreviation for Backus-Normal Form or Backus-Naur Form, which was developed by J.W. Backus[2] for describing a high-level language called ALGOL. To understand the BNF format, we must first distinguish between terminal and non-terminal symbols. The non-terminal symbols are enclosed in brackets to represent units used as intermediate steps in the description process. The terminal symbols are the final symbols from which the generated description is eventually defined.

The symbol :: = is used to specify the term "is replaced by". The symbol | is used for specifying alternative symbols. For example, consider a sentence composed of a subject and verb. This grammar is specified by the form

<sentence> :: = <subject> <verb phrase>

A subject may be either a noun or pronoun, so

<subject> :: = <noun> | <pronoun>

Consider the method of describing the sentence, "The computer is fast."

<sentence> :: = <subject> <verb phrase>
<subject> :: = <article> <noun>
<article> :: = the
<noun> :: = computer
<verb phrase> :: = <verb> <adverb>
<verb> :: = is
<adverb> :: = fast

The terminal symbols are: the, computer, is, fast.

[2]Naur, P., "Revised Report on the Algorithm Language ALGOL 60" *CACM 6*, (January 1963): 1-17

Let's now look at a way to describe the BASIC instruction
5 FOR I = 1 to 10

<line> :: = <line number> <instruction>
<line number > :: = <digit>
<digit> :: = 1|5|0
<digits > :: = <digit> <digit>
<instruction> :: = FOR <variable> = <digit> TO <digits>
<variable> :: = I

For this case, only the one BASIC statement which consists of a line number and an instruction is to be specified. The line number consists of a digit. A digit for this one instruction language is 0, 1 or 5. The instruction, then, consists of the key word FOR, the variable I, the key word =, a digit, the key word TO, and two more digits. The <digit> <digit> notation is the way of specifying the two digits that may be a combination of any numbers specified by <digit>.

The BNF format represents program statements in a form that compilers can systematically interpret.

Thus, we can see that BNF provides a way of describing a language. Not only does this format provide a convenient method of specifying the language, but it also provides an organized means by which syntax and instruction interpretation can be easily accomplished in the compilation process. The above example was simple since only the grammar of a one instruction language needed to be described. Obviously, the grammar of a language such as BASIC, PL/I, Pascal, etc., requires a more lengthy set of specifications.

There are methods other than BNF to describe the grammar of various computer languages with essentially the same function; that is, to describe the language in a form so that the compiler can easily interpret the instructions.

Let's next see how languages are compiled.

COMPILERS

Recall that a compiler is a program that translates a high-level language to machine language. High-level language statements are much more difficult to convert to machine language than assembly language programs. For many instructions, for example, the assembly language instruction is simply a symbolic form for the actual machine instruction. On the other hand, a high-level language statement can be quite involved and result in a translation to many machine instructions.

In general, the translation process for compilers involves a number of basic steps which include:

1. Lexical analysis
2. Syntactical analysis
3. Transformation
4. Intermediate language production
5. Machine language production

We will briefly describe each of these steps now, then in later sections, more detail will be presented.

Lexical Analysis

A language compiler first scans the program statements to identify tokens (variables, arithmetic and logical operators, and key words). Then it checks the tokens for proper syntax.

In lexical analysis, the statements are scanned and the basic tokens defined. Consider the following high-level language statement.

$$F = A * B + C$$

For this statement, the variables F, A, B, C and the operators =, *, + are identified as tokens.

Syntactical Analysis

The second step of processing, syntactical analysis, ensures that the syntax is correct. That is, syntactical analysis ensures that the tokens of the program language (variables, operators, and key words) are used in the proper relationship with each other, just as words of the English language must be related according to rules of grammar to be understood. If not, error messages are generated. Suppose the following statement was processed: $F = A * B \ C$

Assume that for the high-level language being considered, there is no operator between B and C. Therefore, during syntactical analysis, this missing symbol would be detected as an error and a syntax error message printed.

Transformation

Next, the compiler uses the variables and operators to produce an intermediate (machine-independent) code. This code is the source of the final machine code.

In the third step in the compilation process, transformation, the variables and operators are used to form a tree in which an intermediate language can be constructed. Recall from the previous chapter that the tree is a linked list with multiple pointers that show the relationship between the various variables and operators.

Intermediate and Machine Language

After the tree has been formed, an intermediate or machine independent code is developed in step four of the process. From this code, the actual machine code can be constructed and this object module is the actual output of the process. Thus, we can see already that the compilation process is much more involved then an assembly process.

Let's next look in more detail at the compilation process and see how these steps are actually performed. We are only going to investigate one of the many existing methods of compilation. One of the primary differences between the various compilers is the compromise made between memory and CPU optimization.

For instance, the compiler which generates the most efficient machine code often requires much more execution time and much more memory than another method. On the other hand, once the compilation is performed, the object module of the compiled user program may require less storage and execute faster than one generated from a different compiler. If you are interested in further study of compilers and assemblers, there are several books devoted to these subjects.

Lexical and Syntactical Analysis

The compiler initially handles all tokens as variables. It then sorts them by class and arranges them in tables of uniform symbols for syntax checking.

The process of breaking out the basic tokens of a source program is usually referred to as *lexical analysis*. This process involves simple string processing methods where the different kinds of variable strings are indentified.

Consider the following block of statements.

```
BEGIN
F = A*B + C;
TEMP = F**2;
END ;
```

The first step in lexical analysis of these statements is to identify the variables as illustrated in *Figure 8-7*.

**Figure 8-7.
Identifying Variables in
Lexical Analysis.**

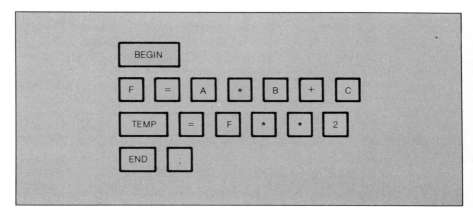

As the variables are identified, they are also classed and a table of uniform symbols for each class constructed (*Figure 8-8*). The uniform symbol table organizes the variables so that syntax checking and instruction interpretation are much simpler. Syntax checking in accordance to a language specification such as the BNF form can be more easily accomplished because the number of characters per symbol to be scanned is always uniform or the same. That is, the symbol ; is classed as a terminal symbol and is given the name TRM while the variable A is called an identifer and given the name IDN. Each symbol is placed in the table in the order processed. This makes the scanning process much easier since the algorithm used for scanning these instructions and interpreting their function will often need to look ahead one or more symbols. All comments and blanks are extracted from the program statements.

**Figure 8-8.
Uniform Symbol Table
Example.**

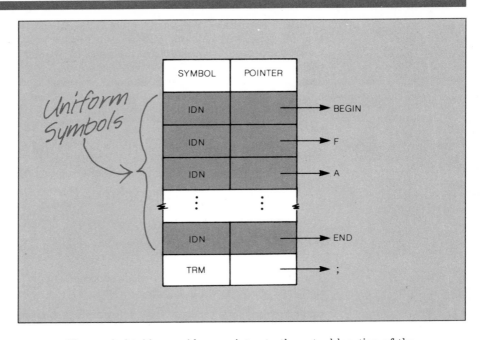

The symbol table for lexical analysis, with pointers indicating the actual memory locations of the symbols, is the basis of the transformation tree from which the intermediate code is produced.

The symbol table provides a pointer to the actual location of the symbol so when the actual variable name is needed, the link in this table is used. From the symbol table, a transformation tree can be constructed and from the transformation tree, intermediate or machine independent code can be generated for interpreting the instruction.

This brief look at the process of lexical and syntactical analysis is summarized in *Figure 8-9*. The detailed procedures that are used for syntax checking and code generation are beyond the scope of this book and, again, the interested reader is referred to books devoted to these subjects.

Let's next look at the procedure for interpreting the high-level instruction and generating the appropriate machine code.

**Figure 8-9.
Summary of Lexical and
Syntactical Analysis.**

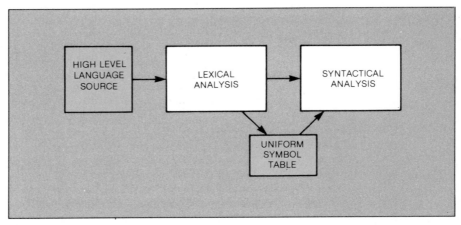

Transformation and Intermediate Language Production

In the third step of the compilation process, a linked list or tree transformation is constructed. This list structure can be used in the fourth step for generating intermediate code and in the fifth step for generating the machine dependent code.

The transformation and intermediate language production is implemented by use of a stack. You remember from the previous chapter that a stack is a first in last out data structure. This structure turns out to be useful in implementing the transformation process. Also during the process, the uniform symbol table discussed in the last section (*Figure 8.8*) will be referenced.

To describe the development of intermediate code, two operations are involved. In the first operation, the entries in the uniform symbol table are each processed. Consider, for example, the arithmetic statement

$$F = a + b*c$$

To evaluate the expression, notice that there are three parts; a variable on the left-hand side, an equal sign, and an expression on the right-hand side. It is easy for a program to scan and locate the equal sign. The right-hand side expression then will be evaluated and assigned to the left-hand side variable.

Reverse Polish Notation

Before generating intermediate code, the compiler rearranges arithmetic expressions into reverse Polish notation (operators follow operands).

In order to evaluate the right-hand expression, it must be reconstructed in a special way. To evaluate an arithmetic expression, a method called reverse Polish notation is often used. Polish notation, which was invented by the Polish logician Lukasiewicz, is sometimes called prefix notation. Prefix notation is where the operator is listed before its operands. For example, the prefix notation for b*c is *bc. Postfix notation is where the operator is specified following its operands or in this case bc*. Postfix notation for an expression is referred to as *reverse Polish notation* (RPN).

RPN has the advantage that neither parenthesis nor operator priority is needed to determine the order in which operations are to occur. For instance, with no established operator priority, the expression

$$a + b*c$$

may be mistaken for

$$(a + b)*c$$

or what about

$$a + b/c*d$$

which could be mistaken for

$$(a + b)/c*d$$

However, RPN insures that the desired order is accomplished. It is used for processing on many of the small hand-held calculators.

Although there are well-defined algorithms for generating RPN which can easily be programmed, essentially they all apply the rule that an operator must always immediately follow its operands.

In our earlier example of $a+b*c$, we note that the + operator is to be applied to the operands a and b*c, thus the first step in reconstructing the expression in RPN yields,

    ab*c +

Next we see that the multiplication symbol * involves the operands b and c so we get,

    abc* +

Another example expression such as,

    a − b*c + d

yields,

    abc* − d +

The abc* − portion is similar to the first example. Since the + operation must follow its operands, the + must follow the d as shown.

After the RPN list has been constructed, intermediate code can be generated. The RPN list is usually a list of links with each entry simply a pointer to the appropriate symbol. Other information regarding variables, such as if it's integer, real or string, is also indicated by pointers from each symbol. If you are getting the impression that the compilation process involves many linked lists and tables, you are right.

Using the Stack

The compiler pushes operands onto a stack to evaluate RPN expressions. The top two operands are used for any operation detected, and the result is pushed back onto the stack for the next operation.

We mentioned earlier that the stack structure is used in this process. We'll now see how the stack is used to process the algorithm of generating RPN from the uniform symbol table and to process the RPN list.

The rule used for evaluating an RPN expression proceeds as follows. First the RPN expression is scanned from left to right. If an operand is detected it is pushed on the stack. When an operator is detected, the top two elements on the stack are used as the operands for the operator and the specified operation performed. The result of the operation is then used to replace the two operands leaving the result operand at the top of the stack. The process continues until the expression is evaluated. Let's consider our preceding example.

The RPN expression is:

    abc* +

The operations are indicated in *Figure 8-10*. During the first step the variable a is placed in the stack. Next the variable b is placed at the top of the stack followed by c being placed at the top of the stack.

**Figure 8-10.
Expression Evaluation
from RPN.**

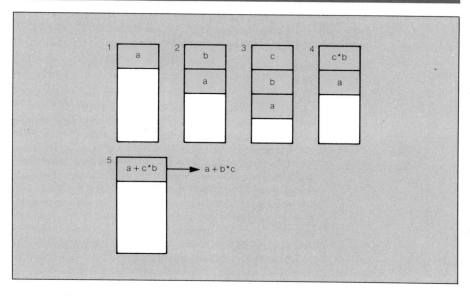

When the * is encountered, the multiplication of b*c is performed
and the result placed at the top of the stack. Next the + operator is
encountered and the final operation a+b*c is performed.

Try to step through the second example problem,

abc* – d +

and you should get the desired evaluation,

a – b*c + d

The compiler generates intermediate machine code as it evaluates the RPN expressions.

As the RPN expressions are evaluated, intermediate machine
independent code is generated. Some compilers generate intermediate code
directly from the transformation tree and bypass the generation of RPN.
Often compilers use pseudo instructions consisting of an operation and
three registers for the two source operands and the destination (result) as
shown in *Table 8-1.* R_1, R_2, R_3 are the registers; A, S, M, D, T are the
operations.

**Table 8-1.
Intermediate Machine
Independent Code.**

OPERATION	PSEUDO-INSTRUCTION
+	A R_1,R_2,R_3
–	S R_1,R_2,R_3
*	M R_1,R_2,R_3
/	D R_1,R_2,R_3
=	T R_1,R_2

FROM THE EXPRESSION F = a + b*c THE FOLLOWING CODE IS DEVELOPED.

OPERATION	INSTRUCTION	COMMENTS
b*c	T R_1,b	b ⟶ R_1 (b to R_1)
	T R_2,c	c ⟶ R_2 (c to R_2)
	M R_1,R_2,R_3	b*c ⟶ R_3 (b*c to R_3)
a + b*c	T R_1,a	a ⟶ R_1 (a to R_1)
	A R_1,R_3,R_3	a + b*c ⟶ R_3 (Sum to R_3)
	T F,R_3	F = a + b*c (Result to F)

Machine Language Production

The compiler's final task is to modify the intermediate machine code to run on the intended computer.

The next step of the transformation process is to convert the intermediate code to actual machine code. The code at the intermediate level closely approaches most machine codes so that the final operations are fairly straight forward. During the code optimization phase, operations that have previously occurred, such as reloading registers that have already been set, are deleted. In fact, optimization is usually performed at both the intermediate code generation level and the final code generation level. The final code optimization level includes the utilization of as many registers as possible and deletion of all redundant instructions.

The overall compilation process is summarized in *Figure 8-11*. As we said previously, the compilation process can be complex and we have only given brief examples to introduce you to the concepts. As you now know, the compiler is a program and, as such, must be written by someone. You may be surprised to know that during the 1970's much work was done to develop still other programs which write compilers. These programs are called compiler compilers or compiler writing systems and we'll turn our attention to them next.

**Figure 8-11.
Summary of Compilation
Process.**

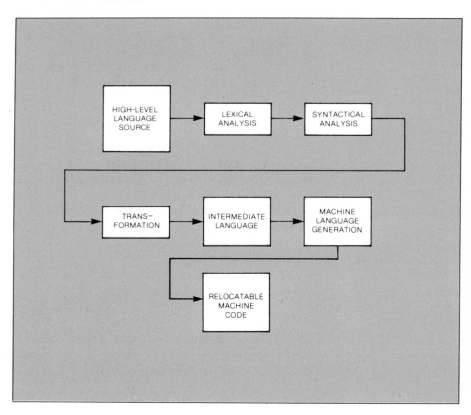

COMPILER COMPILERS

Programs that generate compilers from BNF descriptions of high-level languages have been developed in recent years.

As mentioned in the preceding section, much work has been done in developing programs which generate compilers. These programs are often referred to as translator writer systems, TWS, or compiler compilers. One method which is used involves the use of three separate programs. The first is called an ANALYZER which is a program that translates a language described by BNF to generate a set of syntax tables. These tables are next read into a program called SKELETON which is a table driven translator. SKELETON is a set of XPL routines which describe a compiler. Finally, a program called XCOM translates the XPL routines to System 370 machine code. The combination of the three programs thus forms a useful method of constructing a compiler and has been used successfully for a number of different applications. More on this method is described in a Prentice-Hall book, *A Compiler Generator* by McKeeman, Horning and Wortman.

WHAT HAVE WE LEARNED?

In this chapter we have learned about language translators. First we learned that a linking loader is a program that links relocatable object modules generated by assemblers and/or compilers and loads these modules into memory. The absolute loader simply reads absolute code directly into memory and passes control to this program.

Next we examined assemblers and discussed the way an assembler converts the symbolic machine instructions of assembly language into machine code. Finally we talked about compilers and discussed the various operations involved to translate a high-level language program to machine code.

WHAT'S NEXT?

In the next chapter we will leave our discussion of systems software and examine programming applications for some practical uses of the computer in business. In particular, we will look at a billing and inventory program and see how it can be implemented on a small micro or minicomputer system.

Quiz for Chapter 8

True-False or Multiple Choice

1. A translator which converts one high-level program to another is called a compiler.
   True/False

2. An assembler can generate code which may be relocated to different memory locations.
   True/False

3. A translator which converts a high-level language directly to machine code is called a compiler.
   True/False

4. A cross-compiler generates object code for a machine other than the one on which the cross compiler is executing.
   True/False

5. Loaders which must link the various modules to be loaded and perhaps relocate the final object module are called linking loaders.
   True/False

6. Linking loaders do not require anything of the compiler except the text file and the location where the program is to be loaded.
   True/False

7. Which of the following instructions is always a memory reference instruction?
   a. MOVE R_1 to R_2
   b. LOAD R_1 with contents of 100
   c. SUBTRACT R_1 from R_2
   d. None of the above

8. The primary difference between a linking loader and an absolute loader is.
   a. The linking loader has more pointers
   b. The absolute loader is only for microprocessors
   c. The linking loader may relocate an object module
   d. They are the same
   e. None of the above

9. The absolute loader uses an external symbol table for linking various modules.
   True/False

10. A relocation directory may not be needed if a bit is used in each instruction to indicate a memory reference instruction.
    True/False

11. The external symbol table is used primarily for linking modules.
    True/False

12. The symbol table and the external symbol table have essentially the same function.
    True/False

13. The assembler must essentially convert symbolic machine instructions to actual machine instructions.
    True/False

14. Generally two passes are required by an assembler so that all symbols can be identified before processing.
    True/False

15. A directive is a machine instruction.
    True/False

16. The END directive is used to terminate the assembly process.
    True/False

17. BNF is a method of describing a high level language.
    True/False

18. The primary function of the uniform symbol table is to aid in the scanning process for syntax checking and code generation.
    True/False

19. Reverse Polish notation is used for evaluating arithmetic expressions.
    True/False

20. Translator Writer Systems have not proved to be very useful for compiler construction.
    True/False

(Answers in back of book.)

Systems Analysis

WHAT IS SYSTEMS ANALYSIS?

Systems Analysis is the analysis of system requirements for the purpose of either designing and implementing a new system or to increase the efficiency or capability of an existing system. A system is a collection of components which work together as one to perform a specified function or task as shown in *Figure 9-1*. The components have common relationships and normally interact with each other.

Figure 9-1.
A System is a Collection of Components.

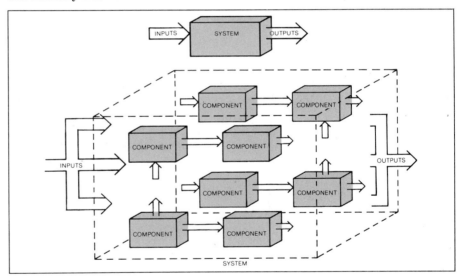

A systems analyst designs, implements, and maintains computer systems.

Systems analyst is the name usually given to individuals or professionals who perform the system analysis. The systems analyst is responsible for designing, implementing and maintaining a system. This person must be able to identify the components and their relationship to the overall function. We know that any system is only as strong as its weakest link. The systems analyst has the responsibility to identify any weak links and to make corrections to prevent a weak link from adversely affecting the desired operation of the system. Some of the requirements for a good computer systems analyst are:

1. A background in engineering, computer programming, or other related technical areas.
2. Several years experience with computer hardware and/or software.

3. Experience in designing one or more subsystems of a system.
4. Good communication skills to talk and listen effectively to other people in order to gather information and to instruct people how to use the system.
5. An effective organizer to sort through the many details that apply to system requirements to determine their order and priority in system design.

Systems Design

The top-down approach to program design described in chapter 3 applies to system design as well.

In a way, the approach we have discussed for writing a computer program is the same general approach that is taken by the systems analyst in solving a complex problem. You will recall that when we discussed top-down design for programming we said that the top-down design method can be used as an aid to solve any problem. The systems analyst also uses this method to identify the components and structure of a system. First the overall functions are identified, then the next lower level functions are listed, followed by the next level, and so on.

In order to define the problem, the systems analyst must have good communication skills as well as technical skills because he or she must be able to talk to people who will use the system to be designed or are using the system that is to be improved. Often the levels of the problem can only be defined by talking with these people. This part of system analysis is usually referred to as the data collection phase.

Data Collection Phase

Defining a system's tasks requires data from various sources.

Sometimes data cannot be directly obtained and simulation may be required, that is, a particular subsystem operation can be described mathematically but cannot be directly solved. Simulation is the process by which typical inputs are randomly input to the system and the output recorded. This is illustrated in *Figure 9-2*.

Figure 9-2.
System Simulation.

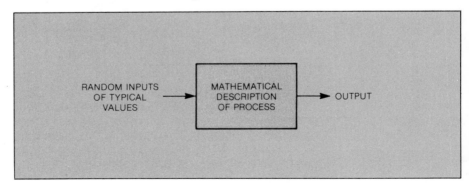

RANDOM INPUTS
OF TYPICAL
VALUES   MATHEMATICAL
DESCRIPTION
OF PROCESS   OUTPUT

Statistics are also often used in the collection process. Statistics allow the systems analyst to define the system or subsystem outputs by using only one or two numbers instead of a hundred. For example, the mean (similar to the average) or variance (an indication of how values vary about the mean) may be used.

These methods, that is, the personal interview, simulation, and statistics are often referred to as tools of the systems analyst. These tools are used in the data collection phase and again in the system analysis and design phases.

Analysis and Design Phases

Once data has been collected regarding a system, it must be organized or classified so that decisions can be made. This is the analysis phase. After the data is analyzed, the system design can begin. After the system is designed, it can be implemented and the success of the design or improvement can be determined. The systems analyst is responsible for all these phases of the system analysis.

Many books or articles on systems analysis usually concentrate on designing or improving a large computer system for some particular application. In this chapter, we will show how to use the tools of the systems analyst to determine how to use a small computer system to solve a problem. In particular, let's see how we can design a system using one of the fourth generation microcomputer systems to handle an application for a small business.

SYSTEMS ANALYSIS EXAMPLE

To illustrate systems analysis, let's design a system for a small business application. The first thing we need to do is to define the problem that we want the system to solve.

The Problem

A typical problem: designing a billing and inventory system for a small company.

The owner of a small computer equipment rental firm has asked us to develop an automatic billing and inventory recording system using one of the small personal computers. The company provides various computing equipment such as terminals, modems, microcomputers, etc. for rent. The problems of billing each day of the month and also keeping track of equipment is time consuming and reducing profits.

To begin the analysis, we need to define the desired functions, that is, the inputs and outputs. This information is obtained by personal interview with the owner and the overall function is shown in *Figure 9-3*.

**Figure 9-3.
Overall System Function.**

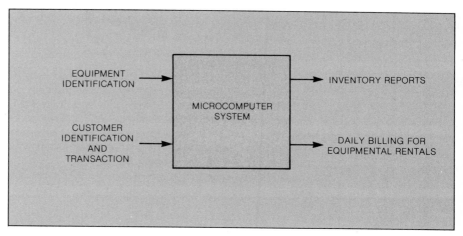

The company has about 100 different devices which can be rented and currently over 1000 customers rent devices during a month. Each day, as the day of the month that equipment was rented arrives, the customer must be sent a bill. The customers must be billed with the invoice illustrated in *Figure 9-4*.

Figure 9-4.
Billing Form.

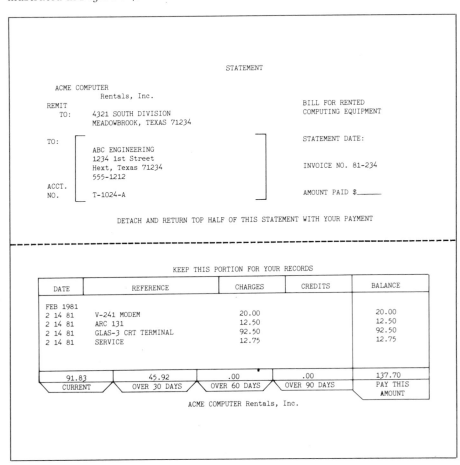

Currently, office personnel have to manually keep track of the day of the month each equipment is rented. The problem is further complicated by the fact that the same customer may rent more than one device on the same day. Furthermore, the same customer may rent other devices during the same month but on a different day. Therefore, a customer may have more than one bill issued per month and, when a payment is received, it must be credited to the correct bill.

The owner is also interested in keeping records of the rental equipment; for example, purchase date, cost, identification number, last maintenance date, etc.

Just a few years ago, the kind of functions desired by this businessman could only be provided on a fairly large computer system; but now these functions, and more, can easily be provided by one of the small microcomputer systems. Analysis of the desired functions show that there are no involved mathematical algorithms or operations which a small computer system can't handle. The main question then is whether the small system can support the data storage requirements. To determine these requirements, the desired functions must be specified further.

System Functions

With the problem defined, the next step is to identify the system procedures necessary to produce the desired results.

Before determining the equipment requirements, the next step following the problem definition is to determine the various procedures for providing the desired functions.

We can state the problem as follows:

Develop an automatic billing and inventory reporting system. The major tasks are broken down into five levels:

1.0. Developing the data base structure
2.0. Entering and updating the data base.
3.0. Billing
4.0. Posting
5.0. Inventory Reporting

First, we have to define the structure of the data base required to keep track of customers and equipment. To determine the data base structure, the data record and file organization must be defined. Next we must define the method of entering, deleting and updating records, and the frequency of updates. We must determine how the billing and posting are to be implemented, and finally, we need to decide what type of inventory reports are desired and the frequency of such reports. From this information we can determine the hardware requirements and software design.

The Data Base

The nature and organization of the information to be maintained determine the structure of the data base.

In order for the system to provide an automatic billing to customers and to provide an inventory report on existing equipment, we need some type of data base. Since only one person will rent and use a particular piece of equipment at a time, and because we want information about both the equipment and those who are renting it, we will organize the data base by equipment type. The data base will consist of files. Each file will have a collection of records and each record will have a set of fields, each one of which have some common characteristics.

Determining Records and Fields

Before establishing the number and names of the fields, the invoice or billing form as shown in *Figure 9-4* should be examined. Upon examining *Figure 9-4*, we see that the billing form requires the customers full name, identification number, complete address, and telephone number, and a list of each equipment type rented along with the corresponding rental date.

The data base file must contain this information. In addition, the owner wants other information about the customer and the rental transaction for his records and to generate reports for business analysis and future planning.

After determining all the information that the owner wants, we can determine the needed fields and their widths (number of characters) as shown in *Table 9-1*. The fields are shown grouped into two classes — those fields related to customer characteristics and those fields related to equipment characteristics.

The field widths listed give the maximum number of characters allowed for each field. For example, the maximum number of characters allowed for a last name is 20 which should provide for most names. The same is true for the first name and middle initial. The number of characters allowed for customer sex is only one as a simple M or F for male or female can be used. The customer posting link field will be used to link payment transactions related to each bill.

Determining File and Record Organization

The files in the sample data base need to keep track of whether equipment is rented, equipment characteristics, and customer information.

The location of equipment is determined by whether it is in stock or rented. If it is rented, we indicate that it belongs to one of the customer files. If the equipment is in stock, we indicate that it belongs to the in-stock files. When equipment is rented we can transfer an available unit from the in-stock file to the customer file. Conversely, when equipment is returned by a customer, we can transfer it back to the in-stock file.

Looking at *Table 9-1*, we see that each record can have a maximum of 302 characters or 302 bytes (recall that each character takes 8 bits). Recall from Chapter 2 that records can be fixed length or variable length although most small systems provide only fixed length records. *Figure 9-5* illustrates the record organization.

**Figure 9-5.
Record Organization.**

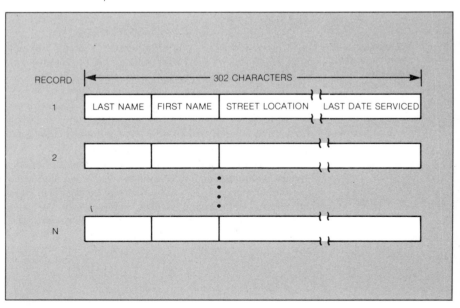

**Table 9-1.
Record Structure.**

RECORD CLASS	FIELD TYPE	FIELD WIDTH
CUSTOMER CHARACTERISTICS	LAST NAME	20
	FIRST NAME (MI)	20
	LOCATION STREET	15
	CITY	20
	STATE	2
	ZIP	6
	SEX	1
	BIRTHDATE	8
	PHONE	10
	CUSTOMER IDENTIFICATION NO.	20
	DATE RENTED	8
	APPLICATION	100
	SALESMAN	20
	CUSTOMER POSTING LINK	6
EQUIPMENT CHARACTERISTICS	EQUIPMENT CODE	8
	MANUFACTURER CODE	8
	EQUIPMENT COST	8
	RENTAL RATE	6
	DATE PURCHASED	8
	LAST DATE SERVICED	8
		302

Since we plan to use a microcomputer we will use floppy disks for each file. *Table 9-2* illustrates how the floppy disks (floppies) can be used for the customer files and the in-stock files. The alphabetical range of groups as indicated in *Table 9-2* can be determined by examining the file of current customers to determine the percentage of customers within each last name grouping. For instance, suppose that in general, ⅓ or 33% of the customers had last names in the range A through D, 33% in the range E through R and 33% in the range S through Z. This is the basis for file organization shown in *Table 9-2*. Therefore, it is desirable that each disk hold approximately 333 records (1000 customers/3). (The 5¼ inch mini-floppies can hold around 100,000 bytes with the actual amount depending on the tables used by the disk operating system and the disk format scheme. If 100,000 bytes are available, each disk can hold around 331 of the records that we defined in *Figure 9-5*.)

**Table 9-2.
File Organization.**

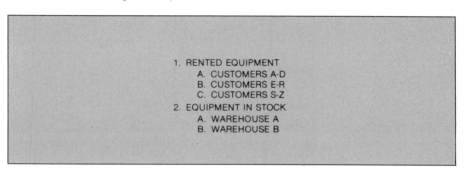

1. RENTED EQUIPMENT
   A. CUSTOMERS A-D
   B. CUSTOMERS E-R
   C. CUSTOMERS S-Z
2. EQUIPMENT IN STOCK
   A. WAREHOUSE A
   B. WAREHOUSE B

Actually, an extra field will be required in our record organization for implementing a linked-list structure because the records will need to be ordered within the data base. A four-byte pointer field reduces the total number of records as defined in *Table 9-1* per disk. The maximum amount will be based on the actual characteristics of the hardware system selected, however, we now have a good estimate for planning purposes. So, with the added pointer field to each of the 1000 records, we need to change the organization shown in *Table 9-2* to allow for four disks for the customer file. Thus, you see that the exact structure depends on the actual system selected.

Routines

The software in the example system should support data base entry and maintenance as well as billing, posting, and inventory reporting.

As indicated earlier, four different routines are necessary for the system program. These are: data base entry and updating, billing, posting, and inventory reporting.

In the first, data base entry and updating, which has been defined as the level 2.0 task, the following functions are needed.

2.0 Data Base Entry and Updating.
2.1 Initialize data structure
2.2 Build entries
2.3 Delete entries
2.4 Modify entries
2.5 List entries

In the first, 2.1, the initial data structure must be set up. Since entries are going to be created, updated or deleted, a linked list organization is needed. Thus an initial space list needs to be structured as illustrated in *Figure 9-6*.

**Figure 9-6.
Initialization of Space
List.**

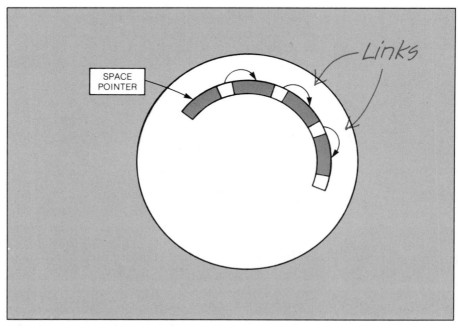

The data base permits random access to individual records. For file analysis, records are linked together by a customer pointer.

Function 2.2 is used to build the data base. Function 2.3 allows items to be deleted and the corresponding free disk area returned to the space list. Function 2.4 permits changing various field entries. Function 2.5 gives the capability of examining various data base records or entries. Once the size has been defined, an individual record can be accessed by its record number. This type of accessing is called random accessing.

The second program type, billing, at level 3.0 provides automatic billing on the form shown in *Figure 9.4*.

The third routine, posting, at level 4.0, provides a way of keeping track of bills that have been paid. As noted earlier, one field in the record is reserved for the customer posting link. This field links all bills paid for the year for each customer for a particular equipment type as in *Figure 9-7*. Each time a bill is paid, a new entry is made giving the date paid, the invoice number, and the amount paid. This transaction is then attached via the customer posting link for that piece of equipment. These transactions are maintained throughout the year for record keeping purposes.

Figure 9-7.
Transaction Linking.

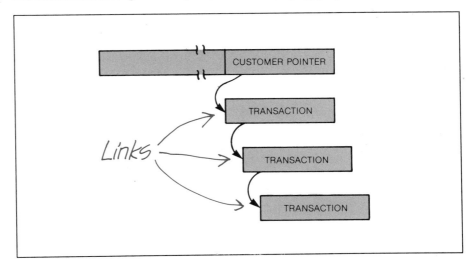

The last routine, inventory reporting at level 5.0, is used to keep track of both rented and in-stock equipment. This routine produces a report as shown in *Table 9-3*. However, various fields can be used for searching or sorting. For instance, a list of all equipment purchases before January 1 of a particular year, or perhaps a list of all equipment that was last serviced before a given date may be printed as a report.

Table 9-3.
Inventory Report.

EQUIPMENT CODE	MANUFACTURER'S CODE	INITIAL COST	DATE PURCHASED	LAST TIME SERVICED	LOCATION
A-4215	PJ5	$375	11/10/1980	11/10/1980	IN STOCK-1
.	.	.	.	.	
.	.	.	.	.	
.	.	.	.	.	

We will look at the data structure next to see how we can keep track of such information.

Data Structures

A straightforward way to organize files in the sample problem is by customer name and by day of the month.

By now you may have thought of several ways to organize the data files so that the desired functions can be carried out. One way to organize the files is by day of month in which the equipment was rented and alphabetically by customer name as illustrated in *Figure 9-8*.

Figure 9-8.
Data Structure.

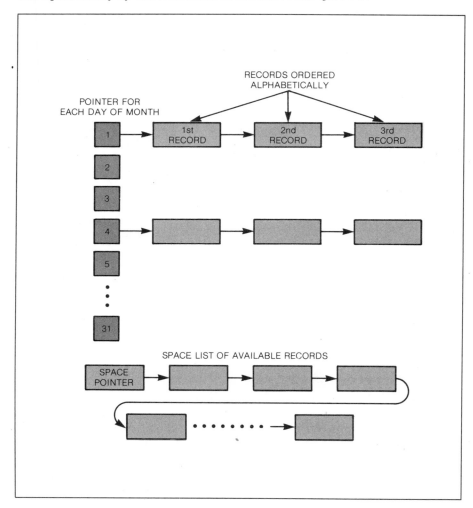

Day-of-the-month organization simplifies billing.

The file organized in this manner has several advantages for the desired functions. First, one of the primary activities is billing which is to occur daily. This list has a separate pointer for each day of the month so that the entire month's file will not have to be read when searching for a specific file.

Alphabetical organization of customers' names simplifies the processing of multiple rentals to a single customer on the same day.

A second advantage deals with relating equipment rented on the same day during the month to the same customer. For instance, say four different equipment units were rented on the fifth day of the month to J. R. Jones. Each unit or equipment type has a separate record, but the group rented by J.R. Jones is linked together since they are linked alphabetically for day 5. The only caution which must be observed is to insure two customers don't have the same name. This problem could be handled by an additional ordering by customer identification number. This linking is illustrated in more detail for a particular day in *Figure 9-9*.

**Figure 9-9.
Linking Detail by Day of Month.**

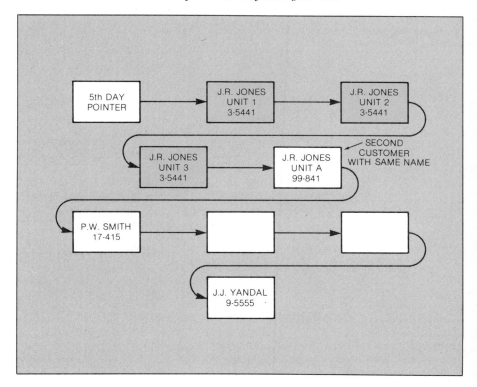

Another advantage to this structure is that bills will be generated by alphabetical order. However if billings in zip code order were required to presort mail, this could be a disadvantage.

To search by customer name to generate a list of all equipment rented by a particular customer requires a complete search of the data file because a customer may have rented equipment on more than one day. Also, since billing is daily, such a customer will receive more than one bill per month. If searching by customer name is to be done often, it would be desirable to add another pointer so that records for the same customer are linked throughout the month. Recall from Chapter 7 however, that updating and particularly deleting a record, becomes much more involved when multiple pointers are used.

Pointers link invoices in the order of payment.

There is an additional pointer for keeping track of customer payments. This pointer is associated with each record as payments to each equipment type must be recorded. Because multiple bills are possible, and because several months could pass before payment is received, care must be taken to ensure that a payment is credited to the correct bill. This is done as illustrated in *Figure 9-10*. Here invoices are linked in the order paid. The invoice number indicates payment order where the first two digits give the year. The invoice records are then inserted in the string at the appropriate location to maintain an order by billing date.

**Figure 9-10.
Accounts Received
Links.**

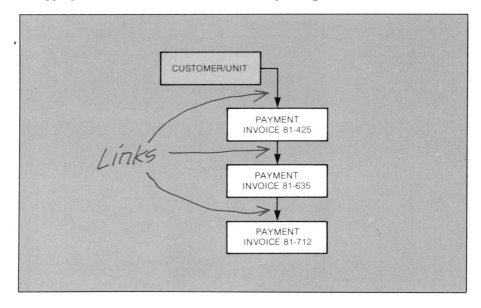

Sorting Records

Sorting becomes necessary if outputs need to be arranged in an order other than the sequences used by the data base program.

The output reports of a program are usually requested to be in a specified order. The billing program output provides the rentals that occurred on a specific day and who the customers were, in alphabetical order. This is necessary to keep the rental of different types of equipment by the same customer grouped together so that only one bill is made per person for a given date.

Suppose however, that the inventory reporting program is to be printed according to the ascending order of the equipment code. Since the data base records are not arranged in this order, all the records have to be read and sorted according to the equipment code value.

Bubble Sort

A simple sorting technique called the *bubble sort* could be used. Let's discuss it so that we can see how easily sorting can be accomplished. The bubble sort is only efficient when there are 10 or so items to be sorted. For a larger number of items, much better sorting procedures are available, however, we will discuss the bubble sort because it's easy to understand.

The bubble sort, most useful with lists of 10 or fewer elements, compares adjacent items and switches them as needed until the list is in the correct order.

The bubble sort is an exchange sorting scheme which essentially involves going through a list and comparing adjacent entries. If they are out of order, they are simply exchanged. In *Figure 9-11*, the numbers shown in the left column are to be sorted in ascending order. During scan 1, items 5 and 2 are compared first. Since they are out of order, their positions in the list are exchanged. Next 5 is compared with 9 and no exchange is necessary. Now 9 is compared with 1 and an exchange occurs. The next comparison is for 9 and 8 and once again an exchange occurs. Nine is now compared with 6 and the last exchange for the first scan occurs.

**Figure 9-11.
Bubble Sort Example.**

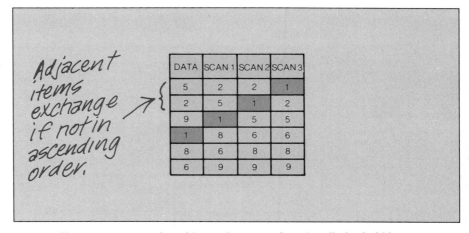

You can see now that this sorting procedure is called a bubble sort because the smaller values appear to 'bubble up' on each scan.

Now let's look at the second scan. Here 2 is compared with 5 and no exchange is necessary. However, 5 and 1 must be exchanged. The numbers 5 and 8 are not exchanged, but on the next comparison 6 and 8 are exchanged. The values 8 and 9 require no change.

The third and final scan needs only one exchange for the first two numbers, 1 and 2, to complete the sort of the list. A BASIC subroutine to perform this sort is as follows:

```
1000    REM  ASSUME THE N ITEMS TO BE SORTED ARE
1010    REM  IN ARRAY A
1020    SW=0
1030    FOR I=1 TO N-1
1040    IF A (I) > A(I+1) THEN SW=1:
          TEMP = A(I) : A(I) = A(I+1) : A(I+1) = TEMP
1050    NEXT I
1060    IF SW = 1 THEN 1020
1070    REM SORT COMPLETE
1080    RETURN
```

This subroutine assumes that the N items to be sorted are given in array A. A variable SW is used to specify if an exchange occurs during a scan (SW = 1). If no exchange occurs (SW = 0) then the sorting of the list is complete. The FOR loop on line numbers 1030 to 1050 is performed N − 1 times. In line number 1040, adjacent items are compared. The BASIC statement in 1040 is a little different from those presented in Chapter 4. Here multiple statements are specified with one line number and the colon is used to distinguish or separate the individual statements. Furthermore, statements following the test of A(I) and A(I + 1) with the same line number 1040 will be executed only if A(I) > A(I + 1). Otherwise, line number 1050 is executed. BASIC interpreters permitting this syntax provide a block capability similar to the following Pascal statements.

```
IF A(I) > A(I+1) THEN
    BEGIN
        SW=1 ;
        TEMP=A(I) ;
        A(I)=A(I+1);
        A(I+1)=TEMP ;
    END ;
```

Actually many BASIC interpreters do provide this capability. Note that this makes the program more readable and, in fact, fewer statements are required, than would be without the block capability. The rest of the subroutine is straight-forward.

As mentioned, the bubble sort is one of the least efficient sorting methods. If the list is completely out of order, then n(n − 1)/2 exchanges are required but if they are in order, then no exchanges are necessary.

Shell Sort

The shell sort, a faster variant of the bubble sort, compares items located at regular intervals from each other.

The number of exchanges can be reduced considerably by using a variation called the shell sort. In this method comparisons between d_i adjacent items are made first rather than immediately adjacent items. For example, if we have 12 items to be sorted, then the first scan compares the first item with the sixth item, then the second item with the seventh etc. On the next pass, d_i is selected as 3. The last scan is a bubble sort. In other words, each set of scans divides the list into sublists which are more nearly sorted.

There are several other sorting methods and some are better than others for different data arrangements. The two sorting methods discussed are called internal sorts; that is, the items to be sorted are in memory. External sorting methods deal with sorting items on disks or other auxiliary storage devices.

Since many applications, particularly business applications, require that data be sorted, sorting algorithms are commonly available already written and tested for most high-level languages for most computers. Therefore, it is easy to simply select the one you need and insert it in a program as a subroutine that is called as needed by the program.

With the system processes and data structures defined, the next stages of development are to specify the program functions, hardware configuration, and man/machine interaction necessary to implement the design.

System Implementation

Now that the system functions have been defined and the data structures needed have been identified, actual implementation can be next considered. The implementation phase involves the following activities:

1. Program Specifications
2. Hardware Specifications
3. Operation Specifications
4. Testing Specifications
5. Software and Hardware Maintenance

Program Specifications

The program specifications must be well defined, particularly if someone else is actually developing the program. With these specifications you can be protected by contract to insure the system does the kinds of things you want it to do. If you don't specify all desired functions, then it is most likely that they all will not be implemented. For example, suppose you decide later that you want records ordered not only by date, but also by name and identification code as we discussed previously. If this is not stated at the outset, then it's unlikely that it will be implemented unless additional money is given for these extra features. Also, don't expect to be able to do some of the things yourself very easily, because, typically, only the person who wrote the program can quickly and easily make small changes. The language the program is written in should also be specified and structured programming methods should be insisted upon.

Hardware Specifications

Hardware specifications include those that define the memory and I/O devices (disks, printer, CRT, etc.). For most small systems like the TRS-80 or Apple, you should specify as much memory as possible to provide for future expansion. Additional memory can usually be bought for a relatively small increase in the system price and you can usually find a use for it later.

Operation Specifications

The next activity, number 3, in the implementation phase defines the operational considerations, that is, the actual mechanics of using the system. Operational procedures must be fairly straight forward and the capabilities of the operators or office personnel must be taken into consideration. Each of the various functions that have to be accomplished by a person must be carefully examined and made as easy and goof-proof as possible.

For example, how does an operator enter information, delete information, or perform a billing function? By defining the operational procedures, the software specifications for operator program interactions are also determined. Often, these interaction routines in the software can be more involved than the routines that perform the actual billing functions because of the many prompts and error checking. Appropriate information must be displayed on the CRT Screen to instruct or aid the operator to correctly perform the desired functions. A selection list or menu should be displayed on the CRT when a user turns on the computer and mounts the appropriate program disk. This menu should list the various program functions such as billing, posting, etc. and allow easy selection of the desired one.

Another operation consideration is that of the filing procedure for the floppy disks containing the data. Procedures must be established for storing these disks and for how often backup copies should be made.

Testing Specifications

The next activity in the implementation phase involves specifications for testing the system to insure that it performs properly. Once again, if someone else does the program development and hardware purchasing, you want to make sure the program and hardware function properly so that the system does everything you want it to do and does it correctly. Thus, much thought must be given to how you want to test the system to prove that it is operational.

Software and Hardware Maintenance

Once in place, the system must be maintained. Local vendors may be preferable to distant ones for maintenance service.

Finally, the last phase in implementation is maintenance. Hardware and software will need maintenance and this phase insures that it can and will be done. You know that the hardware is not always going to work properly. Of course, your system is covered initially, say for three months, by the manufacturer's new equipment warranty, but after that period, you are on your own. Thus, it's often desirable to buy equipment from local vendors because they can usually provide fast, reliable service. Software maintenance is also important. If bugs are found later in the system, or if improvements to the software are developed, you want to ensure that your software is updated. Careful consideration should be given to the location of a software vendor and how long the firm has been in business. It is also advisable to ask a software firm for a list of their customers for reference.

WHAT HAVE WE LEARNED?

In this chapter we discussed systems analysis concepts and methods. We then discussed how these methods could be used to set up a personal microcomputer system for a small business. We quickly noted that, even though the business and computer system were relatively small, the design and implementation problems were not. An application example for implementing an automated billing and inventory reporting system for a small business was used to explore systems analysis. The overall design specifications and implementation phases of this application were discussed. We also learned about sorting procedures which can be used in the billing and inventory reporting applications as well as other sorting applications.

WHAT'S NEXT?

What are the hardware and software trends of the future and what does the future hold for computer science? These subjects will be discussed in the next chapter.

Quiz for Chapter 9

1. Which of the following people would most likely be selected to perform a systems analysis function for a large computer system?
   a. A recent graduate in business systems analysis.
   b. A programmer with 10 years experience in writing programs for similar systems.
   c. An engineer responsible for hardware and software maintenance for a similar system.
   d. A business manager with 10 years experience as a personnel director.
   e. A computer operator with 10 years experience.

2. Which of the following techniques would typically not be used by a system's analyst in designing a computer system?
   a. Statistics
   b. Top-down design
   c. Simulation
   d. Verbal communication methods
   e. All of the above could be used

3. The application described in this chapter involved what class of computer?
   a. Large general purpose
   b. Midicomputer
   c. Minicomputer
   d. Microcomputer

4. Which data structuring scheme was not discussed as a possible application in structuring the data base for the problem of this chapter?
   a. Hashing
   b. Linked list
   c. Sorting
   d. All were discussed

5. Which of the following items was not a task in the computer billing and inventory application?
   a. Data base structure
   b. Billing
   c. System tuning
   d. Posting
   e. Inventory reporting

(Answers in back of book.)

6. Which of the following items was not a field in the record description of the data base in the application problem of this chapter?
   a. Name
   b. Address
   c. Phone number
   d. Place of employment
   e. Equipment code

7. What role did the invoice form of Figure 9-4 play in the application of this chapter?
   a. Determine the simulation requirements
   b. Determine the number of record links
   c. Determine the number of records required for the data base
   d. Determine some of the fields needed in each record
   e. Determine the tree structures implemented

8. Which routine would probably not be included in the final billing and inventory reporting program?
   a. Modification of data entries
   b. Addition of data entries
   c. Space list initialization
   d. Simulation routine
   e. Listing of data entries

9. Which of the following might be considered a searching disadvantage because of the data structure proposed for the equipment and customer entries?
   a. Billing only requires searching one sublist.
   b. Multiple equipment per customer per day of month rented could be identified.
   c. Searching for all equipment rented to a particular customer.

10. Which of the following items were discussed during the system implementation phase of the application of this chapter?
    a. Program specification
    b. Statistical analysis
    c. Simulation
    d. Software specification
    e. Software maintenance

Computer Science and the Future

ABOUT THIS CHAPTER

Thus far we have dealt with computer events that have occurred up to the present time. In this chapter, after spending a little more time reviewing these events, we'll turn our attention to the future. We'll discuss current trends and possible advances in hardware, software, and computer science.

HARDWARE REVIEW

In a single generation, computer refinements have produced drastic reductions in size accompanied by enormous gains in performance.

Throughout this book we have discussed many computer developments in both hardware and software. It is difficult to comprehend that within the span of only the last 30 years, hardware developments have increased the computational capability (computing power) of a system while reducing the physical size. The computational power that used to take a room full of equipment is now available in a self-contained cabinet and the computational power formerly contained in several desk size modules may now be held in one hand — the hand-held calculator. All of this with the advantages of increased overall performance, lower power requirements, and higher reliability.

Larger systems designed to handle business and scientific problems capitalized on these developments to increase their capability to handle larger and larger problems at faster and faster speeds. Where before many company or government computer systems at many different geographical locations around a state, the nation, or the world were used to handle the computing task, now a single central computer with its encompassing capability can be used. Inputs to the computer arrive via communication links from the outlying locations and outputs are sent back to these locations over similar communications links.

Reductions in size and cost have made computers more accessible to more people than ever before, leading to many new computer applications in industry and business as well as in everyday life.

Because of the increased capability in a smaller package, smaller computers (minicomputers) were designed to handle manufacturing tasks on the production line, to monitor and control processes, to provide instrumentation for an electric generating plant, to provide inventory control for the warehouse, to handle sales transactions for the department store, to generate business reports for the small business, etc., etc. The use of computers mushroomed.

Increased capability in a smaller package (microprocessors and microcomputers) and decreased cost brought computer system computational ability to hand-held calculators, electronic toys, electronic games, microwave ovens, thermostats, and yes, to you personally through the personal computers and home computers now available on the market.

HARDWARE OF THE FUTURE

Future progress in technology and software should make computers more commonplace than ever, and may change the patterns of our lives at home and at work even further.

A strong emphasis of a large portion of the hardware development has been to bring more computing capability to the individual. Call it what you want — increased computer fan out, computer system distribution, increased computer communications — computer systems are going to be distributed closer to the individual using the equipment.

It can be envisioned that computing will be distributed such that the individual becomes more self sufficient in the place where that person is located. Information from many sources and many locations will be available to the person due to access to large data bases with pages and pages of entries. Direct information from the person's business in the way of sales, personnel, financial, and marketing reports; supplemental information from market research, libraries, polls, financial community, weather, travel, entertainment — all will contribute to psuedo-independent operation by individuals located miles from the center of their business operations.

Automated and computerized operations of machines in factories, warehouses, power plants, retail stores, grocery stores, and maintenance depots will help to increase worker productivity and contribute to uniform, high quality, high reliability products.

This will be made possible because standard systems of hardware (which may even be called families) will evolve to be used in many applications by simply changing the program — the software.

And individualized computing will also extend into the home. The personal computer like the TI Professional Computer shown in *Figure 10-1* and the home computer like the TI-99/4 shown in *Figure 10-2* will bring the individualized computing system into the home. Information will no longer reside only in books in the library but will be available for viewing on a TV-type screen at the press of a few keys on the computer keyboard.

**Figure 10-1.
Personal Computer.**

**Figure 10-2.
Home Computer.**

Pre-programmed software designed to make the computing system easy to use will lead the user step-by-step through financial decisions, budget planning, educational drill and practice, vacation planning, tax reports, electronic games, and at the same time provide heat and cooling control, security control, record a favorite TV program from around the world, control food preparation, select the house music, and deliver the world news electronically to the breakfast table spoken out instead of recorded on a screen. Truly an exciting demonstration of the pervasiveness of the computer system and techniques. Now, the personal and home computers have brought computers from large businesses to the home, from universities to the elementary school. For it is very likely that children will practice on their home computer screens the same lessons they had at school on their classroom screen; or they may even stay at home and receive their lessons on their screens.

SOFTWARE REVIEW

Applications programs were not originally transportable from one machine to another.

Coupled closely with hardware development, and even a very part of it, were the advances in software development.

Each early large computing system required various software packages to use the system effectively. Unfortunately, even though a large number of users would use the software; the operating system, the loaders, and the compilers were developed more around a particular manufacturer's hardware than for general use. There was not a great need for developing large numbers of operating systems, compilers, and language translators because not very many systems were being developed each year. Almost all programs written were for the application of the system, that is, application programs. Applications programs were written for nearly every conceivable application from space shots to time-sharing programs for small businesses.

Unfortunately, the programs were not transportable. The software written for one application had to be rewritten to apply to the next even though the applications were similar in function. In addition, it was a difficult job to modify the programs and even to maintain them (debug them). Few people understood a particular program except for the people who wrote it.

As the application of computers expanded, the need arose for programs to be transportable, relocatable, and maintainable. Why should a programmer have to write over again a subprogram for recognizing input from a keyboard when one has already been written by another programmer? Why shouldn't a program written by one programmer be easily understood by another programmer who knows the same language? From these questions, the emphasis centered on software developments of high-level languages for structured programming, programming for ease of maintenance, programming so that subprograms could be used again in new applications without rewrite.

As computers became more numerous, the advantages of transportable, systematically written software became evident.

Of equal importance was the expansion of the opportunity to design varied types of software. Since smaller systems were applied in a wide variety of applications, many types of systems were designed. Programmers now had the opportunity to develop monitors, operating systems, loaders, linkers, and language translators because each new system needed one. And, of course, as the applications grew, the need for more application programmers grew.

More applications and more programs produced libraries of software for particular systems. These were shared and even sold by original developers to other users.

Programmable calculators ushered in a new era — pre-programmed software — programs that were already programmed by the manufacturer to make it easy to use his machines for many applications. Alternate programs could be simply "plugged in" to alter the base machine to handle problems in electrical engineering, real estate, business and finance, statistics, navigation, etc. Now the user could utilize the system much faster and easier because the tedious job of learning the initial programming was eliminated. After only a few hours of study, the user could have the system solving problems.

This same emphasis is continuing in personal computers and especially the home computers.

COMPUTER SCIENCE OF THE FUTURE

Career prospects in the field of computer science should be bright.

All of the developments up to now and all the developments that will occur in the future will need and use people. People to design hardware, people to design software, people to recognize the need and use of the computer (systems analysts), and people to develop application programs. So the need will be great for people who know computer science.

The opportunities are almost mind boggling. Some university placement agencies have stated that there were over twenty job offers for every doctoral candidate graduating in computer science over the past several years. A rather staggering statistic. The job opportunities for persons with BS and MS degrees are as equally plentiful in computer science. Less than twenty years ago, few universities recognized computer science as a program directed toward a degree. That has changed. Almost all major colleges and universities now offer full degree programs in the field and many to the doctoral level.

With the spread of computer systems and the emphasis on distributed computing, the opportunity to develop and gain a wide variety of experience will continue. In fact, with semiconductor companies now developing a microcomputer on a chip; operating systems, compilers, and cross-support software must all be developed for these units just as for the larger computer systems.

A major challenge in the future will be the development of more flexible and economical applications software.

More universal software will be the guideline. Development of subprograms, subroutines, routines, modules, new high-level languages, and new programming techniques will be directed to using an application program that is being written for one application again in some other application.

As the home computer comes into more use, and as more and more people have contact with other programmable products, the need becomes even greater for pre-programmed software to make these complex technical products easy to use. As a result, programmers will be asked to develop solutions to problems in personal business, personal finance, personal entertainment, personal education, personal games, etc. The applications are almost limitless.

In like fashion, opportunities in the future for people with computer science experience will be almost limitless.

Whether computer system hardware advances and innovations continue at the same pace for the next 30 years is debatable. However, one thing is clear. Significant advances certainly will occur, especially in providing more computing capability in a small space.

Similar advances in software have not yet occured. In fact, what is needed now is to learn how to more effectively use the hardware advancements already made. The hardware and electronic techniques available now are technically ahead of the software. It is most important that much better use of systems be accomplished through software.

However, it's not enough just to develop software. The development must also be done effectively. Software cost in a system application now far exceeds the cost of the hardware and is the largest percentage of the total system development cost.

Effective use of hardware and software, the reuse of software, and the control of development costs are the tasks for the computer scientist of the future.

Bibliography

Chapter

1   D. Cassel and M. Jackson, *Introduction to Computers and Information Processing* (Reston 1980)

G.B. Davis, *Introduction to Computers* (McGraw-Hill 1977)

2   H.W. Gschwind and E.J. McCluskey, *Design of Digital Computers* (Springer-Verlag 1975)

M.M. Mano, *Digital Logic and Computer Design* (Prentice-Hall 1979)

W.D. Simpson, G. Luecke, D.L. Cannon and D.H. Clemens, *Microprocessors/Microcomputers System Design* (McGraw-Hill 1980)

3   B.W. Kernigham and P.J. Plauger, *The Elements of Programming Style* (McGraw-Hill 1978)

E. Yourdon, *Techniques of Program Structure and Design* (Prentice-Hall 1975)

4   J.E. Sammet, *Programming Languages History and Fundamentals* (Prentice-Hall 1969)

Krietzberg and Schneiderman, *FORTRAN Programming A Spiral Approach with WATFOR/WATFIV Standard Form* (Harcourt, Brace, Jovanovich 1975)

Hugh, *PL/I Structured Programming*, 2nd. ed. (John Wiley and Sons, Inc. 1979)

4   Organick, Forsythe and Plummer, *Programming Language Structures* (Academic Press 1978)

Grauer and Crawford, *COBOL: A Pragmatic Approach* (Prentice-Hall 1978)

5 & 6   J.J. Donovan, *Systems Programming* (McGraw-Hill) 1972)

S.E. Madnick and J.J. Donovan, *Operating Systems* (McGraw-Hill 1974)

Shaw, *Logical Design of Operating Systems* (Prentice-Hall 1974)

7   D.E. Knuth, *The Art of Computer Programming, Volume 1 Fundamental Algorithms* (Addison-Wesley 1973)

D.E. Knuth, *The Art of Computer Programming, Volume 3 Sorting and Searching* (Addison-Wesley 1973)

8   D. Gries, *Compiler Construction for Digital Computers* (John Wiley & Sons Inc. 1971)

Aho and Ullman, *Principles of Compiler Design* (Addison-Wesley 1977)

9   Gore and Stubbe, *Elements of Systems Analysis for Business Data Processing* (W.C. Brown Co. 1975)

W.S. Davis, *Information Processing Systems* (Addison-Wesley 1981)

Glossary

Adder: A building block which provides a sum and a carry when adding two numbers.

Address: A pattern of characters that identify a unique storage location.

Algorithm: A term used to describe a set of procedures by which a given result is obtained.

ALU: Arithmetic and Logic Unit, a subsystem that can perform arithmetic and logical operations on words sent to it.

Analog: Analog circuitry, also called "linear" circuitry, is circuitry that varies certain properties of electricity continuously and smoothly over a certain range.

AND Gate: A device or circuit with two or more inputs of binary digital information and one output, whose output is 1 only when all the inputs are 1.

ASCII: (American National Standard Code for Information Interchange, 1968). See USASCII.

Assembler: A computer program that prepares a machine language program from a symbolic language program.

Base Address: A given address from which a final address is derived by combination with a relative address.

BASIC: (Beginner's All-Purpose Symbolic Instruction Code) — A high-level language developed to provide an easy to use and easy to learn interactive language for time-sharing or dedicated computer systems.

Binary Coded Decimal (BCD): A binary numbering system for coding decimal numbers in groups of 4 bits. The binary value of these 4-bit groups ranges from 0000 to 1001, and codes the decimal digits "0" through "9".

Binary Number System or Code: A method of writing numbers by using two numeral digits, 0 and 1. Each successive bit position in a binary number represents 1,2,4,8 and so forth.

Bit: The smallest possible piece of information. A specification of one out of two possible alternatives. Bits are written as 1 for "yes" and 0 for "no."

Borrow: An arithmetically negative carry in subtraction operations.

Branch: A program is said to "branch" when an instruction other than the next instruction in the program sequence is executed.

Bus: Two or more conductors running in parallel used for carrying information.

Byte: A sequence of adjacent binary digits operated upon as a unit — usually 8 bits.

Carry: When the sum of two digits is equal to or greater than 10, then 10 is subtracted from this sum, and 1 is added to the next more significant digit of the sum.

Central Processor Unit (CPU): Part of a computer system which contains the main storage, arithmetic unit, and special register groups. It performs arithmetic operations, controls instruction processing, and provides timing signals.

Character: A symbol whose image is formed by a display system for representation of information. Examples are numerals, letters, decimal point, punctuation marks, and special symbols indicating status of an electronic system.

Clear: To remove data and return all circuitry to an initial condition, usually "0."

Clock Input: An input terminal on a building-block typically used for receiving a timing control-clock signal, but used in some applications for a control signal or even data.

COBOL: (Common Business Oriented Language) — A high-level language developed in the early 1960's and used primarily for business applications.

Code: A set of meanings or rules assigned to groups of bits. Each combination of bits has a certain meaning based on following certain rules.

Compiler: A program that prepares a machine language program from a program written in a high-level language.

Complement: Usually means the "ones complement" of a bit, which is simply the inverse of the bit. To "complement" a number means to subtract it from a certain number (from one, in the case of ones complement).

Computer: A digital computer consists of at least one CPU, together with input, output and memory units.

Conditional Jump: A jump that occurs if specified criteria are met.

Cross Assembler: A program which converts symbolic machine instructions to the actual machine instructions. However, the machine language generated is for a different machine than the one on which the assembler was executed.

Cross Compiler: A program which converts a high-level language to machine language. However, the machine language generated is for a different machine than the one on which the compiler was executed.

Cycle: 1. An interval of space or time in which one set of events or phenomena is completed. 2. Any set of operations that is repeated regularly in the same sequence.

Data: Another name for information.

Data Bus: One method of input-output for a system where data are moved by way of a group of wires forming a common bus.

Data Structures: A study of methods to more efficiently structure data in a computer system so that the data can be kept and then easily referenced.

Decimal Digit: In decimal notation, one of the characters 0 through 9.

Decimal Number System or Code: Also called "Arabic" number system. A method of writing numbers by using ten numeral digits. The "decimal digits" are 0,1,2,3,4,5,6,7,8, and 9.

Decoder: A combinational building-block receiving several parallel inputs, which "recognizes" one or more combinations of input bits and puts out a signal when these combinations are received.

Digital: Information in discrete or quantized form; not continuous.

Direct Addressing: Method of programming that has the address of data contained in the instruction that is to be used.

Effective Address: The address that is derived by applying any specified indexing or indirect addressing results to the specified address and that is actually used to identify the current operand.

Error: Any discrepancy between a computed, observed, or measured quantity and the true, specified, or theoretically correct value or condition.

Exclusive-OR Gate: A device or circuit with two (not more) inputs of binary digital information and one output, whose output is 1 when either input is 1 and 0 if neither or both inputs are 1.

Execute: That portion of a computer cycle during which a selected instruction is accomplished.

Execution State: A state in which jobs are placed in a computer system when the job is either using the CPU, or having once used it, waiting for its use again.

Fetch: That portion of a computer cycle during which the next instruction is retrieved from memory.

Flip-Flop: A building-block having two stable states that stores one bit by means of two gates (ordinarily NAND or NOR gates) "cross-coupled" as a latch, with the output of each forming an input to the other.

Flow Chart: A graphical representation for definition, analysis, or solution of a problem, in which symbols are used to represent operations, data flow equipment, etc.

FORTRAN: (FORmula TRANslating system) A language primarily used to express computer programs by arithmetic formulas.

Frequency: How often regular waves or pulses occur in a circuit or other transmission medium such as radio. Frequency is measured in hertz (cycles per second).

General-Purpose Computer: A computer that is designed to handle a wide variety of problems.

Immediate Address: Pertaining to an instruction which contains the value of an operand.

Indexed Address: An address that is modified by the content of an index register prior to or during the execution of a computer instruction.

Indirect Addressing: The initial address is the storage location of a word that contains another address used to obtain the data to be operated upon.

Input/Output Devices (I/O): Computer hardware by which data is entered into a digital system or by which data are recorded for immediate or future use.

Instruction: A statement that specifies an operation and the values or locations of its operands.

Instruction Cycle: The period of time during which a programmed system obeys an instruction.

Integrated Circuit ("IC"): A small package with electrical terminals, containing a chip of silicon. The surface of the silicon is processed to form hundreds or thousands of transistors and other devices that are connected to make an electronic circuit.

Interrupt: To stop a process in such a way that it can be resumed.

Inverter: A binary digital building-block with one input and one output. The output state is the inverse (opposite) of the input state.

Job Turn-around Time: The time required to process a job from submission to final output.

Jump: A departure from the normal sequence of executing instructions in a computer.

Label: One or more characters used to identify a statement or an item of data in a program.

Language: A set of representations, conventions, and rules used to convey information.

Language Translators: Programs which convert or translate one language to another.

Light-Emitting Diode (LED): A semiconductor two terminal "light bulb" made of semiconductor material (such as gallium phosphide) that makes light when electric current is passed through it in a particular direction.

Linked List: A data structuring method for linking data items. Each item has one or more pointers for linking these items with one another.

Load: In programming, to enter data into storage or working registers.

Logic Gate: See "AND, OR, NAND, NOR, NOT, and Exclusive-OR."

Logic Symbol: A symbol used to represent a logic element graphically.

LSB or LSD: Least-significant bit or digit. The bit or digit at the end of a number which has the smallest numerical value.

Machine Code: An operation code that a machine is designed to recognize.

Mask: A pattern of characters that is used to control the retention or elimination of portions of another pattern of characters.

Memory: In a digital system the part of the system where information is stored.

Microcomputer: The name usually given to a small computer which uses a microprocessor for its CPU.

Microprocessor: An IC (or set of a few ICs) that can be programmed with stored instructions to perform a wide variety of functions, consisting of at least a controller, some registers, and some sort of ALU (that is, the basic parts of a simple CPU).

Minicomputer: A small computer system with limited resources and most often used for specific applications.

Monitor: Usually a set of routines which enable a user to use a computer system. See Operating System.

MSB or MSD: Most-significant bit or digit. The bit or digit at the end of a number which has the largest numerical value.

Multiprocessing: The process of having two or more programs actually executing at the same time in a computer which has more than one CPU.

Multiprogramming: The process of having two or more programs in an execution state at the same time in a computer system.

NAND Gate: A binary digital building-block that acts as an AND gate followed by an inverter.

NOR Gate: A binary digital building-block that acts as an OR gate followed by an inverter.

NOT Gate: Occasionally used to mean "inverter."

Object Code: Output from a compiler or assembler which is itself executable machine code or is suitable for processing to produce executable machine code.

Operating System: A set of programs which monitors and controls the execution of various user programs.

OR Gate: A device or circuit with two or more inputs of binary digital information and one output, whose output is 1 when any one or more inputs are 1.

Output: An information signal going out of a system or part of a system.

Parity Check: A check to see if the number of ones in an array of binary digits is odd or even.

Pascal: A high-level language developed to teach good programming methods. It is well suited for many applications and enables structured programming.

PC: Program Counter.

Personal Computer: A microcomputer system marketed for home and small business application.

PL/I: A very powerful high-level language well suited for most applications.

Priority Interrupt: A method of providing some commands to have precedence over others.

Program: A series of actions proposed in order to achieve a certain result.

Programmable Read-Only Memory (PROM): A fixed program, read only, semiconductor memory that can be programmed after packaging.

Programmed System: A system that operates by following a series of stored instructions.

Pushdown Stack: A set of registers which implements a pushdown list.

RAM: A random-access memory where words may be "written" (stored) or "read" (recovered) in any order at random.

Register: A certain type of temporary storage unit for digital information.

Relative Address: The number that specifies the difference between the absolute address and the base address.

ROM: A read-only memory containing a program or data permanently stored when the unit was made.

Routine or Programmed Routine: A series of instructions followed by a programmed system in doing a particular job. Usually contained within a main program.

Serial Data Transmission: Two or more bits of a group are said to be transmitted "in series" when one at a time is transmitted through the same wire.

Shift Register: A register in which the stored data can be moved to the right or left.

Significant Digit: A digit that is needed to preserve a specific accuracy or precision.

Simulator: A computer program that represents the behavior of a system.

Software: A set of computer programs, procedures, and possibly associated documentation concerned with the operation of a data processing system, e.g., compilers, library routines, manuals, circuit diagrams.

Source Code Program: A computer program written in a high-level or in assembly language.

Stored Program: A set of instructions in memory determining the order of the problem solution.

Structured Programming: The construction of programs in a well-disciplined modular (subprogram or procedure) fashion. Each module is designed primarily to be independent of others and communication between modules well defined.

Subroutine: A routine that is part of another routine.

Subsystem: A smaller system inside a larger system. Each subsystem can be thought of as a separate system with its own job to do.

Terminal: A computer terminal is an input (usually a keyboard) or output device (usually a printer or CRT screen) operated by a person.

Top-down design: A systematic procedure for problem solving which consists of first specifying a problem solution in rather broad or general terms (the top level). The next level and each succeeding level involves a more detailed solution until no more detail is necessary.

Truth Table: A table showing the logic state of each output that results from each combination of logic states at the inputs. The logic states are 1 (yes,true) and 0 (no,false).

Word: A group of bits handled as a unit usually stored at a certain address in a RAM.

Index

Answers to Quizzes

Chapter 1

1. **a-4, b-5, c-3, d-1, e-2, f-6**
2. **a-5, b-4, c-1, d-2, e-3**
3. **a-T, b-F, c-T**
4. **a-T, b-F, c-F, d-T, e-F**
5. **b**
6. **a-3, b-2, c-1**
7. **a-3, b-1, c-2, d-1, e-3**
8. **a-T, b-F, c-F, d-F**
9. **c**
10. **a-4, b-3, c-1, d-7, e-2, f-5, g-6**

Chapter 2

1. **b**	9. **d**
2. **T**	10. **T**
3. **d**	11. **c**
4. **F**	12. **d**
5. **c**	13. **b**
6. **b**	14. **b**
7. **d**	15. **F**
8. **F**	

Chapter 3

1. **T**	7. **T**
2. **T**	8. **T**
3. **F**	9. **F**
4. **F**	10. **T**
5. **T**	11. **a**
6. **T**	12. **b**

Chapter 4

1. **c**	9. **F**
2. **c**	10. **b**
3. **d**	11. **c**
4. **e**	12. **T**
5. **b**	13. **T**
6. **a**	14. **F**
7. **c**	15. **T**
8. **c**	

Chapter 5

1. **F**	9. **F**	15. **T**
2. **T**	10. **d**	16. **F**
3. **a**	11. **1-c, 2-a,**	17. **a**
4. **T**	**3-e, 4-b,**	18. **d**
5. **c**	**5-d**	19. **T**
6. **T**	12. **b**	20. **F**
7. **F**	13. **T**	
8. **T**	14. **F**	

Chapter 6

1. **1-b, 2-c,**	5. **b**
3-a, 4-b,	6. **b**
5-d, 6-c,	7. **a**
7-e	8. **b**
2. **b**	9. **T**
3. **c**	10. **b**
4. **1-a, 2-c,**	
3-d	

Chapter 7

1. **T**	5. **b**
2. **T**	6. **b**
3. **c**	7. **c**
4. **a-4, b-1,**	8. **a, a**
c-3, d-5,	9. **a**
e-2	10. **b**

Chapter 8

1. **F**	8. **c**	15. **F**
2. **T**	9. **F**	16. **T**
3. **T**	10. **T**	17. **T**
4. **T**	11. **T**	18. **T**
5. **T**	12. **F**	19. **T**
6. **F**	13. **T**	20. **F**
7. **b**	14. **T**	

Chapter 9

1. **b, c**	6. **d**
2. **e**	7. **d**
3. **d**	8. **d**
4. **a**	9. **c**
5. **c**	10. **a, d, e**

UNDERSTANDING COMPUTER SCIENCE